Reflections on the Gospel of John

VOLUME 2
The Bread of Life
John 6–10

Leon Morris

BAKER BOOK HOUSE
Grand Rapids, Michigan 49506

Unless indicated otherwise, Old Testament quotations are from *The Holy Bible: New International Version* © 1978 by the New York International Bible Society, used by permission of Zondervan Bible Publishers. New Testament quotations are the author's translation.

Printed in the United States of America

Contents

Preface

This is the second volume in this series of *Reflections on the Gospel of John* and carries on in the same style. It is my attempt to convey to the general reader something of what John is saying. I have tried to bring out for those who do not know Greek some of the things I see in my Greek New Testament. For that reason I have made my own translation of New Testament passages. It is not a particularly good translation, but it may help to show some of the things I see in John's Gospel. In quoting from the Old Testament I have normally used the New International Version.

Leon Morris

25

The Miracle of
the Loaves and Fishes

*After these things Jesus went off to the other side of the sea of
Galilee, that is of Tiberias. A great crowd followed him because
they saw the signs he was doing on the sick people. Jesus went
up into the mountain and sat there with his disciples. Now the
Passover, the feast of the Jews, was near.*

*Jesus then looked up and saw that a great crowd was
coming to him. He said to Philip, "Where will we buy bread in
order that these people may eat?" He said this by way of testing
him; for he himself knew what he was going to do. Philip
answered him, "Two hundred denarii worth of bread would not
be enough for each of them to have a little." One of his
disciples, Andrew the brother of Simon Peter, said to him,
"There's a little boy here who has five barley loaves and two
small fishes. But what are these among so many?"*

*Jesus said, "Make the men sit down." Now there was a lot of
grass in that place so the men sat down in number about five
thousand. Jesus then took the bread and when he had given
thanks he distributed it to those who were seated, also as much
as they wanted of the fishes. When they had had enough he
said to his disciples, "Gather up what is left over so that
nothing be wasted." They gathered it up therefore and filled
twelve baskets from the fragments of the five barley loaves
which were left over by those who had eaten.*

*Therefore the men who had seen the sign Jesus did said,
"Truly this is the prophet who is to come into the world." Jesus*

*then perceived that they would come and seize him in order to
make him a king and he withdrew back into the mountain, by
himself, alone* (John 6:1–15).

Apart from the resurrection, this is the only miracle
found in all four Gospels. Clearly it made a great appeal to the early
church. We may wonder why, and it is perhaps worth reflecting that
bread occupied a greater part in the life of people in first-century
Palestine than it commonly does with us. We may speak of bread as
"the staff of life," but in practice it occupies a small place in our diet. It
was otherwise for most people in Bible times. The wealthy might have
a variety of foods, but for ordinary people bread was the most significant daily food. And getting enough to eat was not a matter of course;
the poor man often went hungry. Eating and drinking could be used
metaphorically of the good life: ". . . nothing is better for a man under
the sun than to eat and drink and be glad" (Eccles. 8:15a). God's blessing on the poor can be described in terms of his giving them bread (Ps.
132:15). It is interesting that the New International Version here (and
in many other places) translates the Hebrew word for "bread" as
"food." We think naturally of a variety of foodstuffs; the ancients
thought equally naturally of bread.

Eating and drinking may symbolize blessing, for example the blessing that would follow when the people entered the Promised Land: it
would be "a land where bread will not be scarce" (Deut. 8:9). On a day
that was "sacred to the LORD" Nehemiah called on the people to "go
and enjoy choice food and sweet drinks" (Neh. 8:10). Ezekiel looked
forward to a great time in the future when among other things the
prince will "sit inside the gateway to eat in the presence of the LORD"
(Ezek. 44:3). In such a moment as the vision of God we would be
inclined to concentrate on some "spiritual" aspect, but when the elders
of Israel were given their great privilege "they saw God, and they ate
and drank" (Exod. 24:11). More could be cited, but this is enough for us
to see that in first-century Palestine a meal could have much greater
significance than it normally does with us. Food could be a symbol
pointing to many blessings, and when Jesus met the need of the great
crowd this pointed to him as the One who could supply their deepest
need.

The Gathering of the Crowd

John tells us that, following the events of chapter 5, Jesus went off to
the other side of the lake. His "after these things" (v. 1) is not precise. It

does not mean that what now follows took place immediately. John uses the expression with a meaning like "some time later." He gives the lake two names, "the sea of Galilee," which he follows with "of Tiberias." The former would be the name by which it was known in the Christian church and also in all probability locally. The other name would derive from the fact that on its shore there was a town named Tiberias, after the Roman emperor. This town was founded about A.D. 20, so it does not seem likely that people called the sea by this name during the lifetime of Jesus. It may have been the official name and the name by which it was known when John wrote his Gospel. For whatever reason, he gives two names for the body of water and thus ensures that his readers know what he is talking about.

John does not say much about it, but he refers to a sustained ministry of Jesus. His verbs in verse 2 are all continuous, and we would get the force of the statement if we understood it in the sense that the crowd "kept following him because they kept seeing the signs he continually did. . . ." John knows of a large number of miracles Jesus did, though he tells his readers of only a few. These he has selected for his own good reason (20:30–31), but incidental references like this show that Jesus did many wonderful things of which we know nothing. Jesus' compassion for the sick is specially to be noted.

As often in this Gospel, the miracles are called "signs." For John the important thing about the miracles was not the element of wonder, the fact that Jesus was doing things that people could not explain, but that these things were sign-ificant. They had meaning. They pointed beyond themselves. This does not mean that all the people who saw them saw them as signs. The people seem often to have been impressed by the element of the miraculous and to have followed Jesus simply because some of the things he did were so wonderful. John consistently takes the line that it is better to follow Jesus for some inadequate reason than not to follow him at all. But it is better to follow him for what he is, rather than because the signs were so wonderful.

On the occasion on which he is about to concentrate John says that Jesus went up "into the mountain" (v. 3). This expression may mean simply mountainous country in general, in which case the thought will be that Jesus went up from the land around the lakeshore into some more hilly place. But I am intrigued by his use of the definite article, "*the* mountain," especially as it occurs elsewhere (e.g., Matt. 5:1; Mark 3:13). I wonder whether there was some place that Jesus and his followers frequented, so that they spoke of it in this way. If so, we have no way of knowing where it was. But in any case the expression need mean no more than that they went into hilly country.

John adds a little time note. It was near the Passover, and for his Gentile readers he adds that this was a Jewish feast (v. 4). John has a great interest in the Jewish feasts; he has more references to them than has anyone else in the New Testament (he uses the word for "feast," *heorte*, seventeen times, whereas no other writer has more than three). He mentions three distinct Passovers and it is this that gives us the clue that Jesus' ministry lasted for about three years. John does not tell us why he mentions the feasts so often, but the probability is that he saw Jesus as fulfilling all that the feasts pointed to. The Passover was a memorial of a great deliverance in Israel's past, but Jesus would bring a greater deliverance and one available to people everywhere, not just those in one nation. At this point we might also reflect that the original Passover led to the wilderness wanderings and God's gift of manna to sustain his people. The manna will be before us later in this chapter, and the mention of the Passover may be in part to prepare us for this. In passing we may notice that in this verse we have three characteristic marks of John's style, a time note, a reference to a feast, and his mention of "the Jews."

The Problem

John concentrates his attention on the miracle. He does not tell us that Jesus had withdrawn with his disciples in order to be alone, nor that the multitude saw where he was going and followed, so that he spent the day in teaching them and healing those who were sick. He does not tell us that what he narrates took place at the end of the day. These things we find out from the accounts in the other Gospels. John starts at the point when Jesus looked up at the crowds and thought about feeding them.

He lets us see something of the difficulty in the situation by telling us of Philip's suggestion and of Andrew's finding of a small boy who had a little food. Philip was a native of Bethsaida (1:44), and we learn from Luke 9:10 that these things happened near that city. Thus Philip would be the logical person to know what food resources there were in the area and how they could be employed to meet the needs of the hungry people. John wants us to know, however, that this was not a serious attempt on the part of Jesus to obtain the necessary food supplies through Philip. Jesus knew what he was going to do. His question was apparently meant to show that there was a real problem. What he was about to do was to meet a genuine human need, which normal human resources were unable to satisfy. He was "testing" Philip, and the result of the test would be to show that from the apostle's point of view the problem was insoluble.

Jesus asked where they could get the bread, but Philip does not even try to answer that question. Instead he points to the sheer impossibility of feeding the people. They were, of course, in wilderness country. There were no bakers' shops and thus they could not buy bread. But Philip concentrates on the matter of purchase. If they had a lot of money (which presumably they did not) and if they were able to spend it all in buying bread (which in the circumstances they could not do), they would not have enough to give everyone a little taste (v. 7). That was Philip's contribution to solving the problem!

Plainly he had in mind a great deal of money, but just how much is not clear. Early translations often specified a number of dollars or pounds as the equivalent, but these days most do not. Presumably the fluctuations of currencies in modern times are such that any amount that sounds reasonably possible at the date of publication may be wildly erroneous a few years later. Philip specified two hundred denarii, and we can best understand his meaning if we reflect that one denarius was the normal wage for a workman for one day. It was the wage agreed upon, for example, by the owner of the vineyard and his workmen in Jesus' parable (Matt. 20:2). When we allow for Sabbaths on which men did not work, two hundred denarii would be the wages for something over thirty-three weeks, about eight months. When we put it this way we see that Philip was talking about a considerable sum of money.

Clearly he was not giving a possible solution but saying in effect, "It can't be done!" From another point of view so was Andrew, but his approach was not mathematical. Andrew is called Simon Peter's brother, just as he was when we first met him, back in chapter 1 verse 40. Again we see him in the shadow of his great brother. He may not have been an outstanding person and thus may be known more because of this relationship than from his deeds, but we should not overlook the fact that Andrew has a consistency of his own and that consistency is his bringing of people to Jesus. He did it at the beginning with his brother Simon and he does it now with a little boy.

John does not tell us who the boy was, nor how Andrew found him. He does not say whether the lad offered his lunch or whether Andrew persuaded him. Throughout this narrative John concentrates firmly on what he sees as the essential points and passes over a number of things that we in our curiosity would like to know. But his procedure means that the essence of the story stands out in massive simplicity.

The boy, Andrew told Jesus, had five barley loaves and two little fish (v. 9). We should not misunderstand the word *loaves*. Andrew is not referring to the kind of loaf that we might buy in a modern bakeshop. He is talking about something much smaller, like a roll or a biscuit or a scone (the different terminologies in different parts of the English-speaking world make it hard to find one expression that we can all understand; but it should be clear that it was a small piece of bread). John tells us (as the others do not) that these little loaves were made of barley flour. This was cheaper than wheaten bread, and it means that the little boy came from a poor family.

The word we translate "fish" is not the usual word for fish swimming in the water *(ichthus)*, but a word that really means prepared food, usually cooked food. It was used of anything eaten with bread and often of a "tidbit." But what was mostly eaten with bread was fish, and that is the meaning the word has in this place. The five little loaves and the two little fish were, it would seem, the provisions the boy had made (or had had made for him) for his own meal. Now he was offering it to Jesus. But, while Andrew is quite prepared to bring the boy and his offering to Jesus, he does not see this as anything of a solution to the problem before them. "What are these among so many?"

The Miracle

Jesus is not recorded as having said anything to either Philip or Andrew. They appear in the narrative simply to show the impossibility of meeting the situation from human resources and with human wisdom. Jesus began by getting the crowd seated (v. 10). We speak of being "seated," but of course the verb means "recline." At that time people reclined when they went to their tables for meals, and it was this posture that they naturally adopted when they used the grass as their resting place. John tells us that there was a good deal of grass in the place, so it would have been a comfortable enough posture.

John uses two different words for "men." The first time he has *anthropos*, which may mean "human being," and the second time it is *aner*, which may mean "husband." Some see a difference in the meanings here, with John first of all speaking of the totality of the crowd and then speaking of only the men as seated. But this seems highly unlikely (why would Jesus have the women and children stand?). If the change is significant, the meaning rather will be that, while Jesus told them all to recline, the number of men involved was five thousand. This would agree with Matthew's account, for that Evangelist expressly says that there were five thousand men apart from women and children (Matt. 14:21). But John often uses synonyms with no great difference in meaning and this may be another example. While he is certainly not contradicting Matthew's version, he may not be writing about the number of men apart from women and children, but simply varying his terminology.

John describes the miracle very simply. Jesus took the bread and gave thanks over it in the manner of any host beginning a meal (v. 11). Then he distributed it to the people and did likewise with the fishes. From the other Gospels we learn that it was the disciples who actually gave the food to the people. John, of course, does not mean that they did not do this and that Jesus did it all himself. But his way of expressing himself puts the emphasis on Jesus' action. It was what he did in multiplying the loaves and the fishes that mattered, not the actions of the disciples as he permitted them to share in the wonderful event.

John's verb for Jesus' giving of thanks is *eucharisteo,* and to some students it seems significant that he uses this verb rather than *eulogeo,* which is used in the other Gospels. John's verb was used in the early church with respect to the Holy Communion and indeed gave it one of the names whereby it came to be known, "eucharist." It is suggested that John wants us to see a reference to the Holy Communion here. But against that we should notice that Matthew and Mark have John's verb when they refer to the feeding of the four thousand (Matt. 15:36; Mark 8:6), so it has no particular application to this miracle. Further we must bear in mind that John never refers explicitly to the communion. While he has far and away the longest account of what went on in the upper room on Jesus' last night, he does not tell us that Jesus then began this service. Again, he uses the verb *eucharisteo* of Jesus' prayer of thanksgiving at the time he raised Lazarus (11:41). There is no reason at all for thinking of a sacramental reference here.

John goes on to say that Jesus gave the people as much fish as they wanted. A meal of bread and fish would have been very satisfying to those Galileans, and John goes on to speak of them as being "filled" (v. 12); this was no token meal but a substantial repast.

What Happened?

In modern times there has been a good deal of discussion of this miracle, and many scholars have asked the question "What really happened?" While a variety of answers have been given, three in particular stand out.

A favorite with those who are sceptical about Jesus' miracles in general runs like this. There was really plenty of food there, for many people had brought lunch packets with them. But they were selfish. They did not want to share with those who had nothing. So they all kept their food to themselves and refrained from eating. But when the little boy brought his lunch to Jesus they were all put to shame and began to produce their food and to share it. When this was done it proved to be enough and more than enough. Everybody had enough to eat and there was a good deal left over. This makes a big appeal to some, but it has the fatal objection that it is not what John says (or for that matter any of the other Evangelists). It originates in the fertile imaginations of modern people, not in the story told in the Gospels.

A second view is that what took place was something like a service of Holy Communion. It was not really that service, because Jesus had not yet begun it. But the suggestion is made that we have a kind of forerunner. Fellowship was important for Jesus and his followers, and eating together was a significant mark of fellowship. So it is suggested that from time to time Jesus may have had a token meal with his followers. They took a little piece of bread (and here of fish) and ate together as a sign of the fellowship they enjoyed before God. It is pointed out that the verb *eucharisteo* used here is that used of taking a token piece of bread in the communion and thus quite appropriate in a token meal. Again, Moses gave the manna and Elisha fed a hundred men with twenty barley loaves (2 Kings 4:42–44); it is suggested that it was proper that Jesus likewise be seen to be the provider of what was needed and that this was done in a symbolical way. But again it is important to see that this is not what the Gospels are telling us. This view originates in the mind of modern people, not in the Gospel story. There we read of people being "filled"; the meal was not a token, but a genuine reception of a satisfying quantity of food. And the verb *eucharisteo* simply means "to give thanks"; it has no necessary reference to food, nor to a small quantity. Its use proves nothing.

So we come to the third view. What happened was a real miracle. Jesus, being the incarnate Son of God, was able to do things that others cannot, and on this occasion he provided the food that was needed to satisfy the hunger of a large number in a way that we can only call miraculous. If we see Jesus as really God Incarnate, this will provide no difficulty. And if we do not so see him, then we will not see a creative act, whatever the evidence.

What Was Left Over

Jesus was able to use his powers to supply the needs of a great number of people. But that did not mean that he was indifferent to waste. He told the disciples to gather up what the people had left so that nothing be wasted (v. 12). Good food was important. It must not be lost.

When the disciples did this they filled twelve baskets with the pieces of food that remained over (v. 13). This shows plainly enough that John is talking about a miracle; it is astounding that there should be so much at the end when there was so little at the beginning. There is more than one Greek word for "basket," and some maintain that the word used here *(kophinos)* means a small basket, such as a traveler might use to carry his food. They contrast it with the word used in the accounts of the feeding of the four thousand *(sphuris)*, which they hold means a large basket; it could be large enough to hold a man, for it was in such a basket that Paul was lowered from the wall at Damascus (Acts 9:25).

But in fact the difference between the two words appears to refer to the material of which the baskets were made, not to size. The *kophinos* was made of stiff material, like wicker, whereas the *sphuris* was rather made out of some flexible material, like hemp. The *kophinos* may indeed have been small; but, if so, we gather this from the probability that the reference is to baskets that the disciples might have had with them to carry their food, not to the use of this word rather than another. John, incidentally, speaks only of fragments of the bread, but Mark makes it clear that there was fish to spare as well.

Prophet and King

The people were impressed. They may not have understood all that is involved in what John calls a "sign," but they did see that what Jesus had done was wonderful. So they gave their verdict, "Truly this is the prophet who is to come into the world" (v. 14). They do not speak of "a" prophet, but "the" prophet, which points us to that great prophet that Moses said would come in due course, a prophet like himself (Deut. 18:15–18). It is perhaps curious that they thought of Jesus as this prophet rather than as the Messiah, for the Jews in general seem to have distinguished the two (the Jews asked John the Baptist whether he was the Messiah, and when they found that he was not they asked whether he was the prophet, 1:20–21). But perhaps this group of Galileans was somewhat confused about the finer points of theology and put the two together.

Jesus saw that they wanted to make a king out of him, so he withdrew (v. 15). The Jews in general hated being under Roman rule and longed for the day when they would be free and would have their own king to rule over them. There is no doubt that many people of this time looked and longed for a militant Messiah who would lead an army and defeat the Romans. It would seem that the people who had just seen the miracle felt that Jesus would be just the man for this. If he could make five barley loaves and two small fish into a meal for thousands, what could he not do in the way of military supplies and army tactics?

But Jesus was not a king of that kind. He regarded the setting up of an earthly kingdom as a temptation of the devil (Luke 4:5–8) and he would have no part in it. He is king in the hearts of his followers, but that is a very different thing. The tragedy of these Galileans was that they tried to make Jesus into their kind of king. They did not get what they wanted and in the process they lost the kind of king Jesus really is. People still make that mistake. They insist that Jesus be the kind of king (or savior or whatever) that they want. They try to force him into a mold of their own choosing. They can never succeed, but while they are trying they lose the wonderful gift that Jesus is offering. Let us learn to see him as he is and to submit to his kind of kingship.

26

The Miracle
on the Sea

When evening came his disciples went down to the sea. They
embarked in a boat and were going across the sea to
Capernaum. It had become dark already, and Jesus had not yet
come to them. A strong wind was blowing and the sea was
rising. When they had rowed about twenty-five or thirty stadia
they see Jesus walking on the sea and getting near the boat.
They were afraid, but Jesus says to them, "I am. Don't be
frightened." They wanted to take him into the boat, and
immediately the boat came to be at the land to which they
were going (John 6:16–21).

Both Matthew and Mark have the story of the storm
and of Jesus walking on the sea right after the feeding of the multitude.
Their accounts are somewhat fuller than that of John and, for example,
Matthew includes the incident of Peter's walking on the water. Many
have found in John's account an edifying story meant to teach that
Jesus comes to us in our trials when we least expect him. It is edifying
and we may profitably engage in such reflections. But we should not
think of the story as a pious invention. A comparison with the other
Gospels leads us to see that John included the story at this point because it happened straight after the feeding of the five thousand. His
narrative is brief and lacks anything superfluous. He is apparently not

trying to point a moral but giving in the simplest terms a brief account of what happened. Many have pointed out that this story is a very suitable introduction to the teaching in John 6, but that is another matter.

The Disciples' Departure

The previous incident concluded with an attempt by some in the crowd to make a king out of Jesus, so that the Master withdrew into the mountain to get away from them. John says nothing about the disciples in that connection, but we learn from Matthew and Mark that Jesus "compelled" them to get into the boat and go across the lake. Their verb is a strong one; its meaning is given in Abbott-Smith's lexicon as "*to necessitate, compel* by force or persuasion, *constrain.*" Clearly Jesus was determined to get the disciples away from the scene as quickly as possible, and once in the boat they would have been effectively removed from the scene.

None of the Evangelists tells us why Jesus did this, but it is not hard to see. We know that the disciples were not immune from the temptation to see Jesus as a king like earthly kings. There was that occasion when James and John and their mother came to Jesus to ask that the young men might sit one on Jesus' right and the other on his left in his kingdom (Matt. 20:20–23). Even in the upper room at the very end of Jesus' earthly ministry, there was a quarrel among them as to which of them would be the greatest (Luke 22:24). It took the death and resurrection to teach them what sort of kingdom Jesus had in mind, but right up till then they were looking for some form of earthly empire. And they had the natural, healthy ambition of young men. Each wanted a big place in the kingdom when it came.

Many who profess to follow Jesus have surprising ignorance about what is involved. I am reminded of the new minister who in the Sunday school decided to ask a few questions to test the knowledge of the students. He asked one boy, "Who made the walls of Jericho fall down?" and received the answer "It wasn't me, and that's for sure."

The minister turned to the somewhat embarrassed teacher. "What do you think of that?" he asked.

"Tommy's a good boy," she said. "He doesn't tell lies. If he said he didn't do it, I believe him."

The minister thought his church council ought to know of the appalling incapacity of the Sunday school so that he could rely on their support in a program to improve matters. So he reported what had happened. They considered the matter and in due course sent the result of their deliberations to the minister: "We see no point in making an issue of this incident. It will be best simply to repair the walls. We are prepared to pay the cost and charge it up to vandalism."

The story is no doubt apocryphal, but it reminds us that people who call themselves Christians often show surprising ignorance of what they might be expected to know of the Christian way. The disciples in due course gave the church magnificent leadership, but at this point they were certainly lacking in a full understanding of what Jesus was doing for our salvation. At least some of them would have been glad to see him as an earthly king.

It is obvious that the kingmakers among the crowd who had been so impressed by the miracle would have had some active supporters among the apostolic band. The hotheads in the crowd and the hotheads among the disciples would have formed a strong alliance. Jesus wanted none of that sort of trouble and he sent the disciples off early. Without their involvement he dealt with the crowd and went back into the hill country. Accordingly there was no nonsense about starting a rebellion against Rome.

So as the day was ending the disciples came down to the sea. They got into their boat and started off across the water to go to Capernaum. John tells us that it was already dark and that Jesus had not come to them. But, if they were in the boat going across the water, how could he come to them? They were certainly not expecting him to join the boat in the middle of the lake, so these words are unexpected. It would seem that Jesus probably told the disciples to start off immediately and to put in at a certain place along the shore where he hoped to join them. But evidently the instruction included the provision that they were not to wait beyond a certain time. Getting rid of the kingmakers and going into the mountain country took time, so that Jesus did not in fact join them. So they set off across the lake without him.

A Storm

The sea of Galilee is not a large body of water, and there are some considerable mountains close by, which can cause strong wind squalls. It is possible for storms to arise suddenly and evidently that was what happened on this occasion. With a strong wind blowing and a rising sea, the voyage came to be a difficult one. Mark tells us that the wind was contrary and that would have made their rowing a hard task. Rowing is not the easiest of pastimes and rowing against a strong wind can be wearying. Clearly the disciples were in an unenviable situation.

John tells us that they saw Jesus when they had rowed about twenty-five or thirty stadia (v. 19; Mark simply locates the boat "in the middle of the sea," which is not precise but shows that they were still a long

215

way from land). A stadion was about six hundred feet. The lake was about sixty-one stadia wide at the greatest breadth, but they were not crossing at this point, so their voyage would have been somewhat shorter. How much shorter we do not know, because of our ignorance of their precise route. But they were certainly well on their way and may have been about three-quarters of the way across.

They saw Jesus. John's language becomes vivid and he uses the present tense: "They see Jesus, walking. . . ." It was near Passover, so that the moon must have been near to the full and thus there would be light. The wind may have blown up clouds and therefore we do not know how much light, but plainly there was no difficulty in seeing Jesus.

Walking on the Sea

According to most translations Jesus was walking on the sea, though perhaps we should notice that there are some scholars who think we should understand the Greek as "by the sea." They point out that the identical expression is found in 21:1 where it must mean "by the sea." They maintain that with twenty-five or thirty stadia covered the journey must have been nearly over. Further, at the end of the story, when the disciples wanted to take Jesus into the boat, "immediately" the boat came to be at the land. They suggest accordingly that there was no miracle and they see what happened in this way: The sailors were in a difficult position in a storm at sea and in fact were terrified. They thought they might well be wrecked; their lives were in danger. In the dim light they saw Jesus walking on the shore and in their over-wrought state thought he was walking on the waves. But, in fact, the reasoning goes on, he was not, and in a few minutes there they were on the shore, safe and sound.

But the matter is not as simple as that. The Greek preposition *epi* is rather like the English "on." The basic meaning refers to one thing being on top of another, though it is not impossible to use it of "being close by." Thus if you say, "I live on Fourth Avenue," you really mean that your house is beside Fourth Avenue; you do not mean that it is in the middle of the avenue. But the fact that "on" may have more than one meaning does not bother us. The context shows us which one is meant, and we cheerfully use the word in whichever way the need of the moment dictates.

So the fact that in 21:1 the expression means "by the sea" does not give its meaning here. We must take the context into account. It is relevant also to see what the other accounts say, and we find that Matthew has exactly the same expression as John. In his case the subsequent request of Peter that he be bidden to come to Jesus "on the waters" (Matt. 14:28) employs the same preposition *epi*, "on," which makes it very plain that in this story the meaning is "on the sea" and not "by the sea."

There is also the fact that the disciples were afraid. Some of them were skilled fishermen; their trade was to catch fish on that very lake. They knew it intimately and must have been familiar with its storms. There is no indication that their fear was due to the wind and the waves. It was the sight of Jesus getting near the boat when they were well out from land that scared them. Men do not approach ships in the middle of the sea, so it did not occur to them that this was their well-known and well-loved Master; they thought they were seeing a ghost (Mark 6:49). There is no reason at all for associating their fear with the storm; it was the sight of Jesus on the water that made them afraid. They could not explain it, and the unknown filled them with fear.

Reassurance

Jesus reassured them immediately (v. 20), though it is not quite certain how we should translate his words. The traditional way of doing this is "It is I" (KJV); the words simply identify the speaker. However we understand the passage, it certainly includes this. Jesus calmed his followers by assuring them that what they were seeing was no wild phantom, but their well-loved Master. And it is not easy to see how else he would say the equivalent of our idiomatic "It's me!"

But the words may have a further meaning; they are emphatic words, spoken in the style of deity. In the first volume of these *Reflections* we had occasion to notice that in Greek it is usually not necessary to use the personal pronoun to indicate the subject of a verb. We are familiar with this in our use of the English word *am;* the only possible subject of "am" is "I." The Greeks took this a lot further. Their verbs normally showed (by the forms they took) what the subject was. So they did not use the pronoun as a general rule. But if they wanted to emphasize the subject, if they wanted to say "*I* am" rather than "I am," they used the pronoun.

But there was a difference when they came to set down divine speech, the words of God. The Old Testament is, of course, written in Hebrew, but in time it was translated into Greek, and it was this Greek translation that was normally used at any rate by Jews outside Palestine and often by those inside it. When the translators came to words of God they apparently thought that these should be translated differently from the words of men. They tended to use the emphatic form with the pronoun "*I.*"

It is this emphatic form that John uses here. It is not improbable that he wants us to see Jesus as using the kind of speech that is appropriate to God. It would all fit in. The storm that could not conquer or even impede him, the fear of the disciples, the help he was about to bring them, his coming to them walking on the water as men cannot do, all these things made the language of deity appropriate. John may well have felt that in the circumstances it was only right that he should convey to his readers the fact that Jesus was more than a man, and accordingly he used the language of deity. He does this a number of times (8:24, 58; 13:19; 18:5, 6; cf. Exod. 3:14; Deut. 32:39; Isa. 41:4; 43:10, 25). It is beyond doubt that sometimes John uses the words to hint at the truth that Jesus was more than a man, and it may well be that he is doing this here.

It is this expression that calms the fears of the disciples and forms a suitable introduction to the "bread of life" passage that follows. There again Jesus uses this form of words and there it is made plain that he fully meets the needs of his own.

The End of the Story

John goes on to say that the disciples wanted to take Jesus into the boat. That is very natural, but did they do so? John does not say so, though some translators are so sure that they did that they translate that way. Mark tells us that Jesus went up into the boat and that the storm ceased (Mark 6:51). John may well mean this, but it is curious that he does not say so in set terms. However, the difficulties if we suppose that Jesus did not enter the boat are so many that few adopt that understanding of the passage. We should understand that Jesus did get in with the disciples, even though we cannot explain why John does not say so explicitly.

Then he adds "immediately the boat came to be at the land to which they were going" (v. 21). Does this mean that there was another miracle? It is possible to take the words as meaning there was not. Those who see no miracle, of course, welcome this statement. For them it indicates that the disciples were closer to the shore than they thought, and as soon as they recognized Jesus they found themselves safely arrived at land. But we have seen that this is not a good explanation of what John says. He may mean, however, that the coming of Jesus put new heart into the rowers. Before he came they had been disheartened with their hard rowing against a fierce headwind. Now that they had him on board they bent their backs and it was not long before they found themselves at their destination. This would be all the more likely if we bear in mind what Mark tells us about the cessation of the storm. That would have made their work so much lighter.

But many commentators think John means that there was a second miracle. Godet puts this well: "One can scarcely imagine, indeed, that, after an act of power so magnificent and so kingly as Jesus' walking on the waters, He should have seated Himself in the boat, and the voyage should have been laboriously continued by the stroke of the oar? At the moment when Jesus set His foot on the boat, He communicated to it, as He had just done for Peter, the force victorious over gravity and space, which had just been so strikingly displayed in His own person."

This does appear to be what John is saying (cf. Moffatt, "so they agreed to take him on board, and the boat instantly reached the land they were making for"). We are reminded of Psalm 107, which speaks of God's care for sailors, who see God's "wonderful deeds in the deep" (v. 24). God stills storms and delivers them from their distress, but specially important are the words "he guided them to their desired haven" (v. 30). It is something like this overruling care of God of which John is writing.

Through the centuries this passage has been a source of comfort and strength to God's troubled people. We all go through the storms of life, and these can be discouraging affairs when we are tried to the limit of our strength. It is good to know that at all times we are the objects of God's love and care and that in his own way and in his own time he brings us through our trials.

We should also reflect that Jesus comes to us in ways we do not expect. When the sailors were tossed about on that boat there is little doubt that some of them at any rate thought, "If only Jesus were with us!" That would be just what was needed. He would find some way of seeing them through. But when he came he came in a way that they did not expect, and instead of welcoming his appearance they were frightened. And is that not sometimes our experience, too? Jesus often comes to us in the guise of "one of the least of these, his brothers," and we do not expect to see him like that. Sometimes he comes to us in trials and difficulties, and we do not expect that either. It is well that we look for the spiritual perception that will enable us to recognize him and to welcome him in whatever guise he comes. One thing is certain. The Christian way is full of surprises, and Christ constantly comes to us in ways that we do not anticipate. Unless we welcome him, however he comes, our spiritual experience will always be the poorer.

27

Manna from Heaven

And when they had found him on the other side of the sea (the people) said to him, "Rabbi, when did you get here?" Jesus replied, "Truly, truly, I tell you, you seek me out not because you saw signs, but because you ate of the loaves and were filled. Do not work for the food that perishes, but for the food that remains into eternal life which the Son of man will give you; for him did God the Father seal." They said to him therefore, "What shall we do in order to work the works of God?" Jesus replied, "This is the work of God that you believe on him whom he sent." So they said to him, "What sign do you do then so that we may see it and believe you? What do you work? Our fathers ate the manna in the wilderness as it is written, 'He gave them bread from heaven to eat.'" Jesus said to them then, "Truly, truly, I tell you, it was not Moses that gave you the bread from heaven, but my Father gives you the true bread from heaven. For the bread of God is he who comes down from heaven and gives life to the world" (John 6:25–33).

Curiously the crowd asks Jesus, "When did you get here?" (v. 25). John has told us that they were puzzled about what boat he could have come in, and we might have expected them to ask, "How did you get here?" Indeed, so strong is that expectation that some commentators say that this was what they did ask. We know that it was the significant question. If they had asked that and understood the answer, they would have been in a better position to understand who Jesus was. But like so many of us they asked the wrong question (like the little girl who saw some ballet dancers cavorting on their toes and asked, "Mummie, why don't they just get taller girls?"). They had the opportunity of finding out something wonderful and instead asked only about the time.

Jesus' reply is a solemn one, preceded as it is with the "Truly, truly." This expression indicates that what follows is important, sometimes that it is not what the hearers would expect. Jesus points out that his hearers were not really interested in "signs," sign-ificant happenings, events that showed that God was at work. These people had had a splendid free meal and it was this that made them interested in Jesus. But they had not asked themselves, "What does it mean? What does it tell us about Jesus and about what God is doing in Jesus that he is able to do such a wonderful thing?" If they had given consideration to the sign, they might well have learned an important spiritual lesson and have come to believe in Jesus. Throughout this Gospel faith that is based on the miracles is never seen as the highest kind of faith, but it is better than no faith at all.

But these people did not even have that kind of faith. They were interested in having their hunger satisfied, and it was that that kept them talking to Jesus. It was their need as they themselves saw it and not as Jesus saw it that occupied their whole attention. It is easy to make the same mistake. Most of us are so sure that we know what we need in this life that we pursue it single-mindedly and never stop to ask whether it is this that is important, this that matters in the sight of God.

The food in which these people were interested was a perishable commodity. There was nothing lasting about it. They had had a good meal of bread and fishes but now they needed another meal. Their very hunger was evidence that the food of which they were thinking has no lasting results. They should not keep working for what is at best temporary (v. 27). The verb *work* has a continuous force. Jesus is saying that they are constantly working for what is not lasting.

Guy de Maupassant has a story about a young woman in modest circumstances who was invited to go with her husband to an important function. Not having suitable jewelry, she borrowed a necklace from a rich friend. Unfortunately somehow the necklace was lost and the young couple were in despair. The wife, however, found a duplicate in a shop and, though it was very expensive, bought it with borrowed money so that she could return it to her friend. Then she and her husband had to work for years to raise the money to repay the loans. When they had at last succeeded it happened that one day quite by chance she met her friend and on an impulse told her what had happened. The friend replied, "But my necklace was paste; it was worth only a few francs!"

That is a parable about life for many people. They labor for the food that perishes, for that which has no permanent value. Like the couple in the story they give the best years of their lives in working for what is worthless.

Eternal Life

Jesus counsels his hearers to look instead for "the food that remains into eternal life." There are things that last, and they are more important than the transient things on which we spend so much time and energy. Jesus' words form an unusual Greek expression that appears to combine two meanings: the food of which he is speaking is forever in contrast to the perishable food that so preoccupied his hearers, and further it gives eternal life to those who receive it. While Jesus invites the people to concentrate on this food, he does not say that by doing so they will merit eternal life. Eternal life is his gift. It comes in no other way.

The Father has "sealed" Jesus. In antiquity a seal was much more important than it is with us (even when we allow for the importance of the seal in some commercial transactions). It was an age when many people could not read. It was thus useless to write one's name on one's property. Since the rascals who would be tempted to take what was not theirs could not read, they did not know whose it was. Thus an important man used a seal. He had a device, a representation of a bull or another animal or perhaps some geometric design, something that was distinctive. With a signet ring or the like this mark could be impressed into a soft material like wax, which retained the design when it hardened. The potential wrongdoer could see the design and know what it meant. He might be very wary about tampering with the property of a powerful man.

The seal, then, was a mark of ownership. But it was used more widely. It might be affixed to a document, for example, and then it gave attestation. The man who affixed his seal by that fact declared his agreement to what was in the document. It was a mark of approval.

Jesus is saying, then, that God the Father has given his approval to him. The word order in the original is of interest: "him the Father sealed, the God." While we frequently read of "God the Father," this is the only place in the New Testament that has the order "the Father, God" (8:41 is slightly different). It is not clear why the unusual order is adopted, but we should see at least that Jesus is saying that his Father is none less than God. That God has given his seal means that we are not to think of Jesus as simply a peasant from Nazareth giving an interesting personal point of view on certain religious matters. He was one with God and God was at work in him. The seal means that God has given his mark of agreement, of approval. It is an error to dismiss Jesus as no more than just another man.

That brought from his hearers the question "What shall we do in order to work the works of God?" (v. 28). The fact that they asked the question indicates that they had some real interest in serving God. The fact that they put their whole emphasis on what they themselves would do indicates that they had not understood what Jesus was telling them. Like many people through the centuries they were firmly convinced that their salvation depended on what they themselves did. They put their trust in their own strong right arm. They ask "what shall we do?"; they say "to work the works." They entirely overlook the fact that Jesus has just said that the Son of man "will give" eternal life. Eternal life is a wonderful thing, so wonderful that none of us can ever merit it, no matter how hard we try or how great our human achievement. It is always a gift.

Jesus answers their question in terms of faith. They had asked about working "the works" of God; Jesus replied by speaking of "the work" of God (v. 29). The singular is important, for as Jesus told Martha one day, only one thing is needed (Luke 10:42), and that one thing we find here is "that you believe on him whom he sent." God has chosen to work out our salvation in the life and death and resurrection of his Son, and there is no other way. If we are to have eternal life, we must put our trust in the Son. Characteristically the Son is here described as "him whom he sent." It is important that Jesus was not engaged in some self-chosen activity, but that he was on a mission; he had been sent by God. Both the Father and Son are interested in bringing eternal life to sinners, and it is not possible to separate them. So Jesus speaks of believing in such a way as to involve the Father as well as the Son.

The Manna

That evokes a question about a "sign" (v. 30). It is curious that these people, of all people, should ask, "What sign do you show us?" for they had just seen a marvelous sign in the feeding of the multitude with a few loaves and fishes. They could also have known of the walking on the water if they had made inquiry among Jesus' disciples. And Jesus indicates that they had seen a number of miracles as his plural "signs" (v. 26) shows. It scarcely seems that they would need a further sign.

But that is what they ask for. "What sign do you do," they ask, "so that we may see it and believe you? What do you work?" (v. 30). They imply that if only Jesus produced a satisfactory "sign" they would believe him. Of course, had he done so, they would doubtless have found some other reason for not believing. As Ryle put it, "It is want of heart, not want of evidence, that keeps people back from Christ." But they persuaded themselves, and tried to persuade Jesus, that all that was needed was the proper "sign" and they would become believers. Such a demand was made more than once (Matt. 16:1; Mark 8:11–12; Luke 11:29), but Jesus always refused it.

On this occasion Jesus' interrogators pointed to the manna in the wilderness as the kind of thing they had in mind (v. 31). When the Israelites passed through the wilderness they had problems getting enough food, and Scripture tells us that God met their need, sending them each day (except the Sabbath) "thin flakes like frost on the ground" (Exod. 16:14). The name *manna* was given to it (from the Hebrew for the question they asked, "What is it?"), and we are told that it "was white like coriander seed and tasted like wafers made with honey" (Exod. 16:31). This daily gift lasted through the forty years of the wilderness wanderings (Exod. 16:34–35). The manna was called "bread from heaven" (Exod. 16:4; cf. Ps. 78:23–25).

There was an idea among the Jews that God would send the manna again in the latter days. "It will happen . . . that the treasury of manna will come down again from on high, and they will eat of it in those years" (2 Baruch 29:8). Very importantly, there was an idea that the Messiah would be associated with the renewal of this gift. "As the former redeemer [i.e., Moses] caused manna to descend, as it is stated, *Behold, I will cause to rain bread from heaven for you* (Ex. XVI,4), so will the latter Redeemer cause manna to descend, as it is stated, *May he be as a rich cornfield in the land* (Ps. LXXII,16)" (Ecclesiastes Rabbah I.9).

Plainly the Jews who talked with Jesus had something like this in mind. They read of the manna in their Bible and they looked for the Messiah to be in some respects a second Moses. So they thought that he would accredit himself by bringing down the manna from heaven. The Jews were not content with the sign that Jesus had given. They demanded that the sign be the one that they wanted.

This is a natural human tendency. We seem always to want things our own way. I was reading of a man who went into a restaurant in Sydney and ordered from the seafood list a big mud crab. When the dish arrived the diner found that it had only one claw so he asked why that should be. The waiter explained that these crabs are very pugnacious and often engage in fights in some of which claws get torn off. This crab had clearly had a misfortune in fighting another crab. The diner immediately pushed the plate aside and demanded, "Bring me the winner!"

The Jews were a bit like that. They were not content with what they had seen Jesus do, but demanded what they thought would be something better. In their judgment the Messiah must produce the manna. It did not matter whether the Messiah thought that or not. They were sure that they knew what the Messiah would do. It is easy to put a human limitation on what God must do. We must all learn that God does things his own way, not the way we lay down. We would have thought that Jesus' feeding of the great crowd of people from such limited resources would surely be the kind of miracle that must accredit him. But quite plainly the Jews found it insufficient. After all, Moses fed a whole nation; Jesus merely five thousand people. Moses fed them for forty years, whereas Jesus had given them only one meal. Jesus supplied ordinary bread and fish, while Moses gave them "bread from heaven" and, since there is none of that available for sampling, there is no limit to what people can imagine about its delicacies.

True Bread from Heaven

Jesus refutes the position they were taking up. Again he begins with the emphatic "Truly, truly" (v. 32); what follows is important. He points to three errors they had made and he gives the correct position:

1. Moses did not give the gift; God did.
2. God's gift is not only in the remote past; he gives now.
3. The bread from heaven that matters is a spiritual gift; it is not something physical like the manna. They were in error in looking for such a gift.

It is always a mistake to confuse the divine Giver with the earthly instrument through whom he makes his gift. Moses was a faithful servant of God, but it was not in him to supply the manna and in fact he never did. He simply told the Israelites what God would do and passed on God's commands concerning its use.

And it is important to see that God's gifts continue. It was said of one great man that he believed in a God who lived until the days of Oliver Cromwell. Many of us have an attitude something like that. We do not doubt that God once worked in this world. We are sure that he acted among men in Bible days and we are ready to take that a little further. God attested the preaching of the early missionaries with miraculous signs. Some of us take that down perhaps to the Reformation and think of the way God used spiritual giants to set forward his purpose. Others of us come closer to modern times, depending on whom we see as people through whom God delighted to act in days gone by. But when we look at our own problems and the problems of our church in the modern turmoil and the needs of our modern world, it seems so much easier to concentrate on what people can do and are doing. But that is not a Christian position. Jesus is teaching us that God is a present reality. Continually he gives his good gifts. Continually he acts in the fulfillment of his purpose.

But the most important part of Jesus' answer is that in which he says "the bread of God is he who comes down from heaven and gives life to the world" (v. 33). He speaks of "the bread of God" rather than "bread from heaven," thus putting emphasis on the Giver. But the really significant thing is that the gift is Christ himself, "he who comes down from heaven." The Greek could be understood either as "he who" or as "that which." It is likely that the Jews took it in the second sense, for they were thinking of a material kind of food. But Jesus was speaking of himself, and he points them to the deeper truth that the real heavenly bread concerns a person. God has supplied the need of his people by sending them, not something to eat like the manna, but a Savior.

The Savior "gives life to the world." The manna could satisfy bodily hunger, but it could not give life to the dead. Jesus can and does. Throughout this Gospel there is an emphasis on the gift of life. Sometimes it is spoken of as "eternal life," sometimes, as here, it is "life." There is no great difference. Jesus brings to us the life of the world to come and makes it a present reality.

28

Living Bread

They said to him, then, "Sir, give us this bread always." Jesus said to them, "I am the bread of life. He who comes to me will never hunger and he who believes in me will never thirst, never. But I told you that you have both seen me and not believed. All that the Father gives me will come to me and him who comes to me I will certainly not cast out, because I came down from heaven not to do my own will but the will of him who sent me. And this is the will of him who sent me that I should not lose any that he gives me, but raise it up at the last day. For this is the will of my Father, that everyone who sees the Son and believes in him may have life eternal and I will raise him up at the last day" (John 6:34–40).

The woman at the well did not understand what the living water was, but she asked Jesus to give it to her all the same (4:15). The crowd was a little bit like that. They certainly did not understand that Jesus was himself the living bread, but he had been speaking of bread from heaven and they apparently liked the sound of it, even if they did not really believe in its reality. They may even have been a bit sarcastic when they asked that they might be given the heavenly bread always (v. 34). They had spoken to Jesus of the manna, and it may be that they had in mind something of the kind. When the Messiah came the gift of the manna would be renewed, and Jesus claimed to be the Messiah. "Let us ask him, then, for the food from heaven" seems to be the way they were thinking. "Let us see whether he can give us the bread he is talking about!" The manna had been a constant source of supply, and, while Jesus had done something wonderful in giving a meal to five thousand people out of five loaves and a few fishes, if he were the Messiah he would be able to keep it up. So they ask not only to be given the food, but to be given it always.

"I AM the Bread"

Jesus' reply shows that the gift is not to be separated from the Giver. He is himself the bread of which he has been speaking. When we were considering the walking on the water we saw that in Greek the expression "I am" with the emphatic personal pronoun is the style of deity (p. 217). It is this that we have here. Jesus is claiming that he can give a great gift, and his form of words indicates that he is big enough to give such a great gift. He does not say, "I am divine," but this form of words is such that the perceptive listener will understand what he is saying about himself.

Dr. G. Campbell Morgan links this passage with that which tells of Moses at the burning bush. There that patriarch asked the name of him who spoke to him out of the fire and was told, "I am who I am. This is what you are to say to the Israelites: 'I AM has sent me to you'" (Exod. 3:14). Dr. Morgan thinks that on this occasion Jesus "took the name of the burning bush, and linked it with the symbol of perfect sustenance for human life. 'I am the Bread of life.' Thus He employed the simplest of terms, with sublimest significance." Whether or not there is this definite link with the burning bush, the words certainly convey a high claim.

This is the first of seven great "I AM" sayings in John's Gospel, some of them repeated with slight variations. Jesus says emphatically that he is "the light of the world" (8:12), "the door" (10:7, 9), "the good shepherd" (10:11, 14), "the resurrection and the life (11:25), "the way, and the truth, and the life" (14:6), and "the (true) vine" (15:1, 5). This is a tremendous series of claims, and together they point to someone who is far greater than any mere man. Clearly John has gathered a collection of sayings that show very plainly that the Savior of whom he writes is one with God.

Jesus, then, is "the bread of life." This "I AM" saying is repeated with several variations. Thus we read, "I am the bread that came down from heaven" (v. 41); "I am the bread of life" (v. 48); "I am the living bread" (or "the bread which lives," v. 51). We also have some variations on the theme of bread without the "I AM," as "the bread of God is he who comes down from heaven" (v. 33), and "this is the bread which [or who] comes down from heaven" (v. 50). There are many facets to this teaching. Common to them all is the thought that, just as bread is basic to sustaining this bodily, physical life, so is Jesus basic to the eternal life of which this Gospel says so much.

We should notice that "bread of life" could be understood in more ways than one. The genitive "of life" is not precise, but means something like "a 'life' kind of bread." This might mean bread that gives life or bread that is itself alive. Both are true, and in the Johannine manner it may be that we are meant to understand both.

Jesus adds a statement that brings out what receiving the bread of life means. Interestingly he does not say "He who eats it" but "He who comes to me" (v. 35). He is talking about a spiritual experience, and our earthly metaphors do not describe it with precision. There are more ways than one of putting it. If we use the metaphor of food, then bread is to be eaten, and Jesus speaks a little later of people eating the living bread (v. 51). That is the way they get life. But the life of which Jesus is speaking is a spiritual life and is to be understood in terms of knowing God and Jesus himself (17:3). To know him we must come to him, and this is the way Jesus puts it here. We should not try to put fine distinctions between these various ways of expressing it. They are all ways of saying that eternal life is a gift of God and that it comes through Jesus Christ.

Here Jesus explains it in negative terms: the person who has this life will never be hungry or thirsty. Both expressions are emphatic, with the use of the double negative. The one who comes to Jesus will certainly never hunger; the bread he imparts is completely satisfying. Bread normally has nothing to do with thirst, but eating and drinking go naturally together, and thus Jesus adds the information that this person will never thirst either. In any case he has earlier said that he gives the living water (4:10, 14). This expression is even more emphatic than the one that tells of the bread; in addition to the double negative there is added an adverb, which with a negative means "never, not at any time." Jesus is affirming in the strongest terms the satisfying nature of the life he brings.

Elsewhere Jesus speaks of those who "hunger and thirst after righteousness" (Matt. 5:6), but the emphatic denial that believers will ever hunger and thirst is not in contradiction. In Matthew Jesus is speaking of the yearning that is an inevitable part of entering into the salvation of God. When we know something of his righteousness we long for more. It is so wonderful that we cannot do otherwise.

But this is not inconsistent with a deep satisfaction. It is this of which Jesus is speaking in the present passage. When our soul's deep need has been satisfied we are delivered forever from the emptiness and dissatisfaction that are an inevitable part of the life of the worldly, who may rebel from time to time. They attempt to find alternative lifestyles in the face of the frustration and the futility of so much in modern communities. But in the end such rebellion is rarely successful. As Augustine put it in his prayer: "Thou hast made us for Thyself and our hearts are restless till they rest in Thee." It is in this sense that our need is met in Christ. We still long for more and more knowledge of him. But the world's restlessness has gone forever.

The Will of God

Jesus has been speaking of the wonderful gift of life that those who come to him receive. Now his "but" introduces a strong contrast (v. 36). Those to whom he was speaking had not believed in him, had not come to him, and accordingly they had not received the life he was offering. He says that he had "told" them, though it is not clear when. Some think he is referring to verse 26, but it is perhaps more likely that he is speaking of some quite different (and unrecorded) occasion. What he emphasizes is that they saw him, as indeed they were still seeing him, but they did not understand who it was they were seeing. For them he was just another man, and they put no trust in him. Their failure to believe was the critical factor that cut them off from the blessing he was offering.

Perhaps the reason was that they were not included in "all that the Father gives me" (v. 37). There is mystery here. The New Testament consistently teaches that our salvation is the gift of God. It is not that we do something and then God is able to do something. It is not that God stands on the sidelines, a helpless spectator until we decide that we would like to believe, and only then does he come into the process. No one can come to Jesus unless the Father draws him (v. 44). From first to last our salvation is something that God brings about. That is what is in mind when Scripture refers to predestination. It is the divine activity that is the first and most significant thing.

But, along with this, Scripture affirms our responsibility. We are called on to repent and believe. We are warned that those who do not put their trust in Christ will inevitably perish. Nowhere do the Bible writers give the impression that the saved are just automatons, moving like puppets when the strings are pulled. We are responsible people and must one day give account of ourselves.

Both these truths receive emphasis, but nowhere, I think, do the Bible writers attempt to bring them together. That is not one of the things that has been revealed. And Christian theologians have not been conspicuously successful when they try to harmonize them. They usually emphasize one group of passages at the expense of the other. I suspect that the problem is too big for our little minds.

Here Jesus is not giving a reason for the Jews' lack of faith but assuring those who come to him of the warmest of welcomes. When he speaks of what the Father gives, his word *all* is neuter (= "everything") where we might expect the masculine "everyone." The construction (which occurs elsewhere in John) puts emphasis on the universal application of the words. There is no exception. "All," then, that the Father gives to Jesus come to him, but it is the Father's gift that is important. Without that they would not come.

When they come Jesus always receives them. Again we have an emphatic double negative: "him who comes to me I will certainly not cast out." We may come in confidence, knowing that the Giver and the Receiver of the gift are at one.

In this world this is not so. There was the small boy who just after Christmas went to Macy's in New York to exchange a doll that had been given him as a Christmas present for some water pistols. There was no problem with the exchange, but the assistant asked, "Who would give you a doll?" To which the boy replied, "My uncle. He always does. He thinks I'm a niece!" We constantly make misjudgments of one sort or another, and our gifts do not always work out as we would like. John is telling us that this is not so with the Father and the Son. When God's gift is made to the Son it is always received. "I will certainly not cast him out."

Such casting out is unthinkable because the whole reason for the incarnation was that the Father's will be done. We should not think of Jesus as somehow setting up his will as something distinct from that of the Father and then going ahead to do what his own will suggested. No. He came to do the will of the Father. There is no disunity there.

The divine will is further explained. Not only does Jesus not reject anyone who comes to him, but he sees to it that no such person is lost. This is the will of God, and because it is the will of God Jesus sees to it that it is done. We should be clear that there is no disunity in the Godhead and that our salvation is a matter in which both Father and Son are involved. Sometimes in the history of the church believers have overstressed the activity of one or the other. Some have been so impressed with the love of the Father that they have given the impression that all that is necessary for our salvation is that we repent and believe. God will not let us down. And Jesus is not brought into the picture at all.

Others have gone to the opposite extreme. They have seen God as a mighty God, a righteous Judge who will certainly punish all sinners. Since we are certainly sinners, that means that we are in trouble. Into that picture comes the compassionate Son who interposes himself between the wrathful Judge and the doomed people. We are saved from the Judge because the Son loved us enough to die for us and take on himself the consequences of our sin.

Both these pictures are caricatures of what Scripture says. It is God who so loved the world that he sent his Son. And it is Christ who died on the cross for our salvation. When we believe, it is the Father who has chosen us and drawn us and the Son who never casts us out. We should be clear that both the Persons are involved in the work of salvation. It is the will of God, who sent his Son into the world, that none of those he gives to the Son be lost.

This is all sheer grace. It is not like the lawyer who was rather fond of lecturing his son. The young man, in pursuit of his aim to be a lawyer, in due course worked for his dad during vacation periods. One day the father happened to overhear the lad talking to one of his friends. "I hear you'll be working for your father these holidays," said the friend. "How much is he paying you?" "Three thousand dollars" was the reply. "Seventy bucks a week and the rest in legal advice."

God's good gift is not like that. In his grace he freely gives to sinners what they could never merit, never obtain from their own resources. He gives freely, generously, without finding fault.

The Last Day

Jesus says that he will raise up the saved person on "the last day" (v. 40). He speaks about the last day several times in this chapter (vv. 39, 40, 44, 54); it is an expression found only in John in the New Testament. John puts a good deal of emphasis on present salvation and present judgment. He sees both as operative in the world here and now, and from this some have drawn the conclusion that he is interested only in the here and now. It may well be that he sees more importance in what happens in this life than do some other writers, but it is a mistake to think that this is all he is concerned with. We saw when we were looking at chapter 5 that he looks for a day when Christ will call the dead from the tombs. And here he is sure of a day that will end this world and usher in the life to come. He is equally sure that the believer has nothing to fear when that day comes. Jesus will raise him up, and he will go in to the fullness of the life of the world to come. Far from salvation in this world being all that there is, John looks forward to the end of the world and to Jesus as the one who will raise the redeemed and bring them into life eternal.

This part of his Gospel is greatly taken up with the will of God, and it comes out again here. Life eternal is the will of God. Jesus spoke previously of God as having sent him, now as "my Father." The two, of course, go together. It is because he is the Father (with all that this means) that he sent the Son. It is because he sent the Son that we see what it means that he is the Father.

The saved person here is the one "who sees the Son and believes in him." It is not common to have "seeing" connected with salvation. The Jews were earlier blamed for having "seen" Jesus and not having believed (v. 36). They saw Jesus but they did not appreciate the significance of Jesus. It may be something like this that is meant here. Jesus wants people to see him for who he is, to have the heavenly vision that is inseparably linked to faith. With the grace of God at work, and with this vision and this faith, the result is life eternal. And as in the previous verse this is linked with being raised on the last day. The resurrection of believers is important, and Jesus repeats it. Eternal life is wonderful here and now. But we should not think that its meaning is exhausted in this life. Its full unfolding awaits the life of the world to come.

29

The Flesh and the Blood

"This is the bread that comes down from heaven in order that anyone may eat of it and not die. I am the living bread that came down from heaven. If anyone eats of this bread he will live forever and the bread that I will give is my flesh, for the life of the world." The Jews therefore began to argue among themselves, "How can this fellow give us his flesh to eat?" So Jesus said to them, "Truly, truly, I tell you, unless you eat the flesh of the Son of man and drink his blood you have no life in you. He who eats my flesh and drinks my blood has life eternal and I will raise him up at the last day. For my flesh is true food and my blood is true drink. He who eats my flesh and drinks my blood abides in me and I in him. As the living Father sent me and I live because of the Father, so he who eats me, that one will live because of me. This is the bread that came down from heaven, not such as the fathers ate and they died. He who eats this bread will live forever" (John 6:50–58).

Throughout this discourse Jesus has continually referred to himself as "bread," and here the thought is that, in contrast to the manna by which the Jews set such store, he came from heaven. Despite the fact that the Jews spoke of the manna as "bread from heaven," it was not genuinely from heaven. It did not exist in heaven before they received it. It could be spoken of in terms of heaven only in the sense that it was God, the supreme heavenly Being, who sent it to them. But its entire existence was here on earth. Its total function was to sustain earthly life, and it did even that only partly, for the whole wilderness generation (with the exceptions of Joshua and Caleb) died before they reached the Promised Land.

Jesus is bringing out the fact that his hearers had some serious misconceptions about the manna. They did not understand its limitations: those who ate it necessarily died in due course. It only delayed death. And they did not understand that the gift he was offering them was incomparably greater: those who received it would never die. It overcame death. Jesus says that the bread of which he is speaking came down from heaven "in order that" *(hina)* those who eat it may not die (v. 50). That bread is given in order that it may be eaten.

We must not think that it does not matter to God whether people are saved or not. It is the very purpose of his sending of the Son that people enter life. So now Jesus says that his coming to earth is for the purpose of bringing people into salvation. The meaning of "die" here is different from that of the same verb in verse 49. There the point is that in the wilderness the manna was not able to sustain life indefinitely. Those who ate it died in due course. But the bread of life of which Jesus speaks is different. Those who eat this bread have eternal life. They never die. They do, of course, die in the sense that they complete this earthly, physical life. But their reception of the bread of life means that they have been given the life that is eternal, the life that goes on in the age to come and never has an ending, the life that is of a different quality from ordinary, worldly life, for it is the life proper to the age to come. In the sense of spiritual death they will not die.

Once again Jesus speaks of himself as "the living bread" (v. 51) though this time with a slight difference, for he speaks of the bread as "living," and not of "the bread of life." In this Gospel there are many occasions when a word or a phrase is repeated with some slight change but with no apparent difference in meaning. It is a mark of John's style; that is the way he writes. So we should not look for any great significance in the fact that he now speaks of "living" bread, whereas he previously referred to "the bread of life." It perhaps ties in the thought that life is specially associated with Jesus (cf. 1:4; 5:26) a little more clearly, but we can scarcely say more. To eat of this bread is to live forever. We have here a typical example of Johannine emphasis. In verse 50 he says will "not die"; here it is will "live forever." He puts the negative and the positive side by side to reinforce one another in such a way as to leave no doubt about the point he is making. The living bread means to its recipient life and not death. Let there be no misunderstanding about this. The kind of life of which the Jews were thinking is not life in the full sense. The kind of life Jesus was offering is.

"Flesh"

Now comes one of Jesus' "hard" sayings: "the bread that I will give is my flesh" (v. 51). It would have been easier for the Jews (and for us) if the bread of which Jesus is speaking were to be understood in a purely "spiritual" way. Then we could think that Jesus is claiming to be a prophet, one who comes with a heavenly message, such that those who receive it will have a profound spiritual experience and find themselves alive with a vibrant new form of existence. There is, of course, a measure of truth in this, but it is not what Jesus is saying. He uses the harsh, strongly physical word *flesh*. He could have said "my body," as he did when he began the service of Holy Communion. He could have said "myself." But he chose to use the word *flesh*, which puts a strong emphasis on this physical corporeality. It was this body of flesh that Jesus would give for the life of the world.

Some see a reference to the Holy Communion here, but it is not easy to see this in the words Jesus used. As we will see a little later, this is not the way the early church referred to that sacrament. Jesus is referring to Calvary, not to any liturgical service, no matter how solemn.

He will give his flesh, he says, "for the life of the world." The preposition "for," *huper*, is one over which there has been a good deal of dispute. Some scholars hold that it means no more than "on behalf of," and they contrast it with *anti*, "in place of." But this is too simple. There is no doubt that *huper* can be used in the general sense of "on behalf of." It is used in this way, for example, when Jesus says, "Pray for those who persecute you" (Matt. 5:44), or that he who is not against us is "for us" (Mark 9:40).

But the word can convey a substitutionary meaning, as when one person does something "in the place of" someone else. This is common in the papyri, when one person says he is writing *huper* another. The second person is illiterate; he cannot write the letter himself, so someone else writes it in his place and in his name. However we choose to translate it, in such a context it means substitution. This usage is undoubtedly found in the New Testament, for example when Paul writes to Philemon and speaks of Onesimus serving *huper sou*, "in your place" (Philem. 13).

There seems not the slightest doubt that John has this usage. He tells us that the Good Shepherd gives his life "for the sheep" (10:11, 15). He reports the words of Caiaphas that it is expedient that one man die "in the place of the people" (11:50) and goes on to explain that in this way the high priest prophesied that Jesus would die "for the people . . . and not for the people only" (11:51–52) but in order to gather together God's people into one. John reminds his readers of this when he characterizes Caiaphas as he who said it was expedient that one should die in the place of the people (18:14). He has Peter's statement that he would lay down his life "for" Jesus if need be (13:37) and Jesus' question with the same expression (13:38). He tells us that Jesus said there is no greater love than to lay down one's life for one's friends (15:13) and that the Lord in his prayer spoke of sanctifying himself "for" his own (17:19).

From all this there seems to be no doubt at all that John sometimes uses the preposition in a substitutionary sense. That is the way we should take it in the present passage. When Jesus gives his flesh "for" the life of the world he is speaking of his death in the place of sinners, that death that would give life to the world.

Not surprisingly, the Jews found this a difficult saying. However, there was not unanimous opposition, for they "argued" or "disputed" among themselves (v. 52). It was not easy to see how Jesus could die "for the life of the world," and some of them spoke of him contemptuously as "this fellow." If anyone could do something "for the world," they apparently thought, it would not be this man. So they argued.

Eating the Flesh and
Drinking the Blood

This led Jesus to repeat what he had just said, but in a stronger form. He prefixes what he has to say with "truly, truly," which we have seen before is a way of putting emphasis on what follows and marking it out as important and significant. He goes on to speak not simply of his giving of his flesh or of their eating the bread of life, but of eating his flesh and drinking his blood (v. 53). This is the sort of thing that would arouse horror in a pious Jew, who would not even eat meat in his daily food unless the blood had been drained from the carcass. But Jesus says that apart from this eating and drinking there is no life. It is a strong and emphatic statement.

This passage is held by many to refer to the Holy Communion. John has no account of the institution of this service, but his language in this part of the Gospel, with its references to eating the flesh and drinking the blood, seems to many people to be so much like the language of the communion service that this must be the equivalent. They think that for reasons of his own John has omitted the institution but has given his teaching about the sacrament in this chapter. Usually no evidence is cited for this. It is taken as axiomatic; the language is held to apply obviously to the communion service, and that is all there is to it.

But there are difficulties with this position. One is that, despite the confident assertions, the language is not that of the Holy Communion. There one reads of eating the body, here of eating the flesh. The difference may not be great but it is real. The early church did not speak of "flesh" in the communion service, but of the "body." It is sometimes said that Ignatius used "flesh" in this connection, but not much can be made of this because of the way this gentleman used language. Thus he says, "I desire the bread of God, which is the flesh of Christ," which many take to refer to the communion. But Ignatius goes on immediately, "and for a draught I desire his blood, which is love incorruptible." The language looks like the communion at first, but the context is concerned with martyrdom, not liturgy, and in any case the ending shows that Ignatius is simply using metaphors to bring out spiritual truth.

There is a similar problem with his statement that "the eucharist is the flesh of our Savior Jesus Christ," which looks explicit enough. But then Ignatius says, ". . . which flesh suffered for our sins, and which the Father of his goodness raised up." He also speaks of the gospel as "the flesh of Jesus" and of faith as "the flesh of the Lord." It is clear that Ignatius does not use "flesh" as a way of referring to the communion. He uses it in a wide variety of ways, most of which are metaphorical.

The Christian writers of antiquity tend to use "flesh" as a way of referring to the incarnation, as when Justin Martyr spoke of Christ as "having been made flesh by the Word of God." When they refer to the Holy Communion they speak of the "body" of Christ. I do not mean that no example at all can be found of the use of "flesh" in this connection. I mean that such usages are very hard to find and must be thought of as distinctly exceptional. We cannot take the use of "flesh" in John 6 as obviously a reference to the communion. It would be a most unusual way of referring to the sacrament, one completely without parallel in the New Testament and extremely hard to document in the early church.

Even more significant is the strength of Jesus' language. He says that without the eating and drinking of which he speaks "you have no life." It is very difficult indeed to think that Jesus is saying that the one thing necessary for eternal life is to receive the Holy Communion. That would be out of harmony with his teaching in all four Gospels. But here his language is unqualified in any way. He allows of no exception. This is the one way into life. To take the sacramental view of this passage is to say something very serious, for it would disqualify from eternal life whole communities like the Salvation Army and the Quakers and a significant proportion of Christian families, and children who have not yet been admitted to Holy Communion. Those who accept the view I am criticizing should examine the calamitous consequences of their interpretation.

They should also bear in mind that the Jews of that day often used the language of eating and drinking when they wanted to refer to taking teaching into their innermost being. It is easy to listen to a teacher's words in a superficial way. We may say, "What a fine teacher!" but take no notice of what he says. We may perhaps say of someone who profits from the teaching that he takes to heart what he has heard: the Jews of the day spoke of eating or drinking the teaching (do we not sometimes also speak of "drinking in every word"?). For example, there is a rabbinic treatment of Proverbs 25:21: "If your enemy is hungry, give him food to eat; if he is thirsty, give him water to drink." This is said to mean: Resist your enemy "with the bread of the Torah [i.e., the Law of God], as you read 'Come, eat of my bread' (Prov. 9:5); and 'if he be thirsty, give him water to drink'—the water of the Torah, as in the verse, 'Ho, everyone that thirsteth, come ye for water' (Isa. 55:1)." Such statements could be multiplied. The word of God is often likened to food or drink, which must be taken within oneself.

Jesus is then using language that people would appreciate and understand as something quite different from Holy Communion. He has already spoken in this discourse of people coming to him as the bread of life (v. 35) and of believing in him (vv. 40, 47), and he is saying much the same when he invites his hearers to take him into their innermost being. There is the addition in this part of his address that the separation of flesh and blood points to his death, as do different words in 3:16. He is saying that he will die for the people and inviting people to feed on him in a heavenly and spiritual manner.

Those who here see a reference to Holy Communion do not explain why Jesus should have given teaching about that sacrament to a group of Jews who were largely antagonistic to him, and moreover why he should have given it long before he instituted the service. They could not possibly have understood him, and Jesus surely intended his audience to understand what he was saying.

Life

For such reasons, then, we must reject the view that Jesus was talking about the Lord's Supper in this passage. We could say that he was speaking of how people should receive him and that when we understand this we can say that this, too, is how we should receive him when we receive the communion, i.e., by faith. But we can scarcely say more.

Jesus is saying, then, that his death is the one means of salvation and that we appropriate his dying for us when we come to him in faith. That is the one way of salvation, for unless we receive him in this way we "have no life" in us (v. 53). This is a strong and emphatic statement. The cross is at the heart of the Christian way, and it is only by the death of Jesus that we are able to enter into the life he died to bring.

In a way characteristic of this Gospel we have the negative, "unless you eat . . . and drink . . . you have no life," followed by the positive, "He who eats my flesh and drinks my blood has life eternal" (v. 54). The twofold form of expression puts emphasis on the truth being stated. We are left in no doubt that the life of which Jesus is speaking comes only in this one way. Without the eating and drinking, we have no life. If we eat and drink, we have life. That is the great, central truth that Jesus is bringing out throughout this entire discourse.

There is a different verb for "eat" in this verse, and we see it again in verses 56, 57, 58. Strictly it applies to a noisy eating, like "munch," and some have held that it must mean a literal feeding and thus refer to Holy Communion. But this makes no sense. It is nonsense to say that the word means literal eating and that therefore we must understand eating the flesh of Jesus to mean eating the communion bread. The communion bread is not literally the flesh of Jesus. To hold that it is his flesh is to abandon the literal meaning. John often uses words of similar meaning without significant difference of meaning, and we must see the same thing here. The change of verb is a point of style, not a change of meaning.

"I will raise him up at the last day," Jesus says (v. 54). In much of this Gospel there is the precious truth that eternal life is something that we enjoy right now. It is a very wonderful part of the Christian way that the moment we believe we enter into life and that in this eternal life we have the constant presence of God with us, whatever our circumstances. It has been the strength of many a Christian in troubled circumstances that he knows that God is with him and will never leave him. That is true and it is important. But it is not the whole story. John also has the thought that at the last day Christ will raise all his people, and he has that thought here.

True Food

Jesus goes on to say that his flesh is "true food" and his blood "true drink" (v. 55). There have always been people who have offered as spiritual sustenance that which does not sustain. In this very chapter we read of people who suggested that the manna that came down in Moses' time was bread from heaven and that if Jesus really was the

Messiah, he would provide bread like this. But the manna was not food for the soul; it did not give eternal life. In the fullest sense it was not "true" food. It sustained the body but did nothing for the soul. The bread that Jesus is offering is different. It is the true food that we all need and that will sustain us eternally if we receive it.

Yet once more Jesus refers to eating his flesh and drinking his blood, this time connecting it with the thought of abiding (v. 56). John delights in the language of "abiding" and has the verb forty times in all. We see something of how important it is to him when we notice that Matthew has this verb three times, Mark twice, and Luke seven times. Clearly it is an aspect of Christianity that appealed to John and to which he kept coming back. It is important that Christians do not simply have a fleeting contact with Jesus but that we "abide" in him, just as he "abides" in us. We do not know what life has in store for us. There may be wonderfully happy experiences or terribly depressing ones before us. We have no way of knowing. But we do know that as our trust is in Christ we will always be in him and he will always be in us. That will increase our joy in the happy experiences, and it will give us strength in our times of difficulty. John's thought of abiding is a part of Christianity that we cannot do without.

This leads on to another characteristic Johannine thought, that of mission. The living Father sent Christ (v. 57). This runs through this whole Gospel, though not usually with that exact language. But Jesus is speaking about life, and it helps us to see that God is "the living Father." We are not to think of some dead idol, but of the living God, who is himself alive and is the source of all the life that others live. We are alive physically only because the living God gives us physical life, and we are alive spiritually only because the living God gives us spiritual life. That living Father is so interested in giving us spiritual life that he sent his Son into the world to live and to die for us.

Jesus says that he lives "because of the Father." This may be understood in more ways than one. There is the sense that it is the Father who has life in himself and he has given to his Son also to have life in himself (5:26). The life of the Father and the life of the Son are inseparable. There would be no life in the Son if there were no life in the Father. We cannot put a difference between them, for example, by appealing to the one against the other. They belong together.

There is also the sense that on earth the incarnate Son lived to do the will of the Father. That is his necessary food (4:34). It is unthinkable that he should be busy about anything but his Father's business.

Which leads to the thought that this should be our business, too. Notice that Jesus speaks now not of eating his flesh and drinking his blood but of eating him, but the difference in meaning is not great.

There is still the thought of taking him into our innermost being. When we do that we will enter into the experience of living for Christ in the same kind of way that he lives for the Father. Both aspects will be true for us. We owe our spiritual life to him; it is not something we achieve by our own efforts. And when we have that gift of life we will live to do service to Christ. We will live "because of" him.

Jesus ends his discourse by repeating the main thought in a slightly different way (v. 58). His hearers had been obsessed with the manna and wanted the Messiah to bring it down from heaven again. Jesus has told them that they have the wrong idea, and he does so again. The bread from heaven is not the manna. Israel of old had that food and Israel of old died in the wilderness. The true bread from heaven of which Jesus has been speaking throughout this discourse is different. Anyone who eats this bread "will live forever." Real bread from heaven has nothing to do with the sustaining of physical life, as his hearers wrongly thought. It is concerned with something infinitely more important: eternal life, life that is a wonderful gift of God now and that will gleam and glow through all eternity.

30

The Spirit Gives Life

Many of his disciples, therefore, having heard this said, "This saying is a hard one; who can hear it?" But Jesus, knowing in himself that his disciples were muttering about this, said to them: "Does this trouble you? If then you see the Son of man going up where he was before—? It is the Spirit who gives life; the flesh profits nothing at all. The words that I have spoken to you are spirit and they are life. But there are some among you who do not believe." For Jesus knew from the beginning who they were who would not believe and who it was who would betray him. And he said, "For this reason I told you that no one can come to me unless it be given him from my Father."

From this many of his disciples went away backward and no longer walked with him. Jesus therefore said to the Twelve, "You don't want to go away, do you?" Simon Peter answered him, "Lord, to whom should we go? You have words of life eternal and we have believed and have known that you are the Holy One of God." Jesus answered them, "Did not I choose you, the Twelve? And one of you is a devil." He was speaking about Judas, son of Simon Iscariot, for this man was going to betray him, being one of the Twelve (John 6:60–71).

Let us begin this study by noticing that John often speaks of "Jesus' disciples" or "his disciples" or the like, and that this is a mark of earliness. When Jesus was alive there were all sorts of rabbis who had disciples, so those who followed him were marked off from all

243

others by some expression that showed that they were following him and not someone else. When the church had settled down and Christians spoke of "disciples," there was no need to say whose disciples they were, "*the* disciples" being, as Bernard puts it, "a Christian phrase which no one would mistake." The earlier expression is found at times in all the Gospels, and John almost invariably has it.

Many disciples found what Jesus had been saying in the discourse about the bread of life a "hard" saying. This probably means "hard to accept" rather than "hard to understand." Some of the sermon is not easy to comprehend, but the real difficulty does not lie there. As Calvin put it, "The hardness was in their hearts and not in the saying." They had their own ideas about the way to God and they were not going to be shaken out of it.

I am reminded of the very modern boy who went off to Sunday school. When he came home his mother asked what he had learned. "Well," he said, "we had a story about Moses. God sent him behind the enemy lines to rescue the Israelites from the Egyptians. When they got to the Red Sea Moses called for the engineers to build a pontoon bridge to get them across. When they were all over Moses saw the Egyptian tanks coming. Quick as a flash he sent headquarters a message on his walkie-talkie radio, asking them to send dive bombers to blow up the bridge. They did and the Israelites were saved."

His rather dazed mother inquired, "Is that really the way your teacher told the story?"

"Well, not exactly," admitted her offspring, "but if I told it the way she did, you'd never believe it!"

We're all inclined to be a little bit like that. We have a firm idea of how God should act, and we persist in seeing his actions the way we imagine them instead of listening to what in fact he has chosen to do. That was the way it was with Jesus' hearers that day in Capernaum. They were sure of the way God acted. Were not they and all the Jews the people of God? Had he not sent his prophets to their nation? Did they not have fine official interpreters of his word? Jesus, they thought, could not possibly be believed when what he said contradicted their understanding of the way God acts. They did not say all this openly, but "muttered" to themselves (as is still often the way with the discontented). But Jesus knew.

The Son of Man Going Up

"Does this trouble you?" he asked (v. 61), where his verb is a picturesque one taken from the practice of trapping birds or animals. The trap would be set with a stick (called a *skandalon*) propping it open.

244

When the bird sat on the stick and moved it the trap was triggered off and the capture made. The verb *skandalizo* means "to trigger off the trap," and it is this verb that is used here (as in a number of places in the New Testament; it is difficult to find a satisfactory English equivalent, and there are many suggestions: "to cause to stumble," "to offend," and others). Matthew and Mark have this verb often, but John has it only twice (again in 16:1). Jesus perceived that what he had said meant trouble, not enlightenment, to his hearers. They would not accept it; they could not imagine that Jesus was in fact the one way of salvation. So they did not accept what he was saying. They found his words too difficult.

Jesus poses a question for them (v. 62), and there is a problem for us in that he does not complete it. Evidently they were able to fill in the missing bit whereas we, from a different background, find it hard to do so. Our translations put in something to make the sentence grammatical in English. Thus the King James Version inserts "What": "What and if ye shall see . . . ?" (similar are NIV, JB, NEB, RSV; GNB has "Suppose, then, that you should see . . . ?). But Jesus says no more than "If then you see . . . ." but leaves his hearers to work out for themselves what would be the result of their seeing. He speaks of the Son of man "going up where he was before." This must refer to his going back to heaven, for Jesus has made it clear in the discourse just ended that he came down from heaven (vv. 33, 38, 41, 42, 50, 51, 58). There seem to be two possibilities. He may be saying in effect, "If you see me returning to heaven, will you not be troubled even further?" Or he may be saying, "If you see me returning to heaven, will not that solve your difficulty?" But there are problems with each interpretation.

Both seem to refer to the ascension, but John does not record this. And if we turn to Luke's accounts of the ascension, it is plain that it was not seen by very many and evidently was not intended to be seen by the public at large. It was apparently meant to give encouragement to the disciples, not to bring conviction to unbelievers. So it is hard to think that Jesus means that the ascension, as such, will be the means of persuading these unbelievers of the truth of his words. But it is not much easier to think that he is saying that the ascension would bring them more trouble. Why should it?

Perhaps we should see the "going up where he was before" as a kind of shorthand summary of the climax of Jesus' way of saving us. It would then include the cross, the resurrection, and the ascension in one great saving act that culminated when Jesus went back to where he was before. This would make it easier to see their being troubled, for to unbelievers it was only the cross that registered. They could not conceive of anyone who was crucified as having the approval of God.

245

Rather, they thought of crucified people as being accursed (in accordance with Deut. 21:23).

Neither view is completely satisfactory. But we should bear in mind that it is only when Jesus has died for sinners and risen and been exalted to heaven again that we can see him for what he really is. Until then, people could have no more than a partial view of who he was and what he stood for. Unbelievers would see the cross and stop there. It was necessary to believe, if people were to see that the cross leads on to the resurrection and the ascension. And it was necessary to believe, if people were to understand what "the living bread that came down from heaven" means. Whatever else Jesus' words mean, they are a reminder that faith is necessary if we are to understand what he is saying and doing. And they are an appeal for that faith.

The Spirit and the Life

Jesus' next words pose a difficulty of a different sort. He speaks of "Spirit" and "flesh" (v. 63), and this would lead us to think of the contrast between our spirits and our bodies. But he speaks of the Spirit as giving life, and that must mean the Holy Spirit, for our human spirits do not give life. But Jesus also speaks of his "words," and this may point to the "spirit" of what he is saying, as against the literal meaning of the words. Plainly several contrasts are possible, and it seems likely that John expects his readers to see more than one of them.

It is clear in the first place that Jesus is saying that life is the gift of the Holy Spirit. This is in accordance with, say chapter 3, with its insistence on the necessity for being born of water and the Spirit, or simply born of the Spirit. It forms a marked contrast with that aspect of rabbinic teaching that insists that it is the Law that gives life. Thus we read, "Great is the Law, for it gives life to them that practice it both in this world and the world to come" (Mishnah, *Aboth* 6:7). Jesus is saying that life is a gift from God. We have life in the most meaningful sense only when the Spirit of God works within us to produce that life. This is a thought to which John gives expression a number of times (see 3:5f., 8; 4:23f.; 7:38f.), and it is of central importance. People always like to think that they can bring about their own salvation by their own efforts. But it cannot be done. The whole purpose of Jesus' coming to earth was to undo the effect of our sins, and the eternal life he made available to us is effected by the work of the Spirit. The "flesh," which is the best of which we are naturally capable, "profits nothing at all." There is no life in it.

Jesus goes on to speak of his words as "spirit" and as "life" (there is a somewhat similar connection in 3:34). We are not to think that a wooden literalism is the way to profit from Jesus' words. We should not take the attitude to them that the Jews so often took toward the Law. But his words, rightly received, bring about the wonderful transformation. As we take in Jesus' words, see them as they are, the words of God (8:26, 28; 12:49f.; etc.), and respond to them, we find new life from the working of the Spirit within us. It is only as we accept the words of Jesus that we know the life that the Spirit gives.

There is an unusual repetition of the verb *are* in this verse. We would have expected "are spirit and life," but we have "are spirit and are life." This means that "spirit" and "life" are not to be regarded as the same thing. They are distinct. It also means that there is some emphasis on "are." Jesus is talking about facts. We should not take the expression to justify a scheme of allegorical interpretation. This has been beloved by many pious people through the centuries, and it is astonishing what meanings some still find in the Bible by allegorizing difficult passages. Jesus is not justifying such approaches. He is saying that his words are creative. Take them as they are meant and they bring about new life in the believer. The Spirit and the words of Jesus are to be seen as in the closest connection.

Unbelievers

But while Jesus thus offers eternal life to those who hear him, he knows that there are unbelievers listening to him (v. 64). They will not respond. The life of which he has been speaking is not for such people. But these words show that the fact that some did not believe did not take Jesus by surprise. He knew that this would be so, and he knew who they were who would not believe.

It is a little surprising that John says at this point that Jesus knew who would betray him. The thrust of the discourse has been on life, on Jesus as the bread of life, and on the importance of receiving him, of believing in him, of eating his flesh and drinking his blood. All this makes it clear that the life of which Jesus speaks is not a gift made to all. Believing is of fundamental importance. And it is important that Jesus was not deceived by an outward profession. He accepted Judas into the apostolic band, but that does not mean that he did not know what sort of person Judas was.

The problem of Jesus' knowledge in this Gospel is not an easy one. Sometimes it is clear that he did not have knowledge of a particular point and asked a question to find out (e.g., 1:38; 18:34). But on other occasions he had unusual knowledge (e.g., his knowledge of the woman of Samaria's five husbands, 4:18). It seems that his perfect humanity meant that there were areas in which, like all mankind, he was ignorant and had to find out in the same way as others. But there were areas of life in which his unique mission demanded unique knowledge, and such knowledge was given to him. So now we find that he knew who would not believe and specifically knew of Judas's future treachery. Judas would surprise the apostolic band in due course, but he would not surprise Jesus.

This brings us to a repetition of the thought we met earlier in this discourse, that it is not a human achievement to come to God (v. 65; see v. 44). Left to ourselves we continue in our sin. It is only as God does a work of grace in us that we have the desire and the strength to turn away from evil and respond to the message of salvation. People come to Jesus, not because they are gifted with unusual spiritual perception, but because it is "given" them from the Father. The whole of our salvation, from start to finish, is a gift of God.

Backsliders

"From this" (v. 66) is ambiguous. It may mean "from this time" or it may mean "arising from this," "because of this." Either makes good sense and perhaps, in the Johannine manner, both are in mind. Up till this time there had been many who had followed Jesus. Here was a new teacher with some fascinating things to say. And he did some amazing miracles. He was certainly worth following. So the crowds were there. But this last discourse has made it abundantly clear that Jesus was not just another rabbi. He did not teach in the way people expected, and in particular his claim to have a special relationship to God and to be the only one who could bring life to sinners proved a stumbling block to many of his hearers. So they ceased to applaud and simply left him. They were not the genuine article and did not appreciate teaching from God when they heard it.

Knowing the genuine article is not always easy. There was an art student who was a bit lost in an exhibition of abstract and cubist works. But he felt that he should get something out of such a fine exhibition to improve his collection and further his acquaintance with this form of art. Some pieces did not appeal to him and some were out of his price range. But then his eye lighted on a work of striking simplicity. There was a black dot on a field of white, framed in brass. He hailed an attendant and asked, "How much is that?" "That, sir, is not for sale," the attendant replied. "It's the light switch."

It is easy to be pretentious without having a genuine appreciation. It was that way with some of the people who followed Jesus. But when in the end they found out something of what he was driving at they left him. John says they "no longer walked with him," which gives us a little glimpse of Jesus' peripatetic ministry. He walked with his disciples. But these people ceased to walk with him.

The Twelve

That raised the question of how far this movement of backsliding was going to go. So Jesus asked the Twelve whether they wanted to join it (v. 67). In Greek it is possible to put a question in such a way as to show whether a negative or a positive answer is expected, and Jesus' question looks for the answer "No." He was confident of his close followers. He looked to them to remain, and though the question had to be asked in view of the defections, he expressed in it his expectation that they would remain. His "you" is emphatic: "Whatever be the case with others, *you* will not go away, will you?" is the thrust of it.

The question is addressed to them all, but as often happened it is Peter who is the spokesman. He has a question of his own, "Lord, to whom should we go?" (v. 68). He and the other apostles had had enough experience of Jesus by this time to be sure that they did not want anyone else. It was unthinkable that they should abandon their fellowship with him for anything else on earth. Jesus had spoken of his words as life-giving, and Peter shows that he and his friends had understood this: "You have words of life eternal." The words that repelled the halfhearted followers were full of meaning to committed believers, and they pointed to a life with Jesus that believers could not think of abandoning.

Peter goes further. "And we have believed and have known," he says, "that you are the Holy One of God" (v. 69). He uses the emphatic pronoun *we:* whatever be the case with others, *we* have believed. The Twelve have made their decision. In both the following verbs Peter uses the perfect tense. The thrust of this is that they have come to a place of faith and they remain in it; they have come to a state of knowledge and remain in it. Peter is emphasizing the certainty he and his friends had, a certainty of both faith and knowledge. They had put their trust in Jesus, and that meant that they would not abandon him as these halfhearted people had done. Their loyalty was beyond question. They also had knowledge. When people come to know Christ they have a piece of knowledge beyond price. To know him is to lose the uncertainties that are so much a part of worldliness.

"The Holy One of God" is a most unusual expression. In fact, it is used of Jesus on only one other occasion, when a demon-possessed man used it in the synagogue at Capernaum (Mark 1:24; Luke 4:34). It occurs occasionally in the Old Testament, as when Aaron is spoken of in a similar way (Ps. 106:16), but it reminds us of the frequent expression "the Holy One of Israel," which is a way of referring to God. There cannot be the slightest doubt that as Peter used it he gave it the fullest possible meaning. It was a way of showing that he and his friends put Jesus in the highest place they knew. This is one of the high points of John's whole Gospel.

Judas

Jesus knew that what Peter said was true, but that it was not true of the whole Twelve. These were the men that Jesus had chosen, and the implication is that they, of all people, might be expected to be faithful. But even here all was not sweetness and light. "One of you is a devil" (v. 70). John speaks of Judas as having his place in Satan's schemes (13:2) and of Satan as entering him as he went about the betrayal (13:27). He was clear that Judas acted in such a way as to set forward the purposes of evil; he was not wholeheartedly committed to Jesus even though he was numbered among the Twelve.

John adds his own words of explanation. He tells us that Jesus was speaking about Judas, and he speaks of him as "son of Simon Iscariot" (v. 71). The word *Iscariot* is apparently a place name meaning "Man of Kerioth," and it thus applies equally to Judas and to his father. We know of two Kerioths, one in Judah (Josh. 15:25) and another in Moab (Jer. 48:24). Either way it would mean that Judas was not a Galilean, apparently the only one of the Twelve of whom this could be said.

John adds his reference to the betrayal, not implying that Judas had this in mind so early, but as saying that the thing that marked Judas out was the fact that in the end he betrayed Jesus. In the Greek there is a touch of certainty about it. That is what Judas would do in due course. The enormity of this is brought out with the words "being one of the Twelve." It was bad enough that anyone should betray Jesus, but that one from this intimate group should do it is horrible beyond words. It is worth noticing that this is the worst thing any of the Evangelists says about Judas. Nowhere do they speak of him as a wicked villain or anything of the sort. They simply record what he did and let the facts speak for themselves. They are interested in letting their readers know what happened, not in passing their own verdict.

31

The Feast of Tabernacles

After this Jesus was walking in Galilee, for he would not walk in Judea because the Jews were trying to kill him. Now the feast of the Jews, the Feast of Tabernacles, was near. His brothers therefore said to him, "Leave here and go into Judea so that your disciples may see the works that you do, for no one does anything in secret and seeks to be known publicly. If you are doing these things, show yourself to the world." For even his brothers did not believe in him. So Jesus says to them, "My time has not yet come, but your time is always present. The world can't hate you, but it does hate me because I testify about it that its deeds are evil. You go up to the feast; I am not going up to this feast because my time is not yet fulfilled." When he had said these things he remained in Galilee (John 7:1–9).

After this" (really "after these things") gives no indication of how long a time had elapsed; it is an indefinite interval. But the previous chapter has been taken up with what happened at Passover time, and this goes on to the Feast of Tabernacles, which we know took place six months later. John is not trying to give a full account of Jesus' ministry. He selects the incidents that will further his purpose and is quite capable of passing over considerable intervals of time without saying anything about them. He tells us those things that will help us see that Jesus is the Christ, the Son of God, the things that will help us believe (as he tells us in 20:31). And he passes over without comment quite long stretches of Jesus' ministry that do not fit his purpose.

The repeated use of "walking" gives us a little glimpse of the way Jesus lived. His ministry was not confined to any one place and he kept moving among the people. But he traveled in the humblest way: he walked. He did not ride in a chariot or even on a donkey. He walked from place to place and those who traveled with him must walk, too.

Notice further that his walking at this time was done in Galilee, not Judea, on account of the hostility of "the Jews." This avoidance of Judea was not due to lack of courage. When the time came Jesus would go up to Jerusalem and die for us all. But he would do this in his own good time. Till the proper moment he would not rush headlong into danger. That was not the way in which the purpose of the heavenly Father would be set forward. John is not saying that Jesus would not go to Jerusalem at all before it was time for him to die. John will go on in this very chapter to tell us that Jesus did go up to the capital to observe the Feast of Tabernacles. He is saying that Jesus was aware of the dangers that beset him and that he acted accordingly. If he chose to go to Jerusalem at this time, he must do so with proper caution.

John Calvin has an interesting comment. He says that it was not right for Jesus to rush into danger but also that "He did not turn aside a hair's-breadth from the course of His duty." This Calvin sees as having a moral for us as we seek to serve God. We too may have to face danger, and we will be tempted to put a high value on our lives. In such a situation he warns us that "we must always beware that we do not for the sake of life lose the purpose for living." That is good advice still.

John uses the expression "the Jews" in more ways than one. Sometimes it is used in a good sense, as when he says, "Salvation is from the Jews" (4:22), and sometimes it is neutral, as it is here when he speaks of "the feast of the Jews." But mostly he uses it to denote the Jews who were hostile to Jesus, especially the leaders of the Jews in Jerusalem. They were "the Jews" *par excellence*. So it is here, when he speaks of "the Jews" as trying to kill Jesus. This does not mean all the Jews, for Jesus himself was a Jew and so were his disciples and those who followed him. But the Jewish leaders, those who were outstanding Jews, were hostile to Jesus and were the ones who were seeking his death. So Jesus stayed in Galilee.

But the danger was very real. John repeatedly speaks of the attempts being made to kill or arrest Jesus (7:1, 13, 19, 25, 30, 32, 44; 8:37, 40, 59). He has concentrated in these two chapters a good deal of what he has to say about the hostility of the leading Jews to our Lord. It seems that in the early days of his ministry the crowds flocked around Jesus. They loved to listen to the new teacher from Galilee and to see the miracles he did. But then, as we saw in chapter 6, they came to understand something of the demands he made on his followers, and they did not like them. So their ardor cooled. The Jewish leaders saw in Jesus a man who might well claim to be the Messiah and in the process start a rebellion that would bring trouble on the province. So they opposed him vigorously.

We saw at the beginning of this study that it was John's aim to show that Jesus was the Messiah. He seems to have used the Jewish hostility to bring out the objections that were urged to Jesus' messiahship and to show that there were answers to every objection urged. Chapters 7 and 8 are thus an important part of the way John accomplished his aim.

The Feast

John proceeds to tell us that the Feast of Tabernacles was near and speaks of it, not as "a" feast of the Jews, but as "the" feast (v. 2). It was the great occasion in the Jewish festal year. Modern Christians are apt to miss this. The feast about which we hear most in the Gospels is the Passover, and when we read about the feasts in the Old Testament it is Passover that grips our attention. It leads us into the fascinating story of the way God delivered his people from their captivity in Egypt, with the suspense built up through the call of Moses, the series of plagues, and the departure of the people in haste when they had observed the first Passover. There is nothing of the kind in connection with the other feasts in the Jewish ecclesiastical year. The result is that we think of Passover as the outstanding occasion of the year.

But that was not the way it seemed to first-century Jews. They did, of course, delight to observe the Passover. That was a perpetual memorial of God's wonderful deliverance of their fathers and of their emergence as a nation. Nothing should be said that would for one moment diminish the splendor of the occasion. But the high point of their year was not there. It was the Feast of Tabernacles. We see what it meant when we reflect that the Hebrews of the Old Testament were an agricultural people. Their lives were closely bound up in the sequence of the seasons. Passover, it is true, was one of the three great festivals for which males were required to appear before the Lord (Exod. 23:17), but the other two were the Feast of Harvest, when the firstfruits were brought in, and the Feast of Ingathering or Tabernacles, when the harvest was completed (Exod. 23:16). It was the great feast at the culmination of the year's activities. At any earlier time there might be a calamity that would prevent the harvesting of the crops, but Tabernacles marked the successful completion of their labors. The harvest was in the barns; the people could relax and rejoice. It was *the* feast for an agriculture people.

The name "Tabernacles" was due to the custom of celebrating the feast in leafy shelters built for the occasion. These might be in courtyards or on the flat roofs that were so common. Goodspeed translates "the Jewish camping festival," which may help us see something of the attitude people would take to this feast, though we should also bear in mind that it had deep religious significance. It was a thanksgiving for all God's mercies in the harvest and the provision that this meant for all the coming year. Living in temporary shelters put rich and poor on a level while the feast lasted and reminded worshipers that all are of equal status before God.

The feast was primarily a harvest thanksgiving. But other associations developed. There was thanksgiving also for all that God had done for the nation of old throughout the wilderness wanderings. And, with one harvest successfully completed, farmers looked forward to the coming year and used the time of thanksgiving as a time of prayer that God would continue his mercies and send the rain that was needed in the year that lay ahead.

There is a little confusion as to the duration of the feast. It was said to last for seven days (Lev. 23:34; Deut. 16:13, 15), but there is also mention of an eighth day (Lev. 23:36). We should probably understand that originally it went for seven days, but that in time an eighth day was added. But, for whatever length of time it was celebrated, it is clear that it was the high point of the year.

Jesus' Brothers

In time Jesus' brothers came to believe in him, and we find them gathered with the apostles and some believing women soon after the ascension (Acts 1:13–14). But during the time of his ministry they appear to have been very sceptical. Certainly that is the way they were at this time. As the Feast of Tabernacles approached they urged him to go on up to Judea (v. 3). It does not appear that they were sincerely interested in setting forward what he was doing. Apparently they were being sarcastic. They said he should go to Judea so that his disciples might see his "works." That word is often used for Jesus' miracles and is its probable meaning here. The brothers seem to be implying that they know what the "works" are, but that the "disciples" do not. This presents a problem, for there do not appear to be any "works" that the brothers had seen but the disciples had not. Perhaps they are implying that they know Jesus far better than the disciples do. And they know how a public figure should act. He should conform to *their* way of doing things.

I am reminded of the bright young lady who, at a time when it was fashionable for everyone to have a "shrink" of their own, said to a friend, "You've never been to a psychiatrist? You must be crazy!" In this spirit the brothers affirm that they know what Jesus ought to be doing.

Or it may be that they are saying that it is important that Jesus become known in Jerusalem. "If you are going to be a Messiah," their thoughts may run, "then go up to the capital and make your claim. You can't be the Messiah of Israel if you stay in the remote countryside, far from all the centers of population and of power." Their unbelief may be impelling them to urge Jesus to go to the big city where (they thought) his claims would be shown as shams.

They point to the impossibility of acting in secret and expecting to be known publicly (v. 4). They knew enough about what Jesus was doing and about the people who were following him to know that he was making a claim to some public status, be it Messiah or something else. "Let him go to where it counts," they are saying. "No public figure is established in Galilee. Show yourself to the world."

The words could possibly be understood as genuine encouragement. The reader might think that the brothers were urging Jesus to do something that would genuinely set forward his cause. But that would be a misunderstanding, so John adds his little explanation that they did not believe (v. 5). Whatever their motive in saying these things, it was not faith.

Jesus' Time

Jesus declines to do as they say. The brothers do not understand what he is doing; they do not believe in him; their advice does not spring from a sincere desire to forward his mission. Jesus begins by saying that there is a difference between him and them, and he expresses it in terms of "time" (v. 6). His word for "time" is *kairos*, a word that often has about it the idea of "the right time," "the appropriate time." In the first volume of these *Reflections* we saw that there is an impressive series of statements throughout this Gospel that inform the reader that Jesus' "time" or his "hour" had not yet come. These references persist until the eve of the crucifixion, when we find that his hour had come (12:23; 13:1). This saying fits into the series and means in part that Jesus was still pressing on towards that for which he had come into the world. But in the context there will also be the meaning that it was not time for Jesus to go up to the feast in the way the brothers suggested.

Some suggest that we should not see here a reference to the coming of the consummation of Jesus' mission, because John normally uses the word for "hour" for that, not *kairos*. This is so, and the possibility must be kept in mind that he means no more than that Jesus was selecting the most appropriate time to go to Jerusalem. But the contrast with the brothers favors the linking of this passage with those that refer to Jesus' "hour."

It was different for the brothers. Their "time" was always present. They were not sent by God on a mission like Jesus. So they did things when and as it seemed good to them. They neither submitted everything to the plan of God nor accomplished any worthwhile and lasting result.

The World's Hatred

In this matter the brothers line up with the world. They lived their lives in much the same way as the world in general, that world that sets itself in opposition to Jesus and all that he stands for. The world in that sense "can't" hate the brothers (v. 7); they belong to it and share its inability to hear the call of God to mission. The world loves its own (15:19), so the brothers are secure from its hatred. They belong to it.

But Jesus does not. John insists on this over and over again. He is "from above" (3:31); the Father sent him (6:38f.) He came on a mission of salvation (3:17). This is not the way of the world. Indeed, when the world sees what Jesus is doing it hates him. It does not share his love for sinners, his deep concern at the plight into which sin has led them. The world is not prepared for the kind of self-sacrifice that we see on the cross. It knows nothing of winning salvation for others at the cost of one's own life. So it is opposed to Jesus because of what he is and does.

It is opposed to him also because he testifies about it. As we read the Gospels we see this again and again. Jesus did not tolerate the world's evil. He denounced it unsparingly. He called down "woe" on the scribes and Pharisees and did not leave this a general denunciation but singled out specific misdeeds (cf. Matt. 23). There is no harmony between Jesus and "the world" as there is between the brothers and "the world." They cannot appeal to a community of interest because they do not understand what Jesus is doing.

So Jesus declines their invitation and urges them to go up to the feast (v. 8). That was the natural thing for them to do, and they should set about it before it was too late. "I am not going up to this feast," he says, and this presents a problem, because a little later he did go up. It also was a problem for the early Christian scribes, because some of them apparently altered "not" to "not yet" (*ouk* to *oupo*) as they copied out this Gospel. Indeed there are some scholars who accept "not yet" as the right reading, reasoning that as Jesus did in fact go up that must have been what John wrote.

But John's point seems to be that when Jesus went up to Jerusalem he did not go up as one of those who kept the feast. He was not a member of a company of pilgrims who went up together in good time so that they would miss none of the wonderful festivities. He went up privately and of set purpose missed the opening part of the celebrations. He went up, not as a pilgrim, but as the messenger of God. He went up, not to keep the feast, but to deliver the message that God had for him to deliver. The feast was the occasion for the message, not the reason for his journey. It was the means of gathering together those that God intended should hear what Jesus had to say. So, in the sense in which the brothers meant it, Jesus never did go up to this feast. And that is what he means when he says, "I am not going up to this feast."

He adds a reason: "My time is not yet fulfilled." The right moment would come and he would then be there. But his "time" was not the time the brothers suggested. So he stayed in Galilee (v. 9).

The People at the Feast

When his brothers had gone up to the feast then Jesus himself also went up, not publicly but as it were in secret. The Jews then were looking for him at the feast and were saying, "Where is he?" And there was a muttering about him among the crowds. Some people were saying, "He is a good man"; others were saying, "No. But he deceives the people." No one, however, was speaking openly about him for fear of the Jews (John 7:10–13).

At an unspecified time after the brothers went up to the feast, Jesus went up to Jerusalem, too (v. 10). But there was a difference. They went up as pilgrims to keep the feast; he went up incognito. People did not know that he was coming. This does not mean that Jesus traveled stealthily, but that he went by himself without being a member of a party of pilgrims. Such a caravan could be quite large. We are told that when the boy Jesus was separated from Joseph and Mary they spent a whole day looking for him among the company (Luke

2:44). Clearly the pilgrims from Galilee traveled in large groups, and it would be impossible to be inconspicuous in such a group. Jesus went up in such a way that he did not attract attention.

At a feast like Tabernacles crowds of religious Jews went up to the capital to keep the feast, and clearly many in Jerusalem expected that Jesus would be among those who attended. "The Jews" were looking for him (v. 11). This probably refers to the enemies of Jesus; it is a favorite Johannine way of speaking of them. They anticipated that Jesus would come up for such an important feast and they kept their eyes open so as not to miss him.

Evidently the hostility was becoming known and people realized that it might be dangerous to speak too openly about Jesus, for John goes on to say that there was a "muttering" about him (v. 12). Not only the leaders but other people as well wondered about him. When John says "the crowds" he seems to mean neither the disciples nor the enemies of Jesus, but the multitudes who were not committed to his cause, yet were not hostile either. Some of them thought Jesus a good man, while others thought of him as a deceiver. These would largely be pilgrims from a variety of places, and probably a good number of them had never seen nor heard Jesus. They would be relying on what they had heard from others, and their verdicts would depend on their source of information. They knew enough to know that it could be dangerous to speak too openly, so they kept their voices low. Clearly "the Jews" were the dominant people, and it was wise not to antagonize them, the pilgrims thought. So, though there was considerable interest in Jesus, there was little open discussion.

32

The Law of Moses

When it was now the middle of the feast Jesus went up into the temple and began to teach. The Jews were astonished and said, "How is this man learned when he has never been educated?" Jesus answered them, "My teaching is not my own but that of him who sent me. If anyone wills to do his will, he will know about the teaching whether it is of God or whether I speak of myself. He who speaks of himself seeks his own glory; but he who seeks the glory of him who sent him, this man is true and there is no unrighteousness in him.

"Did not Moses give you the Law? And yet none of you keeps the Law. Why are you trying to kill me?" The crowd replied, "You have a demon; who is trying to kill you?" Jesus answered them, "I did one work and you are all astonished. For this reason Moses gave you circumcision—not that it originates with Moses, but with the fathers—and on the Sabbath you circumcise a man. If a man receives circumcision on the Sabbath in order that the Law of Moses be not broken, are you angry with me because I made an entire man healthy on the Sabbath? Do not judge superficially, but judge righteous judgment" (John 7:14–24).

We have seen that Jesus declined his brothers' suggestion that he go up to the Feast of Tabernacles (vv. 3–8). He never did go up as they suggested, as one of the throng of pilgrims, going up to Jerusalem to keep the feast. But he did make his appearance at "the middle of the feast" (v. 14). This may be meant to be taken literally and signify the fourth day. But it is more likely to be a general statement and indicate that Jesus came on the scene somewhere about the middle of the festivities.

There was a prophecy that God would send his messenger to his people: ". . . 'suddenly the Lord you are seeking will come to his temple; the messenger of the covenant, whom you desire, will come,' says the LORD Almighty" (Mal. 3:1). The prophet Zechariah puts a great deal of emphasis on the importance of the Feast of Tabernacles (Zech. 14:16–19). Jesus, it would seem, goes to the temple at the Feast of Tabernacles in fulfillment of such Old Testament prophecies. He is not there simply as one of the pilgrims: he is there as the messenger of the Lord. He will speak the message God has for his people at that significant time.

He "began to teach," which appears to mean that he sat with a group of people and instructed them. Later in the feast he will stand and shout a message to the assembled throng (v. 37), but here the meaning appears to be that he engaged in a quieter session of instruction of a smaller group. As they listened they were astonished. It seems as though these people had not heard Jesus before, and this would not be surprising. John has not spoken of Jesus as teaching in Jerusalem before this time. He has done some miracles there (2:23), and we need not doubt that he did some teaching, too. Nevertheless, all the teaching that John has recorded up till now seems to have taken place in Galilee. In any case we should bear in mind that Tabernacles was the greatest of the feasts and that Jews came up to Jerusalem from many places. The people Jesus was teaching would doubtless have been pilgrims, and most of them may never have been in a position to hear him before this.

Education

Their astonishment was apparently at the way Jesus handled his subject. The expression I have translated "How is this man learned?" (v. 15) is more literally "How does this man know letters?" where "letters" will be understood in the sense "sacred letters," i.e., the Bible. There would have been no problem in Jesus' knowing something of the Bible. It was read in worship in the synagogue, Sabbath by Sabbath, and any attentive person would pick up a good deal simply by taking in what was read. And some parts of the Bible were learned by heart. Thus every little Jewish boy was taught to say "Hear, O Israel . . ." (Deut. 6:4f.). Certainly Jesus knew enough to read the Scripture in the synagogue service (Luke 4:16ff.). Some knowledge of "letters" was widespread and would not be surprising.

But more advanced education would take place in the rabbinical schools. The student would attach himself to a rabbi and the rabbi would teach him the accepted lore. This put a good deal of emphasis on memory work. In a day when all books had to be laboriously written by hand, books were always in comparatively short supply and much was necessarily committed to memory. Indeed, for some people it seems that this was held to be all that was necessary. A term of abuse sometimes used was to call such a scholar "a bag of books." He had committed whole books to memory and could at need recite them. But he had no real grasp of what they meant and no wisdom in handling his knowledge. There were others whose learning led them to concentrate on points that other people might well not know, but which were of no great importance. Some of the Jews showed great ingenuity in their handling of the regulations of the Law, seeing the bare minimum that had to be performed in order to comply with the regulations and the ways in which loopholes might be found for those who did not want to be "overrighteous" (Eccles. 7:16).

Jesus had not been through the rabbinic training, and it would not be expected that he could sustain a continuing argument from Scripture. It was this that seems to have astonished his hearers. They would not have expected a man who came from a carpenter's home in Nazareth to have been able to teach like Jesus taught.

This is a fine piece of Johannine irony. He made it clear at the beginning of the Gospel that Jesus is the divine Logos, the Word of God. Now he sees the Jews confronted by the Logos incarnate and calling him "this uneducated fellow" (Moffatt). They could not recognize the divine wisdom when they heard it.

Teaching from God

Jesus' response is to say that his teaching is not his own (v. 16). We should notice here that in the first century there was a different attitude toward teaching from our customary view. We prize highly an original teacher, but the ancients did not. There was a widespread idea that there had been a Golden Age in the remote past and that at that time men had been greater and wiser and stronger than their successors. Indeed, since that time it seems that history had been all downhill. So, if anyone produced highly original teaching, teaching that could not be traced back in some way to the great days of the race, then obviously that teacher must be in error. When an original teacher appeared he had to perform some intricate mental gymnastics to pin his teaching on some illustrious predecessor. If he could do this, he was accepted. If not, no one took much notice of him.

Thus, if Jesus had claimed that his teaching originated with himself, he would have been immediately discredited. Not, of course, that he took the position he did simply because of the effect it would have on his hearers. He took his position because it was true. It is a consistent piece of Johannine teaching that there was a oneness between Jesus and his heavenly Father such that what he said came from God. And that is what he tells his hearers now.

He does not speak of God but of "him who sent me." Again and again we have this truth repeated in this Gospel. God sent his Son. This is something very different from what was normally accepted in the ancient world. The Greeks thought of their gods as remote from ordinary people, living a serene existence on the top of Mount Olympus, and far too great to be affected by what insignificant mortals might do. They were not moved by our sin unless it in some way managed to outrage one of them personally. And their attitude to the human race was not one of love. How could such great and lofty deities love puny, unimportant, mortal humans?

It was better with the Jews, because they had learned well from the Old Testament that God concerns himself with his people, and that through the centuries he had sent his servants the prophets, the psalmists, the lawgivers, and others, and had worked out his purpose for his own. But for the Jews of the first century it seems that all this was in the past. That God had acted in days gone by they accepted. That God would act in the end of time they fully agreed. But now? That was another matter altogether.

But Jesus kept saying that God had sent him. That means not only that God had acted in love in the past and that he would act in love in the future, but that he was acting in love now. The mission of Jesus meant that God was taking action to bring about salvation, and that colored everything he said and did. Specifically, his teaching was the teaching of the God who sent him on his mission of salvation.

Knowing God's Teaching

Jesus, then, is saying that his teaching should be accepted because it was God's teaching. He knows that, but how are his hearers to know it? He says it is a matter of the will. The set of the life is important. If anyone really "wills to do his will," that person will know the truth of Jesus' teaching (v. 17). It is a matter of being completely sincere. It is easy to delude ourselves into believing something that we very much want to believe. And it is not hard to persuade ourselves that something is erroneous if it is going to be uncomfortable to accept it. Self-delusion is widespread and is a source of many errors. Specifically, if someone does not wish to accept the teaching of Jesus, there will always be some reason he can dredge up that will make his rejection of it plausible.

But the genuine person, the one who simply wants to do what is right and who wills to do the will of God, that person will have an inner certainty. The Spirit of God will be at work with his spirit and will lead him into the ways of truth (16:13). He will have a divinely given certainty, and that is above all price. Jesus is emphasizing that the right attitude towards God is all-important. God will never let the genuine seeker be led astray permanently. He may have his difficulties along the way, but he will be in no doubt that Jesus is the One sent by God and that the teaching he gives is from God.

Long ago the great Augustine uttered some wise words. He pointed out that it is faith that is supremely important in the attitude of the Christian. This great African theologian said, "Do not seek to understand in order to believe"; Christianity is not a religion primarily for the intelligentsia. We do not need to fight our way through an intellectual maze before we can become acceptable to God. That is a matter of trust, not of massive intellect. "What is 'If any man be willing to do his will'?" he asks and then answers, "It is the same thing as to believe." But Augustine is clear that faith does not mean the abandonment of intellectual activity. "Believe that thou mayest understand," he wrote. Understanding follows faith, and Augustine's impressive literary output bears ample witness to this truth. But, massive as his intellect certainly was, Augustine was sure that it is faith that is of central importance.

Jesus goes on to the attitude of the teacher (v. 18). He is speaking primarily of himself, for it is his teaching that is being questioned, but what he says applies in lesser measure to all who teach in the name of God. The person who has his eye fixed on "his own glory" will necessarily speak "of himself"; such an attitude is incompatible with speaking the message of God. As we see from Jesus' lowly life and from his lowly service in going to the cross for sinners, he had no self-seeking. His teaching was genuinely from God. And as we seek to speak in God's name the same attitude is sought from us. One wise man has well said that "it is impossible at one and the same time to give the impression that Jesus is a great Savior and that I am a great preacher." If the Christian teacher is anxious to draw attention to himself, he cannot point people to Christ. On the other hand, if he is concentrating on pointing people to Christ, he cannot keep his interest on himself.

The person with this right attitude, Jesus says, "is true." He does not say that he speaks the truth (though that, of course, is also the case), but that he *is* true. Truth can be a quality of people as well as of words. In a special sense this was true of Jesus, for he could say, "I am the truth" (14:6). But there is a sense in which every believer must be a "true" person, one whose faith is translated into a thoroughly reliable way of life. That person will avoid unrighteousness of every kind.

Moses and the Law

When Jesus goes on to speak of the Law (v. 19) he is not turning to a new and unrelated subject. For the Jews of his day it was the Law that Moses gave (the first five books of our Old Testament) that was the special subject of study. They revered Moses as possibly the greatest of men; certainly the giver of the Law was a highly significant figure. The Jews exhausted their superlatives in seeking to bring out the importance of the Law.

Jesus' opponents have been criticizing him and rejecting his teaching. They maintained that they were doing this because they held to what Moses taught, and everyone knew that God had spoken through Moses. Now Jesus points out that their loyalty to Moses was suspect. "None of you keeps the Law," he says. That would have been a shocking accusation to them. The Law was more than a subject that they thought of only occasionally. It was the center of their study and their model for living. Constantly they tried to live as the Law directed.

But now Jesus asks, "Why are you trying to kill me?" This was certainly not in accordance with the Law. He does not mean, of course, that they are all caught up in the plot, but there are enough for his question to have a point. And it certainly shows that there were those who were far from keeping the Law.

The crowd did not understand. As we have seen earlier, the multitude in Jerusalem at that time would have been largely made up of pilgrims for a wide area. It was not they, but "the Jews," those who lived in Jersualem and particularly their leaders, who were trying to get rid of Jesus. The crowds from so many places did not know what the leaders were trying to do. But killing Jesus sounded crazy to them, and accordingly they accused him of having "a demon" (v. 20), an accusation made on other occasions (8:48–52; 10:20f.; cf. also Mark 3:22, etc.).

The Sabbath

Jesus proceeds to develop his point that none of them keeps the Law. The pilgrims did not know of the plot to kill him (which was one way of breaking the Law). But the way the Sabbath was observed was common knowledge, and he goes on to show them that they were not really keeping the Sabbath in the way they should.

He starts with "one work" that he had done (v. 21). He does not explain which work this is, but the context makes it clear that he is referring to the healing of the lame man who had waited for thirty-eight years for healing, healing that he had sought in vain from the healing waters (5:1ff.). That miracle had been performed on a Sabbath, a fact that had caused the powers-that-be a good deal of concern and had led to a spirited discussion with Jesus (5:16ff.). As he often does, Jesus speaks of his miracle as a "work"; what to us is an inexplicable miracle is to him no more than a "work." Being who and what he is, this sort of thing is what he does so naturally. But it was a miracle that made them all "astonished." There was no explanation for it that they could see, and this led to amazement.

Jesus goes on to one of the central requirements of the Law as the Jews practised it, the requirement of circumcision (v. 22). Moses laid it down that this ceremonial act should be carried out, but he did not originate the practice. God had commanded Abraham to circumcise every male child as a sign of the covenant that he was making with that patriarch (Gen. 17:9ff.). This had been done by the patriarchs, so that the command in the Law was to perpetuate what God had commanded long since, not a new provision initiated by Moses. The exact date of its institution is not important; Jesus simply points out that it was not their highly revered Moses who began it, but "the fathers."

Now the Law required circumcision to be carried out on the eighth day of the baby's existence. It also required that people do no work on the Sabbath. Circumcision was regarded as work, so this posed a little problem: What happened when the eighth day fell on the Sabbath? Should the Sabbath be regarded as of overriding importance, so that circumcision be postponed till the next day? Or was circumcision so important that it took precedence over the Sabbath regulations? Should they go ahead and circumcise the baby even though it was the Sabbath? Moses did not say what should be done under such circumstances, but the Jews were clear: "Great is circumcision which overrides even the rigour of the Sabbath," said Rabbi Jose (Mishnah, *Nedarim* 3:11), and this was the accepted understanding. Circumcision was extremely important. The Law was understood to mean that nothing must stand in the way of its performance, not even the Sabbath.

Jesus reminds his hearers of this well-known fact in order to make clear his attitude to the Sabbath. When he healed on that day it was not in an anti-Sabbatarian attitude. He was not saying that the Sabbath should not be kept. Nor was he saying that the rules for the Sabbath were too strict and that there should be some relaxation.

He was saying that his critics did not understand what the Sabbath meant and why it had been instituted. He was saying that if they reflected on the meaning of their regular practice with regard to circumcision, they would see this for themselves. The Law of Moses provided for circumcision on the eighth day, and the need of the little baby to be included among God's covenant people by the use of this rite overrode the requirements of Sabbath observance. Think what this means. Think. The person is more important than the rules. The Law itself bears witness to this.

So with Jesus' healing. It was concerned not with one member of the body (as circumcision was), but with the "entire man" (v. 23). It was unthinkable to Jesus that the man should be allowed to remain any longer in his helplessness and his hopelessness. If his critics understood what the Law meant, they would see that the kind of thing he had done in healing the lame man was not only permitted but required by the Law. The Law was meant for the good of the people who were under the Law. Good deeds, deeds of mercy, *ought* to be done on the Sabbath. His enemies were in the wrong. They were not really keeping the Law at all when they objected to his healing.

There is an interesting change of tenses in Jesus' two uses of the word *judge* (v. 24). The first is a present, which with the negative conveys the force of "stop judging superficially." There is the implication that they have been doing this, and Jesus commands them to stop it. "Judge righteous judgment" employs the aorist (at least in many good manuscripts), which concentrates on the specific case and tells them to make a right judgment about it. They should, of course, do this all the time, but the way Jesus puts it places emphasis on the specific example before them. They should make a right judgment about this, and that would help them to a better understanding of the ways of God.

33

"Where I Am You Cannot Come"

Some of the Jerusalemites therefore said, "Is not this he whom they are trying to kill? And look, he is speaking openly and they are saying nothing to him. Do the rulers by any chance know that this man is truly the Christ? But we know where this man comes from. But as for the Christ, when he comes, no one knows where he comes from." Jesus therefore cried out in the temple as he taught saying, "So you know me and you know where I am from! And I did not come of my own accord, but he who sent me is true, One whom you do not know. I know him, for I am from him and he sent me."

Therefore they tried to arrest him, and yet no one laid a hand on him because his hour had not yet come. But many of the crowd believed in him and said, "When the Christ comes will he do more signs than this man has done?" The Pharisees heard the crowd muttering these things about him and the high priests and the Pharisees sent officials to arrest him. Jesus then said, "Yet a little while am I with you and I go to him that sent me. You will look for me and you will not find me, and where I am you cannot come." The Jews therefore said to themselves, "Where will this man go that we will not find him? He won't go to the dispersion among the Greeks and teach the Greeks, will he? What is this saying that he spoke, 'You will look for me and you will not find me, and where I am you cannot come'?" (John 7:25–36).

267

There are different groups of people in Jerusalem referred to in this chapter. As often, there are references to "the Jews," which normally mean those Jews who were hostile to Jesus and more especially the Jewish leaders in Jerusalem. Then there is "the crowd," which seems to mean mostly the pilgrims who had come up to the capital and specifically to the temple in order to keep the feast. They were uninformed about Jesus, but many of them were ready to listen to his teaching and some of them were so impressed that they believed in him (v. 31). Now another group is mentioned: "the Jerusalemites." This is a very unusual expression, being found elsewhere in the New Testament only in Mark 1:5. Obviously it means people who lived in Jerusalem, but it seems to be used not of the whole population but of the city mob. They had more information than the pilgrims, for they knew of the plot to kill Jesus (v. 25), though it was not their plot; an undefined "they" were responsible.

The mob was impressed by the fact that Jesus was teaching publicly and openly and that nobody was doing anything about it. The word that I have translated "openly" (v. 26) is an interesting one. It is made up of two words, which literally mean "all speech," so that it points to an attitude of being completely at home, a comfortable feeling wherein the words come freely and easily. From this basic meaning the word comes to be used in two common ways. It may mean "boldly," "courageously" (when we feel quite at home we are not afraid); or it may mean "openly" (when we feel at home we feel no urge to cover up and keep things secret). It is the second meaning that is used here, though, the hostility of the enemies of Jesus being what it was, the first meaning might also apply.

Why, then, were the rulers doing nothing about Jesus' public teaching? The Jerusalemites raise the possibility that these rulers knew that Jesus was in fact the Christ. They do not rate this possibility very highly. The way they express it in the Greek implies that a negative answer should be given to their question. There has to be some explanation. So they suggest this one. But they dismiss it; there is no probability in it.

They toy with the idea of "the Christ." Many Jews seem to have held that when the Christ came he would burst on the scene suddenly and people would not know where he had come from. There was certainly the idea that the Messiah would be "revealed," and this seems to have been understood at any rate by some to mean that nobody would know anything about him until the revelation took place. Another view was that he would arise out of the sea, which meant, of course, that prior to his sudden appearance nobody could have any idea of him or of where he would come from. Again there was a rabbinic saying that held that three things come quite unexpectedly: Messiah, a windfall, and a scorpion. It is an interesting trio, but it leaves no doubt that whoever originated it did not see how Messiah's arrival could be forecast. That was completely unknown. Justin, a Christian writer from the middle of the second century, quotes a Jew as saying that even if the Messiah had come, that Messiah would not know he was the Messiah until Elijah came to anoint him.

There was thus no shortage of ideas, and, while we cannot be sure which one these men of Jerusalem held, clearly they were not going to allow the possibility of Jesus being the Messiah. Despite what the rulers might hold, despite the miracles Jesus did, there was always something that could be alleged as an obstacle. There was no satisfying them.

I am reminded of a little family that went to a restaurant for a meal. When the waitress came for their orders the wife said she would like a salmon sandwich with white bread. The waitress said, "You'll like our chicken better. And brown bread is better for you than white." Then when the daughter decided on a green salad with no dressing, and coffee to drink, the waitress responded, "There's not much nourishment in that. Why not have a cottage-cheese salad. And milk is better than coffee." The man in the party, thoroughly cowed by this time, said timidly, "What would you suggest?" To which the waitress snapped, "Suggestions! Who's got time for suggestions?"

You can't win with some people. Whatever line you take, they disagree. It seems that the Jerusalemites were something like this. They did not know as much about Jesus as they perhaps might. But they certainly weren't going to be found out saying that he was the Messiah. If one objection wouldn't do, another could surely be found. As it happened, the one they settled on was that they knew Jesus' origin. This is another piece of John's irony. If they had really known where Jesus came from, they would have known that he was indeed the Messiah. But all that they knew was that he came from Nazareth, an unimportant village in Galilee. They were quite ignorant of the virgin birth, of the truth that Jesus was "from above," and that he was where he was because the heavenly Father had sent him.

Sent by God

Jesus used this as a starting point for some important teaching. He "therefore cried out" (v. 28), and the verb shows that he wanted to give the greatest publicity to an important statement. This verb is used a number of times in this Gospel to introduce important teaching; look at the way it comes in in 1:15; 7:37; 12:44, for example. Jesus begins

269

with an ironical agreement with what the Jerusalemites had just said. They knew where he came from. This was certainly true in the sense that they knew that he came from Nazareth. But it was not true in the deeper sense that he came from God.

So Jesus goes on: "I did not come of my own accord." This does not mean, of course, that he did not want to come, that his own desires lay elsewhere. It is an important part of the teaching of this Gospel that the Father and the Son are one, that in the salvation that Jesus was in process of working out they were in perfect harmony. But his point here is that he is not, as his hearers think, an upstart. There were many who claimed positions of eminence and even some who claimed to be Messiah. But these were all motivated by their own impulse. They came on their own initiative. They had the support of their own adherents, but that was all. The critical thing was that they had no divine mission. They might claim it, but God had not sent them.

It mattered everything to Jesus that God had sent him. It was this that gave him assurance in the face of the hostility of so many people who might have been expected to be genuine servants of God, the leaders, especially the religious leaders of the nation that rejoiced to be "the people of God." But while they might reject him, he rejoiced in the nearness of "him who sent me," of whom he now says that he "is true." Goodspeed translates this "someone who is very real." The "reality," the "truth" of God was very important, but these people did not know God. Because they did not know God they did not know Christ. It is impossible to know the one without the other, and consequently to be ignorant of one is evidence that one is ignorant of the other.

It is another truth insisted on throughout this Gospel that Jesus knows the Father. In fact the three expressions that come together here, "I know him," "I am from him," and "he sent me," sum up a great deal of Johannine theology: knowledge, origin, and mission.

Attempted Arrest

These words of Jesus led to different reactions. Some decided that Jesus had gone too far and that he should be arrested (v. 30). John says "therefore," which shows that this was the consequence of what Jesus had just said. He does not tell us in what the attempt to arrest him consisted, nor who did this. He simply says "they" sought to arrest him, but in Jerusalem the only people with the power to bring about an arrest were the Romans and the temple authorities. There is no question of Roman might at this point, so it must be the priests and their allies. John makes it plain that there was strong hostility and that Jesus' enemies were prepared to take action.

The attempt, however it was made, was completely unsuccessful. Not a hand was laid on Jesus. As we do not know exactly who was trying to make the arrest or how they went about it, we cannot know what went wrong with the attempt. But we do know the basic reason for the failure—Jesus' "hour had not yet come." As we have seen more than once in these studies, John is clear that Jesus had come to discharge a divinely given mission. He must do what was necessary to bring about the salvation of sinners, and in due course that would mean dying for them. But that death would be at the time and in the way that God planned it all. Puny tyrants would not be able to interfere. Till the time came for Jesus to die, nobody could prevent him from going about his business in the service of God. Of course, when his "hour" came, nothing would be able to prevent him from going forward to death either. But that is another matter and it will be developed in another place. Here John is content to leave us with the thought that in the will of God it was not yet time for Jesus' enemies to succeed. So, whatever the attempt they might make to arrest him, it must be unsuccessful.

So much for the reaction of Jesus' opponents. But there were also many of the pilgrims there, "the crowd" (v. 31). These people were more open-minded. They had probably for the most part not known Jesus and perhaps even not known of him before they went up to Jerusalem for this feast. But they were ready to listen to him and to watch what he did. John tells us that many of them came to believe in Jesus, the attitude for which John is looking throughout. He wrote his Gospel, he tells us, so that people would believe. These pilgrims then were doing what people, in John's judgment, ought to do.

But if their faith was praiseworthy, perhaps the reason for it was not quite so admirable. They ask, "When the Christ comes will he do more signs than this man has done?" In this Gospel "signs" is a characteristic word for the miracles; it marks them out as significant happenings. For John faith that is based on the miracles is not the highest kind of faith, but it is better than no faith at all. It was this "miracle faith" that the pilgrims had. To record this in such a context is, of course, to confer high praise, for there was hostility to Jesus and his enemies were taking strong action against him. It must have taken some courage to profess faith in him accordingly, but this these pilgrims did. It is interesting that they think of the Messiah primarily in terms of the doing of miracles. For us it is his love for sinners, his work of salvation, his atoning death, that matters most. But we view what happened in Palestine with the benefit of centuries of hindsight. For those pilgrims it must have been difficult to know how to recognize the Messiah. The miracles were a useful guide.

Though they professed belief, the pilgrims evidently did not speak very openly about it. But the Pharisees heard them "muttering" and took notice of it (v. 32). There is an interesting little mark of John's accuracy here. He speaks of the Pharisees as hearing what the crowd was saying, but of the high priests and the Pharisees as trying to make an arrest. The point is that the high priests were aristocrats. They did not know what the common people were saying. But the Pharisees, the religious leaders, were much more in touch with what was going on. They tried to teach people what they saw as the right way. They were sufficiently in touch to hear these quietly spoken words. But they had little power. They did not control the police; they had no power of arrest. That belonged rather to the high priests. Quite clearly the Pharisees went off to the high priests and told them what was going on. Then, when those who had the power decided on an arrest, the Pharisees are linked with them in sending the officials. They gave their religious sanction to what was being done.

Going Away

Evidently it took a little time for the officials to get busy. It may be that there were no officers immediately available and some had to be sought. Perhaps the crowd around Jesus was thick and it took time for them to make their way through to the place where he was. It may be that their instructions included a warning that the situation was tense and that they should be careful how they went about their work. For whatever reason, Jesus continued for a time with his teaching and we do not hear of the arresting posse again until verse 45, when they report that they had not done what they had been ordered to do. But John says little about them. His interest is in Jesus, not in a posse of policemen.

Jesus' teaching takes a surprising turn. He speaks of being with them for a short time and then of returning to the One who had sent him (v. 33). Perhaps this is a logical follow-up from the last words John has recorded of Jesus, back in verse 29. He said then that he was from God and that God had sent him. Now he speaks of returning to him who had sent him, his mission complete. It is also possible that we should see the words as a reaction to the attempted arrest. It would not be long before Jesus was removed to a place out of the reach of any arresting party. It may even be that the words are a response to the faith John has just spoken of. That faith was based on the miracles, and some hold that Jesus is referring to his death, which was much more significant for faith than the miracles were.

His enemies will look for him, Jesus says, and will not find him; he will be in a place where they cannot come (v. 34). We do not find it overly difficult to understand this, for we are on this side of the cross and the resurrection. But it puzzled those who heard it. How could Jesus possibly go to some place where they could not follow? If he could go, surely so could they?

The speakers now are "the Jews," the enemies of Jesus (v. 35). They express their wonderment at such a destination and proceed to a suggestion, "the dispersion among the Greeks." At that time there were many Jews who lived outside Palestine. Most of the big cities of the Roman Empire had sizable groups of Jews, and there were also many in some countries outside the empire. All these Jews outside their own country were called "the dispersion"; they were the dispersed members of the people of God. They do not suggest that Jesus will teach the dispersion, the Jews scattered abroad, but the Greeks. This may be another example of John's irony. Jesus himself never did go to the dispersion and teach Greeks, but his followers did. In due course the early Christian preachers traveled all over the empire, making the synagogues their jumping-off points in the cities to which they went as they preached the gospel message to the Greeks (and others). What the Jews here dismiss as fantastic became in fact the method by which the Christian way was spread throughout the empire.

It is easy to make blunders based on misunderstanding. I was reading of a shopkeeper who lived next door to his shop. He was often troubled by people using the parking lot alongside his shop, though he saw it as meant for his customers and certainly not as a free public parking lot outside shop hours. Coming home late one night, he saw the lot just full of cars. He felt this was too much, that he must do something about it. So he hunted up a police officer and did not rest until there was a ticket on every car. Satisfied and rejoicing at a job well done, he went inside, only to find that his wife was hostessing an evening for the ladies of the church, who had been very happy to find parking available so close to the home where they were meeting!

So with these people. They did not realize what they were doing when they rejected Jesus of Nazareth and in doing so rejected the incarnate Son of God. Like the man in the little story, they would have been well advised to have made more inquiries before they settled on their course of action. They thought of the Greeks and they thought of the dispersion. But they did not think of the possibility that in Jesus of Nazareth they were being confronted with a messenger sent by God, nor that the going away might be a going away not simply from Palestine but from this whole earth, a going back to God.

So John leaves this part of his story with these people repeating the words of Jesus in puzzlement (v. 36). In this Gospel words are very rarely repeated exactly, and this is one of the few places where this happens. We should see the words as important. Probably John also means us to see that the words haunted these hearers. They knew that they did not understand and they knew that the words did have a meaning. Jesus understood quite well what he was saying. What could he mean? John leaves us with the picture of people who were not willing to submit to the voice of God and who accordingly did not understand. Which is not exactly unknown in our own day.

34

"It Was Not Yet Spirit"

On the last day, the great day of the feast, Jesus stood and cried out saying, "If anyone is thirsty, let him come to me and drink. He who believes in me, as the Scripture said, rivers of living water will flow out of his innermost being." He said this about the Spirit whom those who believed in him would receive. For it was not yet Spirit, because Jesus was not yet glorified (John 7:37–39).

You would think it would be easy to know when "the last day" of the feast was, especially since it is also called "the great day." But this is not the case. In Deuteronomy 16:13 we read, "Celebrate the Feast of Tabernacles for seven days . . ." and this is repeated in verse 15, "For seven days celebrate the Feast to the LORD your God. . . ." But in Leviticus 23:36 we read with respect to this feast, "For seven days present offerings made to the LORD by fire, and on the eighth day hold a sacred assembly and present an offering made to the LORD by fire. It is the closing assembly. . . ." It is not unlikely that an original seven-day festival was at some time lengthened by a day. Or perhaps there was a closing assembly on the eighth day from the very first. We do not know. But the uncertainty leaves us wondering whether John regards the seventh or the eighth as the last day.

At this feast there were ceremonies with the pouring out of water and the lighting of great candelabra, which were said to have illuminated every house in Jerusalem. But these seem to have finished by the seventh day; they were not used on the eighth. So also the leafy shelters in which people lived during this feast were taken down on the seventh day. It can thus be argued that the eighth day was not really a part of the feast, being rather an addendum.

But perhaps we should say that if the eighth day was observed at all, the seventh day can scarcely be called the last day. Moreover, the absence of the water and light ceremonies on the eighth day may have given greater point to Jesus' words about living water and about the light of the world. It seems best to understand John as speaking about the eighth day.

Ceremonies at the Feast

Tabernacles was a very happy feast. It marked the end of the year's work, with the harvest safely in, so everyone was merry. Living in leafy shelters for the duration must have been a lot of fun. People carried bunches of leaves, which they called *lulabs*, in accordance with the way the Pharisees interpreted Leviticus 23:40: "On the first day you are to take choice fruit from the trees, and palm fronds, leafy branches and poplars, and rejoice before the LORD your God for seven days." The Sadducees took this to be an instruction about the material out of which the leafy shelters were to be constructed. The Pharisees, however, took the words as an instruction to the worshipers to carry fronds from the trees named. The Pharisees were closer to the people and had a better reputation as religious leaders, so it is not surprising that their interpretation of the passage prevailed.

A. Edersheim says that the worshiper carried in his right hand the "*lulab* or palm, with myrtle and willow branch on either side of it, tied together on the outside with its own kind, though in the inside it might be fastened even with gold thread." Rabbi Ishmael maintained that the requirements for a *lulab* were three branches of myrtle, two of willow, one palm, and one citron. Whichever was right, the people made their *lulabs* and carried them in their right hands, while each had a citron in the left hand. At certain points in the reciting of psalms they all shook their *lulabs*, which thus featured in the observance. The observances included dancing and the music of flutes. Young branches of willow were brought in and arranged round the altar in such a way that the tops formed a canopy over it.

Each day for seven days a priest would convey water from the pool of Siloam in a golden vessel and bring it in a happy procession marked by the blowing of trumpets till they came to the temple. This was a very joyous occasion about which there is a rabbinic saying: "He that never has seen the joy of the water-drawing has never in his life seen joy." At the temple the water was poured out into a bowl beside the altar, from which a pipe conveyed it to the bottom of the altar, while at the same time wine was poured in a similar fashion on the other side of the altar. This water ceremony was an acted prayer for rain. A saying reputed to go back to Rabbi Akiba (who died in A.D. 134), and which may be much older, asks "Why has the Torah commanded: Pour out water on the Feast of Tabernacles?" and answers "The Holy One, blessed be He, has commanded: Pour out water before me on the Feast of Tabernacles, in order that the rain (of the coming year) may bless you." Whether the saying had been formulated in New Testament times we do not know, but there is no doubt that this is the way the people understood the water ceremonies. Indeed, the idea goes back at least as far as the time of the prophet Zechariah, who associated rain with the observance of the Feast of Tabernacles (Zech. 14:16–19). The reciting of Psalm 118:25 as a prayer for prosperity is also thought to be a petition for rain. Some words from Isaiah were also used, probably during processions: "With joy you will draw water from the wells of salvation" (Isa. 12:3).

Let the Thirsty Drink

It is against this background that we should understand Jesus' words. The people were in a happy mood as they joined in the celebration of this most joyful feast. But the acted and spoken prayers for rain reminded them of their dependence on the goodness of God. They were not able of themselves to provide for the coming year. Unless God sent the rain, the Feast of Tabernacles next year would be a grim occasion.

The water ceremonies had been dutifully carried out for seven days. On this day there were none. But now Jesus speaks (v. 37). It is a solemn occasion and he stands up to issue his invitation. Teachers usually sat with their disciples, so that his posture was unusual. This may be to mark an unusual occasion, and it is also the case, of course, that by standing he put himself in a position to be heard more widely. John says that Jesus "cried out"; the loud shout would mean that the maximum number of people would hear him.

Jesus speaks of the thirsty and invites them to come to him and drink. Clearly he is not speaking of thirst after the water that sustains our physical life, but of thirst after spiritual things. It is that thirst that is of first importance, and it is that thirst that Jesus satisfies. Up till this point Jesus seems not to have given specific teaching of his own at the feast. John has recorded Jesus' replies to questions put to him, but not any teaching he gave spontaneously. That has been reserved until now, the climax of the whole observance, and Jesus brings out the deep significance of the feast. It points to him as the giver of the water that really satisfies. The people have been thinking of their need of rain; Jesus reminds them that they have another and a deeper need, the need of their souls. It is likely that he has in mind God's giving of water from the rock to the people in the wilderness (Exod. 17:6; Num. 20:7–11). After all, at Tabernacles water was poured out by the altar, but the people did not drink it. In the wilderness they did drink the water that came from the rock. Jesus is the Rock from which his people's need is abundantly satisfied.

There is a problem of punctuation here and this affects the sense. There is very little punctuation in the most ancient manuscripts; the reader was expected to supply it himself. Usually this presents no problem, but now and then there is uncertainty. In this place we usually put a comma after "thirsty" and a full stop after "drink." But some suggest that we should put our full stop (or semicolon) after "me" so as to read (with NEB), "If anyone is thirsty let him come to me; whoever believes in me, let him drink." But, though many accept this understanding of the text, there are some strong objections. Thus the words about being thirsty look for something about drinking. It is the thirsty person, not the believing person, whom we expect to drink. The words about faith go better with coming to Jesus than with drinking.

There is also a grammatical point. When we come to the expression "rivers of living water will flow out of his innermost being" (v. 38), the word "his" must refer to the preceding "he," the believer. It cannot refer to "me" (i.e., Christ), as most who adopt this punctuation prefer. Indeed, one of the main reasons for accepting the variant punctuation is that those who adopt it understand the passage to mean that it is Christ who is the source of the living water.

Rivers of Living Water

The question that arises then is "Do the rivers of living water flow from the believer or from Christ?" It is because it seems so obvious that they come from Christ that many scholars take "he who believes" with the preceding verb "drink." And, of course, it must be accepted that it is Christ who supplies the living water, not the believer. But there is a sense in which the believer can be the source of blessing to others, a truth given expression in the prayer of the humble man who prayed, "Lord, I can't hold much, but help me to overflow lots." It has often been the case in the history of the church that people of small capacity have been the source of blessing to many.

We should notice, moreover, that Jesus speaks of the giving of living water as taking place "as the Scripture said." Now it is very difficult to find a passage that meets this situation. People sometimes appeal to the story of the water coming from the rock (Exod. 17:6), but it is not easy to understand this passage as a prophecy that the Messiah would give living water. It is no better with "He opened the rock, and water gushed out" (Ps. 105:41), or with the water coming out from under the threshold of the temple in Ezekiel's vision (Ezek. 47:1), or with Joel's prophecy that "all the ravines of Judah will run with water. A fountain will flow out of the LORD's house and will water the valley of acacias" (Joel 3:18). Each of these passages has been appealed to, but none ascribes living water to the Messiah. The same is true of other passages. If we adopt this understanding of the text, we are left with Jesus' appealing to "the Scripture" in a way that we cannot follow.

It is true that the Old Testament does not say in precise words that rivers of living water will flow from the believer. But it does speak of God's people as the source of blessing to others and uses the imagery of water to make the point. For example, "You will be like a well-watered garden, like a spring whose waters never fail" (Isa. 58:11b). A spring, of course, is outgoing; it is not like a well that simply accumulates water. The spring sends it forth. This may be involved also in calling the heart "the wellspring of life" (Prov. 4:23). Other passages could be cited; the Old Testament often uses water to bring out the thought of God's good gift to his people, and sometimes, as in the passages quoted, there is the thought that the believer is outgoing.

Of course this comes short of producing a proof text that does away with all argument. I am simply saying that there does not appear to be any Old Testament passage that says that the Messiah will be the source of living water, but there are some that are naturally interpreted along the line that the believer can pass on the blessing he has received from God.

It goes without saying that the believer is never thought of as originating the living water, neither in the Old Testament nor in Jesus' words. That is always a divine gift. But Jesus does appear to be saying that when the believer has this gift he will not be a self-centered person. He will be outgoing, and the blessing he has received from God he will pass on to other people.

John Bunyan has the old gentleman, Mr Honest, say,

> A man there was, though some did count him mad,
> The more he cast away, the more he had.

Over against which we may set the "rule" of the pool that takes in but does not give out. Of this rule it can be said, in the words of the poet Wordsworth,

279

> The good old rule
> Sufficeth them, the simple plan,
> That they should take, who have the power,
> And they should keep who can.

But this rule is self-defeating, as the Dead Sea shows. Where water keeps flowing in and none flows out, there is stagnation and death. It is the pool out of which water flows as well as into which water flows that sparkles with life.

The Spirit

John adds the explanation that Jesus was speaking about the Spirit (v. 39). He was not saying that the believer is naturally a source of blessing to others. That is not so. The Christian does not somehow become a great and wonderful person, full of life and vitality in his own right. But the Holy Spirit within him enables him to be outgoing in such a way that he will be of help to others.

Now the Holy Spirit is not given only to great and outstanding people. We are not to think of great saints as empowered by the Spirit while ordinary Christians are left to struggle on as best they can. The Spirit is given to "those who believed in him." Every believer receives this great gift. That is the wonderful thing about the Christian way.

Many of the religions of antiquity had the thought that from time to time a divine spirit would come upon people. But they held that this was a gift given only to the outstanding. The recipients of this great gift would be priests or others standing in a specially close relationship to the god. They would not be ordinary worshipers. It was something new when the Christians said that the Spirit would be given to every believer. Paul can go so far as to say, ". . . if anyone has not the Spirit of Christ, he does not belong to him" (Rom. 8:9; he also puts it the other way round, "As many as are led by the Spirit of God these are sons of God," Rom. 8:14). To be a Christian is to have the Holy Spirit. That is a precious and wonderful truth.

Another difference from the religions of antiquity was the way the Christians understood what the Spirit would do. The worshipers in other religions held that the presence of the divine spirit would be known by ecstatic behavior of some kind. People on whom this spirit was bestowed would engage in "holy roller" kinds of activity; they would speak strange gibberish, and there would be other curious physical manifestations.

But the Christians held that the presence of the Holy Spirit would be known by the way people lived. "The fruit of the Spirit," Paul wrote, "is love, joy, peace, longsuffering, kindness, goodness, faith, meekness, self-control" (Gal. 5:22–23). The Spirit makes people better people. He does not simply make them unpredictable people, as the heathen thought.

So it was that in the first century humble, ordinary people came to believe in Jesus and became different people. The Holy Spirit within them guided and strengthened them so that their lives were transformed. Instead of going in the ways of selfishness and sin they became loving people, doing all they could to help others. The transformation was obvious and left even the heathen saying, "Behold, how these Christians love one another!" The Spirit enabled quite ordinary people to live up to what is meant by being members of "the people of God."

"Not Yet Spirit"

Next John has a very unusual expression, which I have translated "it was not yet Spirit." Most translations have something like "the Spirit was not yet given," which makes a better English sentence and seems to translators to be what John must have meant. But there are references to the Spirit's activities among people in earlier days. Thus Luke speaks of John the Baptist as filled with the Holy Spirit from his mother's womb (Luke 1:15). Elizabeth was filled with the Spirit (Luke 1:41), and the Holy Spirit was upon Simeon (Luke 2:25). As we saw in our study of John 3, Jesus taught that it is necessary to be "born of the Spirit" if we are to enter the kingdom of God (John 3:5). So it is clear that the Spirit was active in people before this time. When John has said things like "So is everyone who has been born of the Spirit" (John 3:8), he surely cannot mean that the Spirit has not yet been given.

He goes on to say that the reason for his statement about the Spirit is that "Jesus was not yet glorified." We have seen in our earlier studies that John uses the concept of glory in an unusual way. He does not see glory in terms of majesty and splendor and the like, but in terms of humble service. When we see someone who could rightfully claim a position of ease and honor leaving all that this means in order to engage in lowly service of the needy, there we see true glory as John understands it. And especially do we see glory in the cross of Jesus, for Jesus' death is the supreme example of taking the lowly place to meet the needs of others. So John speaks of Jesus as being "glorified," where other people would say he was "crucified." Thus, with the cross immediately before him, Jesus says, "The hour has come that the Son of man may be glorified," and again, "Now the Son of man is glorified" (12:23; 13:31).

The New Testament makes it clear that things were very different after Jesus died and rose again. In the second chapter of Acts we read of the coming of the Holy Spirit in mighty power on the early church, and from then on references to the Spirit are frequent, much more frequent than in the Old Testament or the Gospels. It has been said that Acts is wrongly named; it is not so much "the Acts of the Apostles" that the book is about as "the Acts of the Holy Spirit." Throughout that book it is the Spirit who is constantly active. And in the Epistles that follow in our New Testament we see that the Spirit was a vital presence for the early Christians.

Putting all this together, we can see that what John is saying is something like this. It is true that the Spirit was active in some measure in Old Testament days and in the days when Jesus was on earth. But he did not come in all his fullness until the work of Jesus had been done. In the providence of God the work of the Son preceded that of the Spirit. The era of the Spirit, the time when the full scope of the Spirit's work would appear, was "not yet."

Jesus invited people to come to him in faith. That was the way they would enter into salvation. Their sins would be forgiven because in due course Jesus would die on the cross as their Savior. And the Spirit of God would take them and transform them. He would make them into loving, outgoing people, people from whose innermost being blessing would flow to others.

This is still the order. Justification precedes sanctification. We do not find our lives transformed by the power of God's Holy Spirit and after that come to believe in Jesus Christ. First we believe, we appropriate what is meant by "Christ crucified." Only then do we come to know what it means to experience the presence of the indwelling Spirit. John is pointing us to an order that is important in the working out of the Christian life.

35

Pride and Prejudice

Some of the crowd, when they had heard these words, said, "This is truly the prophet." Others said, "This is the Christ." But some said, "The Christ does not come from Galilee, does he? Has not the Scripture said, 'The Christ comes of the seed of David and from Bethlehem the village where David was'?" There was a division in the crowd because of him . Now some of them wanted to arrest him, but nobody laid hands on him (John 7:45–52).

The teaching Jesus gave at the feast made a big impression on some of his hearers. "The crowd" is evidently still the pilgrims who had come up to Jerusalem for the feast, not the Jerusalem mob. They were more open-minded than the people of Jerusalem, but not necessarily well informed. They were not unanimous, and John records two different verdicts that they gave after the teaching.

Some of them were sure that Jesus was "the prophet," i.e., the prophet to whose coming Moses looked forward (Deut. 18:15). In earlier passages in this Gospel we have seen references to this prophet, and it is clear that there were quite a few Jews who expected that prophet to appear. Why they should think of Jesus as fulfilling the role is not clear, but then we have no information about what the Jews of the first century thought that prophet would do. Clearly he would be an important person, for otherwise the great Moses would not have prophesied of him centuries before.

There were others who went further and spoke of Jesus as the Christ (v. 41). This we know to be a true perception, though of course we have no way of knowing what they meant by "the Christ." Some people used the term but had strange ideas about who the Christ would be and the kind of work he would do. Some thought he would be a warrior who would push the Romans out of their country. This was probably a fairly widely held idea, because patriotic Jews hated having the Romans rule them and thought that when the Messiah came he would be a very powerful person. Surely then he would get rid of the hated conqueror? Whether or not these people had such a concept of the Messiah we do not know. But at least they saw Jesus as the Christ and we must appreciate that.

But there was prejudice in the air. There were others there who could not possibly think of Jesus as the Messiah, the Christ, because they were so convinced that he came from the wrong place. They held that the Messiah would come from Bethlehem (v. 42), and as Jesus was a Galilean he could not be the Christ. It did not matter how impressive his credentials, how outstanding his teaching, how wonderful his miracles; he came from Galilee and that was that! So does prejudice blind people.

They ask a question about the Christ and Galilee, but the way they put it looks for a negative answer. They rejected the possibility of a Galilean Christ altogether. They speak of "the" Scripture, which normally means a specific passage from the Bible. But it is difficult to find a passage that says exactly what they claim. We can say that the general thrust of many Old Testament passages is such as to suggest that the Christ would be a descendant of David. There are passages like God's message to David: ". . . I will raise up your offspring to succeed you, who will come from your own body, and I will establish his kingdom. . . . I will establish the throne of his kingdom forever" (2 Sam. 7:12–13). Such words point to a great king descended from David, but later words in this passage are hard to apply to the Christ: "When he does wrong, I will punish him . . ." (v. 14b).

There are passages in the Prophets, such as Isaiah 9:2–7, which speaks of the wonderful child who would be born (though without calling him the Christ) and says, "He will reign on David's throne" (v. 7). Again, "A shoot will come up from the stump of Jesse; from his roots a Branch will bear fruit" (Isa. 11:1). Again we read in Jeremiah: "'The days are coming,' declares the LORD, 'when I will raise up to David a righteous Branch . . .'" (Jer. 23:5).

Another possibility is Psalm 89:3–4, where God says, "I have made a covenant with my chosen one, I have sworn to David my servant, I will establish your line forever and make your throne firm through all generations." But this is not a very promising passage for our purpose. While we may well say that it is only Christ who will rule "through all generations," the passage does not specifically mention him. We can certainly say that the name of David is firmly linked with what God would do when he came in blessing (see, for example, Jer. 30:9; 33:15, 17, 22; Ezek. 34:23f.; 37:24; Hos. 3:5; Amos 9:11). We do not doubt that such passages refer to the Christ, but the difficulty is that they do not mention him in set terms and thus we cannot be sure that any of them is "the Scripture" of which the people speak.

There are also passages that point us to Bethlehem, but there is none that says in set terms that the Christ will come from that village. Most Christians think of Micah 5:2, which speaks of "one who will be ruler" as coming from Bethlehem and which goes on to say that his "origins are from of old, from ancient times." This is enough to convince most of us, and I certainly agree. But the point is that the passage does not mention the word *Christ,* and thus we cannot be certain that the people had these words in mind.

In the end we are left wondering. Clearly these people were certain that their Bible connected the Christ with David and with Bethlehem. And we think they were right. We are sure that our Bible does the same. But we cannot find any one passage that does this, so we cannot be sure of exactly what Scripture they had in mind.

So there was a division among the crowd. Some were sure that Jesus was the Christ and some were sure he was not. The second group was so sure and so much in opposition that they wanted to arrest him. They almost certainly did not have the power to do this: John is telling us of people in "the crowd." But they wanted to do so; they were firmly opposed to Jesus.

Failure to Arrest Jesus

The officials therefore came to the chief priests and Pharisees and these said to them, "Why didn't you bring him?" The officials replied, "Never did man so speak." The Pharisees answered them, "Are you deceived too? Have any of the rulers or of the Pharisees believed in him? But this crowd, which does not know the Law, is accursed." Nicodemus, who came to him formerly, said (being one of them), "Does our Law condemn a man if it does not first hear from him and come to know what he is doing?" They answered him saying, "Are you from Galilee too? Search and see that a prophet does not arise from Galilee" (John 7:45–52).

The mention of failure to arrest brings us back to the fact that earlier the chief priests and Pharisees had sent a posse to arrest Jesus (v. 32). Now John tells us what happened when they reported back. They evidently did not say anything at first, but it was obvious that they had no prisoner, so those who had sent them off asked why.

The manuscripts differ a little in reporting their reply (v. 46). Many read: "Never did man speak like this man," and this is accepted by many scholars. But there is good reason for accepting the shorter reading: "Never did man so speak." The officials would have meant that Jesus' teaching impressed them; there had never been a teacher like him. But John probably means us to see a deeper meaning in the words: Never did *man* so speak. The words of Jesus were such that they are not to be thought of as the teaching of a mere man. They are more than that. They are words that come from God.

This is an interesting defense of their failure. It is curious in the first place that they did fail to arrest Jesus. We know that in the providence of God it was not yet time for him to confront the Sanhedrin. But people who are sent to make an arrest are subordinate people and they normally simply carry out instructions. It is not for them to make the big decisions, so they do what they are told. Of course, sometimes they are confronted with circumstances beyond their control, such as the hostility of the crowd. But there were apparently no such circumstances in this case. As far as we can see, there was nothing that physically prevented them from making the arrest.

And people who fail to carry out instructions usually present some excuse. On this occasion we know that there was a division in the crowd, with some people holding that Jesus was the Christ and some rejecting the idea. The officials could have defended themselves by saying that with the crowd divided there was the danger of stirring up trouble if they made the arrest. But they said nothing of the sort. They simply said that no man ever spoke like this.

It was the Pharisees who answered (v. 47). Evidently the chief priests were not as much involved as the Pharisees were. The Pharisees could not go along with the officials for one moment. The only explanation of such outrageous conduct is that they had been "deceived." But that is incredible. So they put their question in a form that means "You aren't deceived, too, are you?" Earlier we noticed that some of the crowd were governed by prejudice in that their idea of the origin of the Messiah prevented them from seeing Jesus as he really was. They rejected his messiahship, not because anything was lacking, but because their own prejudice ruled out the possibility. Now we see the prejudice of the Pharisees. They were the religious experts. They knew.

In their view the common people or the arresting officers could not possibly be right. Prejudice blinded the Pharisees, too.

They go on to point out the stupidity of believing in Jesus by asking whether any of the rulers or Pharisees had believed (v. 48). For them to ask the question was to answer it; no important person could possibly believe! "Rulers" is a general term, but here it seems to mean people like the Sadducees or the leading priests. It is the politically-minded over against the Pharisees, who were religious leaders. What they are saying is that nobody of any consequence has believed in Jesus. It is true that he has a following of a sort. But for the Pharisees this following comes only from the rabble, from people who have no real knowledge. They are certainly not the kind of people who should influence the officials. Actually the officials had not mentioned the crowd, but the Pharisees are not influenced by that. It is enough for them that their own party and the people they respected, such as the "rulers," had not believed in Jesus. Therefore the officials were in the wrong when they took notice of the nobodies who followed Jesus.

The Pharisees go on to speak of the crowd as "accursed" (v. 49). They perhaps have in mind such words as those of Deuteronomy 27:26: "Cursed is the man who does not uphold the words of this law by carrying them out." Whether or not it was this passage that was meant, there cannot be the slightest doubt about the contempt felt by people like the Pharisees for the common people. Those who gave time to the study of the Law regarded this as the highest good open to man (they did not allow women to study it!). They studied it in minute detail, often, alas, missing its important teaching while they concentrated on things like the number of words in a book. But there is no doubt about the way the Pharisees looked down on people who did not accept their view, people like those in the crowd of pilgrims. So they tell the officials that they are quite wrong to be impressed with Jesus. Only accursed people are influenced by him.

A Hesitant Defense

They must have been greatly surprised to find Nicodemus, one of their own number, speaking up in mild opposition to the rest (v. 50). John tells us that this man had come to Jesus earlier, and he repeats now what he told us then, that Nicodemus was 'one of them,' i.e., a ruler. It was the last thing the other Pharisees would have expected.

Actually Nicodemus's defense is very tentative (v. 51). He simply takes up the reference to the Law, which the Pharisaic spokesmen have made, and points out its relevance to their view of Jesus. He does not even make a categorical statement but asks a question, though the way

287

he puts it looks for a negative answer. It is as though he were saying, "Our Law does not condemn a man, does it, if it does not first hear from him . . . ?" The Jewish laws did not provide for automatic condemnation of the kind of Pharisees were engaging in. A man had to be examined and given a chance to defend himself. The judges had to know what he was doing, not what his opponents thought about him.

There is irony here. The Pharisees' question implied that no important person believed in Jesus, and straightaway Nicodemus, "a ruler of the Jews" (3:1) spoke up. They spoke of the people who did not know the Law as "accursed," and immediately they are reminded that they were not acting in accordance with the Law. They were prejudging the case. In the literal sense they were prejudiced.

Prophets and Galilee

And that prejudice prevented them from paying serious attention to what Nicodemus was saying. They were angry men, and people who have lost their temper do not usually weigh arguments carefully. They use another question expecting a negative answer and an emphatic pronoun to give the sense, "Surely *you* aren't from Galilee, are you?" (v. 52). They recognize that Nicodemus is a resident of Jerusalem in good standing. They do not suggest that he is a provincial from the country districts. But they make it clear that they see it as incredible that anyone who is anyone could think for one moment that Jesus, the Galilean, was worthy of credence.

They go on to invite Nicodemus to search for a prophet from Galilee. He will see that there have never been any. Actually they use the present tense, and it is just possible that they mean that no prophet comes from Galilee in their own day. That would mean little, because there was no prophet from anywhere else at that time either. But they may possibly mean that the Galileans of their day were specially unspiritual. "Look for yourself," they may be saying. "You will see that a prophet never comes from people like these Galileans."

If that is not their meaning, if they are saying that there has never been a prophet from Galilee, they are mistaken, for Jonah came from Gath Hepher (2 Kings 14:25), a town in that district. Other prophets may also have come from Galilee; our knowledge of the origins of the prophets is not as full as we would like. But it is certain that Galileans were looked down on by many of the dwellers in Jerusalem (it is not exactly unknown for other city people in other times and other cultures to have a poor opinion of people they regard as country bumpkins).

This attitude was not universal, however, and some of the Rabbis could do better than the Pharisees in our incident. There is a saying of Rabbi Eliezer: "There was not a tribe in Israel from which there did not come prophets." God, of course, raises up his messengers where he will. Prejudiced and self-opinionated people like these Pharisees are not good guides to what God has done and is doing in his world.

It is interesting to notice another possibility. Years ago Rudolph Bultmann, a great German scholar, suggested that we should understand the text to mean not "a prophet" but "the prophet," i.e., the Messiah. Jonah was so obviously from Galilee that the Pharisees should not have made such a glaring mistake as to say that *no* prophet came from that province. But the context is one in which people are talking about the Messiah, and the suggestion is that they are saying that, whatever be the case with other prophets, *the* prophet, the Messiah, does not come from Galilee.

At the time Bultmann and others made this suggestion there was no support for it in the manuscripts. All without exception read "a prophet." But since then a very old papyrus has come to light (which the scholars call P66) and it does have the definite article: "the prophet." This seemed to some a confirmation of Bultmann's conjecture and they have been inclined to accept it.

That is an interesting incident in scholarly activity. But it still remains that every Greek manuscript except this one reads "a prophet," and no good reason has been suggested why this one manuscript should be right and every other Greek manuscript in existence should be wrong. It still seems that we should accept the reading "a prophet." The Pharisees were making Galilee out to be the kind of place from which spiritual leadership can never come. So does prejudice blind even people as religious as these Pharisees.

36

"Caught in the Act"

*And they went each to his own home, but Jesus went to the
Mount of Olives. Now early in the morning he made his way to
the temple. All the people were coming to him and he sat down
and taught them. The scribes and the Pharisees bring to him a
woman taken in adultery. They stood her in the middle and
they say to him, "Teacher, this woman was taken committing
adultery, caught in the very act. Now in the law Moses
commanded us to stone such women. What, therefore, do you
say?" They said this to test him so that they might have
something wherewith to accuse him. But Jesus stooped down
and wrote on the ground with his finger. Then as they
continued to ask him he straightened up and said to them, "Let
him that is without sin among you be first to throw a stone at
her." And again he stooped and wrote on the ground. Now
when they heard this they went out one by one, beginning with
the elders, and he was left alone, and the woman in the midst.
And Jesus straightened up and said to her, "Woman, where are
they? Did no one condemn you?" "No one, sir" she replied. And
Jesus said, "Neither do I condemn you. Go, and from now on
sin no more" (John 7:53—8:11).*

There seems no doubt that this story forms no part of
John's Gospel. It is found in only one of the oldest manuscripts, and
scholars agree that this one manuscript cannot be held to be right,
against the overwhelming weight of the others. When the story does

begin to appear it is found in various places: it is found after verse 36 or after verse 44, sometimes at the end of this Gospel, or again after Luke 21:38. More manuscripts put it after verse 52 than anywhere else, but the divergence makes it plain that there were scribes who thought the story ought to be retained but did not know where it ought to go. So they put it where they thought best, and their ideas varied.

The language convinces many that the passage does not belong in this Gospel. For example, it speaks of "the scribes" (v. 3), an expression familiar to us from the first three Gospels, but which John does not use at all. There are several Greek words which occur in this little story, but which are found rarely or not at all or which are used in different ways in the Fourth Gospel.

Such considerations seem decisive. There is no real reason for thinking that John included this story in his Gospel. But that does not mean that it did not happen. The story has an authentic ring to it. As we read it we feel, "This is what Jesus would have said!"

If it is not the account of something that actually happened, the question arises, "Where did the story come from?" It is not the kind of tale that the early church would have made up, for it might be taken to mean that adultery did not matter very much, and the early church took up no such position. Indeed, the story seems not to have been very popular in the early church and it would seem to be for this reason. Christian leaders apparently felt that it might encourage people to engage in sexual adventures, which they themselves resolutely opposed. So it seems that this is a true story, a story of something that really happened, which for some reason the writers of our Gospels chose not to include. But it persisted in the early church and in time tended to become attached to John's Gospel. We may profitably study it as an incident in which we see Jesus' compassion and the way he handled ingenious and hardhearted opponents.

The Accusation

Clearly the story once belonged to a longer narrative. As we have it, it starts with a statement that everyone went home, but it does not tell us who these people were, nor from where they went home. It goes on to say that Jesus went to the Mount of Olives, so evidently the preceding narrative was set in Jerusalem. And if we do not know much about the place, neither do we know the time. But Luke tells us that when Jesus was in Jerusalem in the days just before he was arrested, he used to teach in the city during the day and go out to lodge in the Mount of Olives at night (Luke 21:37; Mark speaks of Bethany, Mark 11:11, but this would be seen as part of the Mount of Olives). It would all fit in if we thought of the incident as taking place at Jerusalem during Jesus' last days.

The story goes on to say that early in the morning Jesus went to the temple, and we are reminded that Luke says that the people went to the temple early to hear Jesus teach (Luke 21:38). "All the people" came to hear (v. 2), so evidently there was quite a large crowd. "Were coming" is continuous: it gives a picture of people continuing to come over quite a period. Jesus sat down to teach, for sitting, of course, was the normal posture for a teacher in those times. Standing before a class seems not to have been usual.

Now "the scribes and the Pharisees" come on the scene. Scribes were people who could read and write, quite an accomplishment in a day when the majority were illiterate. We should not exaggerate this, for there were many who could read in the first-century Roman Empire, but we should not read back into the situation anything like the degree of literacy in a modern Western community. Being members of a profession concerned with reading and writing, the scribes themselves did a good deal of reading, and many of them were learned. And as the Law, the first five books of our Old Testament, was the principal subject of study, they tended to be religious men as well. This, of course, formed a natural link with the Pharisees who were wholeheartedly concerned with the way God should be served. While the scribes were not all Pharisees (some were linked with the high priests and their associates, e.g., Acts 4:5), it is never surprising to find them mentioned together.

On this occasion they come to Jesus, bringing with them a woman they said had been caught in the very act of adultery, and they go on to ask whether she should be stoned. This raises some very difficult questions.

Proving Adultery

One of the questions concerns the proving of adultery. Let us notice first of all that in Judaism at that time adultery meant sexual relations outside marriage on the part of a married woman. Her husband was not regarded as committing adultery unless his sexual partner was married. In the male-dominated society of that era there was a wider permissiveness for the husband than for the wife.

But adultery was an offense very hard to prove. This is so in the nature of the case, for lovers the world over and the centuries through tend to seek solitude. In all its forms lovemaking is a private activity of two persons. It is easier to suspect a breach of marriage relations than to prove it. This difficulty was intensified by the way first-century Jews conducted their legal system. They insisted on much more rigorous standards of proof than those accepted elsewhere. For example, it was required that there be two witnesses, and it was not enough for the witnesses to have seen the offenders in a compromising position, such as coming out of a room in which they had been alone. Even lying on a bed together was not sufficient proof. The witnesses must be able to testify that the movements of the people in question allowed no other interpretation. And, of course, the evidence of the two witnesses must agree.

There was moreover a legal rule, "No penalty without a warning." This meant that in the case of any crime it was necessary that a potential offender be warned not to do such and such a thing. He must be aware that a certain action was wrong. He was not regarded as in breach of a law if he did not know what the law provided. An interesting provision is that a scholar need not be warned orally. It is presumed that his study of the Law made him aware of what he should and should not do. But lesser mortals had to be told.

In the case of adultery this meant normally that the husband expressly told his wife, in front of witnesses, of her duty. Of course, it could be argued that even a young bride knows what she should do in marriage and this knowledge made legal arguments possible. But the maxim was there and must be borne in mind in such a situation as the one with which we are dealing. It added to the difficulty of proving adultery, however it be understood. However, on this occasion the scribes and the Pharisees appear to imply that the conditions had been fulfilled. They had the necessary witnesses and the woman had been taken in the very act.

A Trap?

All this leads us to ask some questions. First, it is impossible for a woman to commit adultery all by herself, so the question arises, "Where was the man?" If the woman had been taken in the very act, as her accusers said, then there should have been a male offender who was taken, too. Of course, if there had been a trap set for the woman, arrangements might well have been made to enable the man in the case to make good his escape. It is not easy to see how he could have avoided capture otherwise.

We do not know why a trap should have been set for the woman, but clearly the accusers were bent on having her executed. It may well be that the husband wanted her out of the way and had engaged helpers to secure that end. In Jewish law he could, of course, have divorced her without any difficulty. All that was necessary was for him to write "a bill of divorcement" and send her away. But if she had property she would take it with her when she was divorced, whereas if she died it would revert to her husband. We know nothing of her circumstances, and the situation may have been very different. All that I am saying is that the story reads as though a trap had been set for the woman, and it is not difficult to envisage circumstances in which an unscrupulous husband might seek to entrap his erring wife with a view to having her executed.

Another feature of the story is the lack of proper legal officials. There is no mention of any officer of the court, and the accusers may well have been trying to bring about a lynching. They faced a problem because, while the Law of Moses provided for an execution as they claimed, it was not possible for the Jews to execute anyone without the permission of the Romans (see 18:31), and the Romans would never give their permission for an execution for such an offense as adultery. But if a lynching took place, and if this was discovered and the perpetrators brought to book, they could always claim that they were following the provisions of their religion and hope that they would not be treated too harshly (this was evidently what happened when Stephen was stoned). In any case the Romans would not be able to bring the woman back to life.

But if this is the way the events should be understood, it was well for the lynching party that they should make out as good a case as they could for the woman's guilt and for her punishment according to their law. So they had their witnesses. And they went through the form of consulting Jesus, who was a religious teacher, even if not one recognized by the rabbinical schools.

"What Do You Say?"

But if the participants in the plot had ends of their own to secure, at least some of them were Pharisees and strongly opposed to Jesus. They decided to use the woman to try to score against him. So they submit the case to him and ask for his opinion. It seems that rabbis were often asked to settle knotty points in the interpretation of Scripture. Rabbis were the great expositors of the Law of Moses, and when a difficult point arose it was standard procedure (and very convenient!) to look to the experts for their opinion. There are many such interpretations scattered through the Mishnah and the Talmud. They are not put in the form of decisions in legal cases, but in that of interpretations of passages of Scripture as in the present case.

They begin politely by addressing Jesus as "Teacher" (v. 4). They go on to explain the circumstances. There is apparently no doubt about guilt. The woman was "caught in the very act." The problem was what their course of action should be. They say that Moses prescribed stoning in such cases (v. 5), though it should be noted that they do not quote Moses exactly. In both Leviticus 20:10 and Deuteronomy 22:22 it is provided that both guilty parties be executed, whereas these zealots use the feminine form and confine their attention to the execution of the woman in the case. They also specify stoning as the method of execution, whereas the Law of Moses says no more than that the guilty couple should be put to death. Stoning was prescribed for the couple when a man had sex with an engaged girl (Deut. 22:23–24), in circumstances where her consent could be assumed, but for only the man if circumstances were otherwise (Deut. 22:25–27). It is true that the Jews had come to the view that stoning was to be used where Scripture spoke of the death penalty without prescribing the method. But the point is that here the accusers in their zeal ascribe to Moses words that he did not utter.

For them the position in Scripture was plain. But would Jesus agree? They use the emphatic pronoun, "What do *you* say?" On the surface of it, this is a perfectly normal question. They were about to do something that the Romans might not approve of, and they were consulting a religious teacher to make sure that they were doing the right thing.

But the narrator goes on to tell us that they were not sincere (v. 6). They asked their question as a test for Jesus, with a view to getting him to say something of which they could accuse him. It is not quite certain what the nature of the trap was. Perhaps they thought that if Jesus said, "Stone her," he would be in trouble with the Romans, for only they had the right to execute and they did not execute for adultery. If on the other hand he said, "Do not stone her," he might well lose influence with many of the Jews, for he could then be pictured as urging people not to obey the Law. It is objected that the Romans would not have taken action, but we do not know enough about their views on such situations to be definite.

Another suggestion is that the zealots were simply concerned with Jewish opinion, not that of the Romans. Those who hold this view maintain that, while death was the penalty for adultery in the Law, there was a strong body of opinion that opposed this. There is evidence that adultery was fairly prevalent during the first century, but executions were uncommon. Thus, were Jesus to favor stoning, he would alienate a considerable number of people who thought the penalty too severe. But if he rejected it, he would be held to be soft on sin and a breaker of the Law.

His enemies clearly felt that whichever way he answered they had him. Of course, he could have avoided giving a decision. He was not in an official position. He was not required to make pronouncements and he was not a recognized teacher. He could simply have refused to answer. But if he had taken this option, the woman would certainly have been killed. In any case it was not Jesus' way to avoid hard questions.

Writing on the Ground

But at first he said nothing. He stooped and wrote on the ground with his finger. The narrator does not tell us what he wrote, but Christian expositors have not let this deter them. In the early church it was suggested that he wrote the sins of the accusers, but this does not attract much support in modern times. Some have felt that Jesus was following the practice of Roman judges, who wrote their sentence first and then read it out. On this view what he wrote was "Let him that is without sin among you be first to throw a stone at her." Another view is that Jesus simply did not wish to look at these professedly godly men who were so intent on killing a woman; the writing was incidental.

An interesting modern view is that Jesus wrote some words from the Old Testament. The Hebrew alphabet consists of consonants only, the reader supplying the necessary vowels. A system was devised of using dots and dashes above and below the consonants to indicate vowels, but the text of sacred Scripture is consonantal. Sometimes more than one set of vowels can be supplied to the same consonants, and in the first century it was held that a given set of consonants may be understood to include all the meanings given by the different sets of vowels that might be supplied. If Jesus spoke the words, the reasoning runs, he was limited to the meaning of the vowels he actually spoke, whereas if he wrote them, he could include all the possible meanings of those consonants.

It has accordingly been suggested that Jesus wrote some words from Exodus 23:1: "Do not help a wicked man by being a malicious witness." With different vowels "a wicked man" becomes "wickedness." If this is in fact what Jesus wrote and if this is why he wrote it, he is warning the accusers (a) to be careful lest they be guilty of being malicious witnesses, and (b) to make sure that they are not associating themselves with wickedness, with an unsavory business. People who themselves were not giving false witness might find themselves in legal trouble if they associated themselves with what false witnesses were doing.

Witnesses

The apocryphal Book of Susanna emphasizes the importance of truthfulness in witnesses and the danger attending the bearing of false witness. In the story two wicked elders tried to persuade Susanna to have sexual intercourse with them, and when she refused they accused her of this misconduct with a young man. She was sentenced to death, but as she was being led away to execution a young man called Daniel prevailed on them to go back to the place of judgment. There he examined the witnesses separately and showed that they were lying. The result was that the punishment the elders had tried to have administered to Susanna was inflicted on them and they were executed. This insistence on true witness and the danger of false witness must be kept in mind as we proceed to the next stage of the story.

When Jesus said nothing, but wrote in the dust, apparently his enemies felt that they had him in trouble. They pressed him to give them an answer. His answer has become a classic: "Let him that is without sin among you be first to throw a stone at her" (v. 7). It could not be said that Jesus was soft on law and order. He definitely told them to throw a stone. But, by confining his invitation to the man among them who was without sin, he effectively stopped the execution.

His words invited them to think again. And among the thoughts that went through their minds there must have been the importance of being sure the witnesses were trustworthy. If no proper warning had been given to the woman, for example, the witnesses might well be in danger. And anyone who associated with a false witness could be penalized.

Jesus resumed his writing on the ground while they thought about it. One scholar thinks that this time he wrote, "Have nothing to do with a false charge" (Exod. 23:7). Those who read these words would be able to finish the verse: ". . . and do not put an innocent or honest person to death, for I will not acquit the guilty." These very words had been used by Daniel in the story of Susanna to convict the lying elders and bring about their deaths. Whether Jesus wrote these words or not we cannot know, but the truth they expressed must have occurred to his hearers. At first they had been eager for a stoning, seeing nothing but the opportunity for killing off someone who could not strike back. Now they realized that it was not so simple. If they joined with false witnesses to bring about an execution, their own execution might well follow.

Exit the Accusers

As the realities of the situation dawned on them they went out (v. 9). None of them were guiltless, and they came to see that they were in no

297

position to throw stones. How many of them were deterred by the simple realization that they were sinners themselves, and how many were thinking of the penalty of associating with false witnesses, we have no way of knowing. All that we know is that they went. The elders went first. They would have the greater responsibility. In the culture of the day they would be expected to take the lead, which meant that they had to be very careful. If there was anything amiss, they would be expected to take a stand against it, so their place was more precarious than that of the younger men. But when the elders went off, the younger saw that their position was impossible and they went away, too.

Jesus stood up and saw that the woman alone remained. "In the midst" may mean that Jesus' original hearers were still there and that those who had gone were the people who had accused the woman. But the important point was that there was nobody there who wanted to stone the woman.

Jesus asked her, "Where are they? Did no one condemn you?" (v. 10). "No one, sir" was her answer (v. 11). We could take the last word in the sense "Lord," but there is no evidence that she was a follower of Jesus, so it is probably better to take it in its more usual sense. She is polite and doubtless deeply grateful.

Jesus declined to condemn her, but this does not mean that he countenanced her sin. "From now on sin no more" implies that she had been sinning and is a call to her to amend her ways. Jesus does not say that she is forgiven. She has given no evidence of penitence or faith. She was still an unregenerate sinner. But he had been merciful to her, and his call to her to cease from sin is a way of indicating that the way is open wide if she would but come.

37

The Light of the World

So Jesus spoke to them again saying, "I am the light of the world. He who follows me will certainly not walk in the darkness, but will have the light of life." The Pharisees therefore said to him, "You are bearing witness about yourself; your testimony is not true." Jesus answered them saying, "Even if I do bear witness about myself my testimony is true, because I know where I came from and where I am going. But you do not know where I come from or where I am going. You make your judgment according to the flesh, I judge no one. And if I do judge, my judgment is true, because I am not alone, but I and the Father who sent me. And in your law it stands written that the testimony of two men is true. I am he who bears witness about myself and the Father who sent me bears witness about me." Therefore they said to him, "Where is your Father?" Jesus answered, "You know neither me nor my Father. If you had known me, you would know my Father too." He spoke these words in the Treasury, as he was teaching in the temple, and no one arrested him, because his hour had not yet come (John 8:12–20).

Most scholars hold that this chapter continues to refer to what happened at the Feast of Tabernacles. That was a great festival and its observance was not hurried. The ceremonies with light and with water were picturesque and were clearly the center of attention. As this chapter is taken up at least in part with the importance of light and the way light helps us see something of the significance of Jesus' person and mission, it is thought that it would naturally refer to what happened and what was said at the feast. It would certainly fit in.

But we should notice that nothing is said about the feast in this part of the Gospel. Nothing is said about the crowds either, and the crowds at the feast were large and were a significant part of the celebration. Tabernacles was not a private occasion, but one when the gathering of large numbers of people made it clear that this was a national celebration. Now the crowds are mentioned constantly in chapter 7 (eight times in this one chapter), but John does not mention them again until 11:42. It is, of course, possible that they were there but it just happens that he says nothing about them. But it is more probable that he does not mention them because they were not there. It seems that the feast was over and the crowds had gone off home. This is all the more likely in that throughout this part of the Gospel Jesus is confronted by his enemies. They hassle him and try to trip him up in some way. They are there throughout. We would probably not be far wrong if we thought of the events of this chapter as taking place after the Feast of Tabernacles, though not long after it. The crowds have gone, but people's thoughts are still taken up with the wonderful ceremonies. And without the crowds to inhibit them, the enemies of Jesus use the occasion to try to overthrow him.

Jesus' Great Claim

The "so" and the "again" (v. 12) mean that this followed on some previous incident. As we saw in our last study, there is no real reason for holding that the story of the woman caught in adultery formed part of the original Gospel, let alone that it stood just before these words. And if we go back to what immediately precedes it, we find a meeting of Jewish leaders. There is no obvious connection.

But the last words in that incident were the retort of the leaders to Nicodemus in which they ask whether he is a Galilean and invite him to search and see that no prophet ever arises from Galilee. It may be that we are to take John as meaning that Jesus' great claim is to be understood over against that contemptuous rejection. They saw him as an insignificant provincial, not even a prophet. John immediately records that Jesus is the light, not just of Galilee, not just of all the land of the Jews, but of the whole world. It is the kind of ironical situation that John delights to record.

Jesus' "I am" is in the style of deity (v. 12). In an earlier study I pointed out that in Greek it is not necessary to give the personal pronoun on most occasions (p. 217). The verbal forms differ with different personal subjects. And, as the form of the verb thus showed what the subject must be, people did not bother to state it. They let the verb tell what the subject was.

But if they wanted to put some emphasis on the subject, if they wanted to say "*I* am" rather than "I am," they included the personal pronoun. The use of the pronoun points to emphatic speech.

Now when pious Jews were translating their Scriptures from Hebrew into Greek they evidently thought that they ought to use some emphatic form of speech when they were giving us the words of God himself. We can still feel the force of this when we reflect on the form in which we have traditionally received the Ten Commandments. There is a series of commands beginning "Thou shalt not—" a form we would not normally use at all. But it sounds right in the Commandments. In line with this the translators quite often used the emphatic pronoun when recording words that God himself had spoken. "I am," with God as the speaker, would be the emphatic "*I* am."

This is what we find with the saying "I am the light of the world." The "I" is emphatic. This is the way God speaks. The form of the expression is making a claim, quite apart from the meaning of the words.

Light

And the words do make a staggering claim. We are probably to understand them against the background of the Feast of Tabernacles. The words were evidently spoken not long after that feast, and John has recorded them right after his account of the feast. Now a very spectacular part of the feast was the use of the great candelabra. There were four of them and they were filled with oil by young men who to do this climbed ladders that, according to the Talmud, were fifty cubits high. The light from the lamps was brilliant and the Mishnah says that "there was not a courtyard in Jerusalem that did not reflect the light." Such brilliant illumination was a great occasion and seen but rarely in the ancient city. When the feast was over, of course, the great candelabra were not lit. This formed a marked contrast, and it was in the darkness of the post-festival period that Jesus spoke.

He spoke not only of being a light to Jerusalem, which, spectacular as it was, was all that the light of the feast could mean. He spoke of being a light of the world. The imagery implies that the world is in darkness, in the darkness of sin. Men left to themselves cannot overcome that darkness. But Jesus claims that he can bring them the illumination that will banish the darkness in which they habitually live, and this wherever they are in the whole wide world.

There is some foreshadowing of this in the Old Testament, for example, when the Servant of the Lord is called to be "a light for the Gentiles" (Isa. 42:6; 49:6; cf. 51:4). It seems that the idea did not die out completely in Israel, but on the whole the nation did not make much of it. In the first century the evidence is that most Jews were inward-looking. They were very happy that their nation was the chosen nation and that they were the chosen people. But they saw that as a privilege rather than a responsibility. Such a group as the community in which the Dead Sea Scrolls were written was very particularist. They saw themselves as the people God chose and all outside their sect as lost. Other Jews were not so extreme, but most of them tended to confine the love of God to his chosen people.

So Jesus' teaching that he was the light, not simply of his followers, nor even of Israel, but of the whole world, was breathtaking. It implied that God had a love for all mankind and not only for Israel. No one is beyond the love and the care of God. The coming of the Son of God is to bring light to all people, whoever they may be and wherever they may live. He is the light of nothing less than this whole world.

The Light of Life

People are expected to react to the light. They are not simply to be happy because it has reached them, as the people of Jerusalem were happy in the illumination of the great candelabra. Jesus immediately speaks of people following him. The light is to bring them out of the darkness, and that means that they must now follow the right road; they must follow Jesus.

In first-century Palestine a teacher like Jesus moved about from place to place and his disciples went with him. So to "follow" Jesus for people like the Twelve (and others, see Luke 8:1–3) meant literally following him as he went from place to place. But the word, of course, could also be used in the sense "follow as a disciple." While there was often in Jesus' lifetime a literal, physical following, the term was used from the first in the sense of becoming an adherent of Jesus and seeking to live according to his teaching.

When anyone does this, Jesus says, he will certainly not walk in the darkness. There is an emphatic double negative here, which emphasizes that it is impossible for anyone who follows the light of the world to find himself walking in the dark. Darkness is often used in antiquity, in Judaism and elsewhere, for negative things, things like obscurity, concealment, deception, error, and the like. Sometimes it is used of the darkness of death. Jesus is saying that anyone who follows him is delivered from all such things.

On the contrary, the follower "will have the light of life." This means more than that he will walk in the light. That way of putting it, of course, expresses an important truth, but it views light as something external, an illumination coming from some external source that enables the traveler to see where he is going. To "have" the light means something extra, for now the light is not something external that may or may not be present when it is needed. The follower of Jesus *has* the light.

And this light is "the light of life." That is to say, it is light that excludes death, light that is intimately involved with life. We have seen repeatedly in this Gospel that these two concepts are closely connected. Now we see this repeated and at the same time see that Jesus is the source of the light that means life.

Testimony

But Jesus' opponents are not listening, or if they are hearing the words they are not taking notice of what they mean. They do not concern themselves with light and darkness; indeed, these two great concepts are not mentioned again in the rest of the chapter. Instead the Pharisees turn immediately to the question of the rules of evidence. They say that Jesus is not to be believed because he is talking about himself (v. 13). Of course, when a man talks about himself, his detractors will always think that he has a bias and that what he says must be weighed carefully. But these Pharisees go further than that. They simply reject Jesus' whole testimony because it comes from him personally. "Your testimony is not true," they say. By "true" they seem to mean "valid"; it is testimony that does not conform to the rules and therefore is not to be accepted. They would have agreed in any case that it was not true, but their point is that self-testimony is not valid testimony and cannot be accepted when anyone is trying to establish a point in a court of law.

So they want to talk about testimony. Jesus proceeds to show that they do not really know what they are talking about. He points out that he is qualified to talk about himself whereas they are not. Jesus is aware of his heavenly origin and destiny, but these Pharisees know neither (v. 14). The great point that is insisted on throughout this Gospel is that Jesus is sent by God. The two Greek verbs for "to send" occur with great frequency. In fact John uses both of them more often than does anyone else in the New Testament. And his most frequent use is for the Father's sending of the Son. It is a basic teaching of this Gospel that in Jesus we see none less than the One whom God has sent into the world to do his will and bring salvation to sinners.

But God has not sent him with a blare of trumpets and an army of angels so that it would be impossible to deny his heavenly credentials. The self-satisfied, the proud, the smug, are in no position to appreciate the great spiritual realities, and they do not recognize the Son of God. The lowly in heart are in a different position. They do believe in Jesus and they recognize that God has sent him. They may not know all about him and their capacity to carry on a theological discussion may be minimal. But it is not great intellectual capacity or years of theological education that matter. Such things neither bring people close to Jesus nor compel them to stay at a distance. It is spiritual perception that counts and it is this that the Pharisees lacked. They did not have the humility or the self-knowledge or the close walk with God that would enable them to appreciate what God was doing in Jesus.

Their judgment was "according to the flesh" (v. 15). "Flesh" is, of course, the soft part of the body and in itself is neither good nor bad. In some parts of the New Testament it is used of what is sinful (cf. our expression: the temptations of "the world, the flesh and the devil"), but John does not often have such a usage. The term can refer simply to what is weak about human life, and this human life of ours is inevitably weak in its knowledge of ultimate spiritual things and in its ability to understand and act on them. The trouble with these Pharisees was that they were making a judgment on profound spiritual realities (the Father's sending of his Son into the world) on the basis of human weakness and human limitation. They did not understand Jesus' heavenly origin and destination and were thus unable to judge him.

His attitude was so different from theirs that he says, "I judge no one." In the sense in which they were judging (with their minds closed to fundamental spiritual realities) he was not judging. It would be wrong to use the same verb for two such different activities. So Jesus says simply that he judges no one.

This presents us with a problem, for Jesus later says that he has many things "to speak and to judge" (v. 26), that he came into the world for judgment (9:39). Indeed, the Father has committed all judgment to him (5:22). We should probably understand this in the sense that judgment was not his aim. He came not to judge but to save (12:47), and this is constantly in view throughout this Gospel. But the salvation he died to bring is not something automatic. There were many who refused to have anything to do with Jesus or his salvation. Did he then judge them? In one sense, not at all. They judged themselves. They turned away from the salvation that God was offering them, and that meant that they called down judgment on themselves. We get it all wrong if we think of Jesus as a grim tyrant looking around for people he could send to hell. He came to rescue people, not to sentence them, and John never lets us forget this. This is what is in mind at this point. Jesus, the Savior, judges no one. Those who reject him judge themselves.

The Testimony of Two

So Jesus claims that when he judges his judgment is true (v. 16). This is because he does not stand alone but is to be seen always in conjunction with the Father who sent him. Notice how the Father's sending of the Son is stressed. For John this is one of the great truths and again and again he reports sayings of Jesus that bring this out. So Jesus' judgment is never to be thought of as a merely personal judgment. All he does he does together with the Father.

This enables him to go on to the validity of his testimony, even as judged by the criteria of the Pharisees. They disregarded the testimony of Jesus because it stood alone. Very well. Jesus reminds them that "in your law" testimony is valid when there are two witnesses who agree (v. 17). His "your law" sets him apart from them (cf. the way Nicodemus can say "our law," 7:51). At the same time it reminds them of what was valid even from their point of view. The law required two witnesses (Deut. 19:15), and even when a man's life was at stake two witnesses were sufficient to send him to execution (Deut. 17:6). It was specifically laid down that the testimony of one person is not sufficient (Num. 35:30), and the Jews were so impressed by this that even when the number of witnesses was not mentioned they took it that at least two were required.

Two witnesses would establish a position. Jesus goes on to say that in his case there were two witnesses, the Father and himself (v. 18), and once more the Father is characterized by the fact that he sent Jesus. Mission is very important throughout this Gospel. It was this testimony that carried conviction to Jesus. For him what men said mattered little; it was the Father's testimony that mattered.

But for the Pharisees that was another matter. They asked where Jesus' Father was (v. 19). They were doubtless looking for a human figure, someone they could see and question. Such a figure was not available. But then what difference did it make? They could see and question Jesus and they still refused to believe him. The point was that they lacked spiritual perception. They could not recognize that the wonderful teaching Jesus was giving was true, nor could they recognize that it was endorsed by the Father they professed to serve. As Jesus had just spoken of himself as "the light of the world" (v. 12), it may not be inappropriate to say that the Pharisees' preoccupation with darkness disqualified them from a worthwhile verdict on the light with which they were confronted. They never did come to see that there was a unity between Jesus and the Father. If they had come to see the truth of what Jesus was saying, if they had really come to know him (as his disciples had done), they would have known the Father as well. The two are inseparable. It is impossible to know the one without the other. The Pharisees never did learn this.

Jesus' Hour

John rounds off this section of his narrative by telling us that Jesus was teaching "in the Treasury" (v. 20). This can scarcely mean the place where the temple treasures were actually stored. It must refer to that part of the precincts where people came when they wished to make their offerings. There was a part of the Court of the Women where there were thirteen trumpet-shaped collection boxes into which the devout would cast their offerings. Each one had an inscription to show to what use the offerings cast into that particular box would be put. That the court was called "the Court of the Women" does not mean that men would not be there, for each of the courts was named for the people who could go no farther. Thus Israelites as well as Gentiles were in the Court of the Gentiles, but the Gentiles could not go into the Court of the Women. Israelite males and females could both be found in that court, but women could not go into the next court.

John goes on to say that nobody arrested Jesus. He implies that some would have liked to do this, and in view of the hostility of the Pharisees throughout the section we have been looking at we can see that this was certainly justified. But "his hour had not yet come" and until it had come he was safe from all his enemies. As we have seen in earlier studies, this is a note that begins as early as 2:4 and recurs from time to time throughout the Gospel until we come to the eve of the crucifixion. John is clear throughout that Jesus moves towards his "hour."

38

Dying in Sin

Therefore he said to them again, "I am going away and you will look for me and you will die in your sin. Where I am going you cannot come." The Jews said therefore, "He won't kill himself, will he? Because he says, 'Where I am going you cannot come.'" And he said to them, "You are from below, I am from above; you are of this world, I am not of this world. Therefore I told you that you will die in your sins. For if you do not believe that I AM, you will die in your sins" (John 8:21–24).

We have seen that John has a great interest in life and specifically in eternal life. It is one of his great interests to bring out the wonderful difference Jesus made by bringing to people the news of what God has done to give them life. He emphasizes that the whole purpose of the death of Jesus was to bring life to all who believe. In studying John we must bear this well in mind and indeed put strong emphasis on it.

But the other side of that coin is that there is such a thing as death. People may refuse the offer of eternal life. Some did in John's day and some do in our day. John does not overlook the fact that the offer of life is made against a background of death. If people are not brought into life, then they die. John is a realist. He does not gloss over unpleasant facts. And one such unpleasant fact is that if people do not enter eternal life, they die.

John pays a good deal of attention to this. For example, he uses the verb *to die* twenty-eight times in all, which is more than in any other book in the New Testament. Nearest is Romans, which has it twenty-three times, a book that, like this Gospel, gives serious attention to the issues of eternal life and death. The other Gospels have the verb much less frequently: Matthew five times, Mark nine, and Luke ten times. Clearly John's use of the word is exceptional. He also has the noun *death* more than the other Gospel writers, but as all four come within the narrow range of six to eight this is not specially significant.

John speaks of sin seventeen times, while Matthew has it seven times, Mark six times, and Luke eleven times. This emphasis is not always noticed. For example, one scholar has written, "The fact of sin ceases to be the dominant fact in his theology, but here and there he recognises it and makes some partial attempt to connect it with his own doctrine of the work of Christ"; and again, "the doctrine of sin, in the sense that it meets us elsewhere in the New Testament, is almost wholly absent from the Fourth Gospel."

But this is just not true: it does not square with the facts. John has so many great thoughts that apparently this scholar did not notice that he is not oblivious to the problem of sin. John has his own way of dealing with it, and it would be a mistake to hold that, because he does not treat sin in the same way as does Paul, for example, he does not see it as serious. He does. And in the passage we are studying today we see this clearly. Here he links death and sin in such a way as to make it clear that both are serious and that the one leads inevitably to the other. The only way of escape is to respond to the fact that God sent his Son to be the Savior of the world.

Going Away

"Therefore he said" links the words that follow to those that precede, but the link is not such that we can say exactly how they are related or whether they were spoken on the same occasion. We do not know exactly when Jesus said them, but John knows that they are important and he includes them. The words about going away are similar to what Jesus said earlier (7:33–34), though there he spoke about a short time while here that is not expressed. It may be held to be implied, but here Jesus concentrates on the facts of his departure, their inability to find him, and their death in sin. The verb *to go away* can be used of the ordinary goings and comings of life (e.g., 4:16; 21:3), but John uses it quite often in a special sense. Perhaps that is not the best way of putting it, for this use is never in John's own words, but always when he is reporting what Jesus said.

Several times Jesus said he was "going away," mostly without saying anything about his destination. Sometimes he says he is going to the Father (16:10, 17), sometimes to him who sent him (7:33; 16:5), and once he says he is going to God (13:3). He tells the disciples that he is going away and that where he goes they cannot come (13:33, 36). He assures them also that, though he is going away, he will come back to them (14:28). And, while this going is clearly mysterious, Jesus knows very well what his destination is (8:14).

Thus the idea that is put before the people in the passage before us is not an unusual one in this Gospel, but one that we meet a number of times. And it is clear that it puzzled the hearers. We are not always told of their reaction, but whenever we hear of it they do not understand.

Here Jesus simply says that he is going away. Now the words "I am going away" need mean no more than that Jesus was about to remove to another part of the country. But it would not be true of such a destination that his hearers could not come there, so the words must have a different meaning. In the light of the other passages that refer to Jesus as going to God or the Father or him that sent him, there can be little doubt that here he is referring to his going away from this world in death. Of course, his enemies would die in due course, but their death would not be like his. There was something voluntary about Jesus' death, and it was a death that would restore him to the life with the Father he had enjoyed before coming to this earth. They could not come to God in such a passing from this world.

"You will look for me," Jesus says. This probably is meant to bring out the importance of the passage of time. By then it will be too late. During the time that he moved among them they had ample opportunity for accepting his message, for becoming his disciples, for entering into salvation. But in due course their opportunity would be over. Jesus would return to the Father and, search as they would, they would no longer be able to hear and see him. No matter how hard they looked, they would not find him. There is no substitute for using the opportunity while we have it.

"You Will Die in Your Sin"

Jesus tells them that they will die in their sin. This does not mean simply that they will be sinners all their days until they die. It means that they will face that death that is the due reward of sin (Paul can speak of "the wages of sin" as death, Rom. 6:23). Jesus does not go into detail and there remains something mysterious about the saying. But it is clear enough to be devastating. To die in sin is the ultimate disaster. Jesus speaks of dying "in sin," whereas in verse 24 he has the

309

plural "sins." This may be nothing more than the variation without significant difference in meaning that we have seen a number of times in John. But the words about dying in sin are placed before the verb here, which gives them special emphasis, and it may be that we are to understand that rejecting Jesus is the sin of all sins.

There is an application to physical death. In due course these people would come to the end of their earthly lives and go through the portal we call death. That would mark the end of the time open to them to repent and believe in the Savior. It is the consistent teaching of the New Testament writers that there is something decisive about life here on earth. Here we face the critical choice and we carry the result with us into the afterlife. As the writer to the Hebrews puts it, "It is appointed to men to die once and for all, and after this—judgment!" (Heb. 9:27). It is now that is the day of salvation, and we do well to pay good heed to this aspect of scriptural teaching.

Jesus' words also apply to death in the sense that death is the wages of sin. The link with sin in this saying is plain. Sin cuts us off from that life that is life indeed and shuts us up to the full horror of death. It may be worth reflecting that John has just recorded Jesus' words about being the Light of the World and his assurance that the person who follows him will not walk in darkness, but rather "will have the light of life" (v. 12). The death of which he is now speaking is the reverse of all this. It means a rejection of the Light of the World. It means a refusal of discipleship of the Son of God. It means doing without "the light of life" and doing without that light by one's own deliberate choice. It means shutting oneself up to all that darkness means.

Suicide

It is curious that Jesus' opponents do not give a moment's thought to all this. I suppose that this is the way of the world all through the centuries. It certainly is the case today. The world's tragedy is that with the way of salvation before them people choose to concentrate on the world's fading attractions. It is not so much that they deliberately weigh the claims of Christ and reject them, as that, like the people in this passage, they do not take him seriously. They fix on something quite irrelevant and give no thought to where that leaves them, nor to the magnitude of the opportunity they are slighting.

Instead of facing what it means to die in their sin, the people talking to Jesus wonder whether he will kill himself (v. 22). The form in which they put their question shows that they do not take this very seriously (it expects the answer "No"). But it is the one thing they face out of what Jesus has said.

Suicide was regarded as a very serious matter by first-century Jews. They were impressed by the words of Genesis 9:5: "And for your life-blood I will surely demand an accounting. . . . ." They remembered, too, the dreadful fate of Ahithophel (2 Sam. 17:23). An occasional exception was made, for example in the case of Samson, who slew so many Philistines in a way that brought about his own death. Nearer to New Testament times there was praise and admiration for the defenders of the fortress of Masada who killed themselves and their families rather than fall into the hands of the Romans. But such exceptions were rare. Generally speaking, suicide was thought of as desperately wicked and as inevitably bringing the punishment of hell on its perpetrator.

Josephus, the first-century Jewish historian, speaks strongly about taking one's own life: "But as for those who have laid mad hands on themselves, the darker regions of the nether world receive their souls, and God, their father, visits upon their posterity the outrageous acts of the parents." He goes on to point out that, though even the bodies of enemies are given decent burial, the bodies of suicides remain unburied until sunset (as a form of punishment). He also says that in other nations a suicide's right hand must be cut off, "holding that, as the body was unnaturally severed from the soul, so the hand should be severed from the body." It is interesting that the Jews should take such a strong line when the philosophers of Greece could regard suicide as a permissible, even a praiseworthy, way of bringing to an end a long and honorable life that had now become burdensome.

Even though they strongly opposed him, Jesus' enemies could not think that he was talking about suicide. Hatred of such a crime was too deeply entrenched in the nation for anyone to contemplate it. They mention the possibility only to dismiss it.

But there may be something more. Granted that they did not really think Jesus would commit suicide, why do they raise the possibility? Perhaps as a deliberate misinterpretation with a sting in its tail. They may be reasoning, "He is talking about suicide. That means going to hell. Well, we certainly can't come where he is going, if that is what he's planning."

"From Below" and "From Above"

We should probably understand Jesus' reply in the light of such an understanding. His enemies were talking about hell, about the nether regions. Jesus invites them to reflect on where their real affinities lie. On another occasion he spoke of the scribes and Pharisees as going to great lengths to make a convert, and when they have done so, he said to them, ". . . you make him twofold more a child of hell than yourselves" (Matt. 23:15). His "from below" has a somewhat similar meaning here (v. 23). He is saying that these people who were so ready to sneer at him and to suggest that he would go to hell were in fact speaking of their own domain. They were "from below"; they belonged to hell. Jesus' "you" is emphatic. They were linking him with hell and in so doing they inadvertently showed what their own proper place was.

By contrast, Jesus is "from above." His proper place is heaven. Right through this Gospel John insists that Jesus had come from heaven, from God. He keeps telling us that it was the Father who sent Jesus. His appearance on earth was not because he was of the earth, for he was not. It was because the heavenly One came to this place to save the sinful denizens of earth. They should not misinterpret the reason for his presence.

Almost the same contrast is made in terms of "this world" and "not of this world." There is a great deal about "world" in this Gospel (the Greek word for "world" is used seventy-eight times; the most in any other book is twenty-three, in 1 John). It is used in a number of different ways, but one important way is the one we see here. This world can be a very attractive place for those who live in it, and there is a constant temptation to make it the center of everything in life. To be "of this world" in this way is to miss the greatest good. There is, of course, no reason why we should not enjoy this world. It is a good world, made by a good God, and the people of God legitimately find much of value in it. But when it becomes the focus of the whole of life it is a snare and a source of error. It is this concentration on the things of this life that Jesus is blaming in those to whom he is talking.

We so readily accept the world's values, even when we are seeking to do good. I like the story about the thirteen-year-old boy who, in a time of heavy snow, decided to make a few dollars by clearing driveways. Before he began his father pointed out that there was a good deal of snow in their own driveway and it would be nice if he started there.

"How much is it worth?" asked the boy.

"Son, this is your home" said his father. "I leave it to your sense of honor how much you ought to charge. Or even whether you ought to charge at all. Let your conscience be your guide."

So the youth got to work. With the driveway nicely cleared he confronted his father and said, "Dad, I've made a decision. I will charge you nothing at all. I leave it to your sense of honor how much you ought to pay. Or even whether you ought to pay at all. Let your conscience be your guide."

Despite their high-sounding words we get the feeling that both father and son were moved by a worldly consideration—how to get the
best deal for himself. And is this not rather widespread in our modern
communities? It comes natural to us all to look for the best for ourselves and to avoid, if we can, the kind of confrontation with the challenge of the service of God that will make life a little less easy. That was
what Jesus' opponents were doing.

In both his contrasts, "below"–"above" and "this world"–"not of this
world," Jesus uses emphatic pronouns for both *you* and *I*. He sets
himself in strong contrast with the enemies to whom he is speaking.
They should not blur the difference between them. Jesus is not talking
about a minor difference of opinion. He is taking about the ultimate
cleavage between the people of God and the people of Satan, between
those whose place is heaven and those who belong to hell.

"I AM"

"Therefore," Jesus says, "I told you that you will die in your sins"
(v. 24). The reason for this fearful death is the fearful lives they are
living. They belong to this world, to "below," and thus they disqualify
themselves from being with God in the world to come.

Jesus explains this further with a reference to faith. "For if you do
not believe that I AM," he says, you will undergo this death. The
thought that people must believe is a common one in this Gospel, and
indeed John tells us that he wrote it in order that people might believe
and in believing might have life (20:31). We have noticed in our studies
that he uses a variety of constructions with his verb 'to believe' and may
give expression to the thought that people must trust Jesus, accept
what he says as true, and so on. Here he speaks of believing "that."
Faith has content, and unless we see this we shall never believe as John
understands the term. It is not a matter of producing just any kind of
faith, as though faith were itself a merit. It is faith in Jesus as he is that
matters, faith that recognizes the wonderful truth behind his "I AM."

In earlier studies we have seen that the personal pronoun is not used
in Greek in the way we use it. The form of the verb tells us sufficiently
what the subject is. But where God is the speaker the pronoun is used.
This emphatic way of speaking was seen as suitable when a divine
person is doing the speaking.

In the Old Testament the emphatic "I AM" is used a number of times.
There was an important occasion when God revealed himself to Moses
and sent him to say to the Israelites, "I AM has sent me to you" (Exod.
3:14). "I AM" is the very name of God in this passage. There are other
relevant passages, such as the one in which God says to Isaiah, "I am

he" (Isa. 43:10). We could assemble quite a group of such passages. They make it clear that "I AM" was closely connected with God's revelation of himself.

And that is surely the significance of what Jesus is saying here. He is taking the expression so firmly linked with God's self-revelation in the Old Testament Scripture and using it of himself. He is saying that God is revealed in him in a special way. Unless we recognize this revelation and respond to it in faith, we place ourselves outside the sphere of salvation. As Jesus put it, if you do not believe this, "you will die in your sins."

39

Pleasing the Father

*So they said to him, "Who are you?" Jesus said to them, "Why
do I talk to you at all? I have many things to say and to judge
about you, but he who sent me is true and as for me, the things
I heard from him, these are the things I speak to the world."
They did not know that he was speaking to them about the
Father. Jesus therefore said to them, "When you have lifted up
the Son of man, then you will know that I AM. And I do
nothing of myself, but as the Father taught me, I speak these
things. And he who sent me is with me. He has not left me
alone, because I always do the things that are pleasing to him."
As Jesus said these things many believed in him* (John
8:25–30).

The people to whom Jesus had been talking probably
did not understand all that he was saying, but they understood enough
to see that what he said implied a big claim about his own position. He
was "from above," whereas they were "from below"; they were "of this
world," whereas he was "not of this world" (v. 23). Unless they believed
"that I AM" they would die in their sins (v. 24). This certainly meant
that Jesus was claiming to be on a very different level from the one
where they stood. So they asked him, "Who are you?" They put some
emphasis on "you" by placing the pronoun first; "You, who are you to
talk like this?" is the force of it. One commentator sees the expression
as meaning "Why do you give yourself such airs?" They rejected utterly

any idea that Jesus was different from or better than they were. They saw him as just another Jew, and one from the provinces at that. He could not possibly know more about God and the way God should be served than they did.

Jesus' reply is one of the most difficult pieces of Greek in the New Testament and it is translated in a variety of different ways. The King James Version reads "Even the same that I said unto you from the beginning," and essentially the same translation is given by the Revised Standard Version with "Even what I have told you from the beginning." But this version has an alternative in the margin, "Why do I talk to you at all?" This is not the reading of other manuscripts; it is a different attempt at translating the same piece of Greek. The New English Bible faces the same problem but puts its solution the other way round. In the text it reads "Why should I speak to you at all?" and in the margin it has "What I have told you all along." The Good News Bible has essentially the same translation as the Revised Standard, with "What I have told you from the very beginning" in the text and "Why should I speak to you at all?" in the margin.

The problem is that we have the Greek word that means "beginning," but it is used in a very unusual way. Used in the way John employs it here, it really means "at first," "at the beginning." But "What I am saying at the beginning" is not an easy expression. We see something of the problem translators have if we consult the commentary of C. K. Barrett. This writer notes that the expression means "at first," "at the beginning," but goes on to say that we must choose between "I am from the beginning what I tell you" and "I am what I tell you from the beginning." But the trouble with this is that Barrett substitutes "from the beginning" for "at the beginning," and these two do not mean the same thing at all. And the expression we are thinking of means "at" not "from." John sometimes says "from the beginning" (6:64; 8:44; 15:27; 16:4), but in none of these places does he use the expression we have here.

Now it happens that this expression is sometimes used by the Greeks with a meaning like "altogether." But they use it with a negative. We would get the force of this if we were to see it as "at all" in the phrase "not at all." A great preacher of the early church, John Chrysostom (which means "John of the golden mouth"), explains the passage this way: "What He saith, is of this kind; 'Ye are not worthy to hear My words at all, much less to learn who I am.'" We must always take what Chrysostom says seriously, for Greek was his native language and he read the Greek New Testament in his native tongue. Despite this, not many have gone all the way with him, though the "at all" that he saw is taken up in several translations. Mostly those who take this view see the words as a question, "Why do I talk to you at all?" or the like. The Berkeley version, however, sees it as a statement, "I am exactly what I tell you."

The trouble with this way of taking the expression is that in Greek writings generally it seems to be used with this meaning only with a negative. It is the "at all" in "not at all," but it does not seem to have been used with this significance without the negative. So, while this remains as a possibility, it cannot be said to be without difficulties.

The earliest manuscript of this Gospel that survives, the Bodmer papyrus which the scholars cite as P66, reads "I told you at the beginning what I am also telling you." There is always a great respect for the earliest manuscript of any part of Scripture, and most of us would like to feel that this manuscript is right. The reading is without difficulty and gives a clear and acceptable meaning. The problem here is the question "If this is what John wrote originally, how does it come about that every other manuscript in existence is wrong?" It seems easier to think that the scribe who wrote this manuscript found the reading so difficult that he said to himself something like this: "This does not make sense; someone must have made a mistake. Now what would make better sense? I know. . . ."

Other suggestions have been made. Barclay translates, "Anything I am saying to you is only the beginning" and Rieu, "So we go back to our starting-point!" There are other renderings. But none of them impresses us as an adequate way of putting the Greek into English.

So in the end we must confess that we simply do not know the precise meaning of what John has written. Until some further evidence comes to light we must be content to remain uncertain. There are two main possibilities: it may be the question "Why do I talk to you at all?" or it may be the statement "What I say to you at [or "from"] the beginning." But there is nothing that enables us to say definitely which is right or whether there is a better solution.

Jesus evidently means that there is no point in explaining further what he has said; his hearers have such closed minds that they will not understand. Either way of taking the words fits in with this. So he says, "Why do I talk to you at all?" Or perhaps he is saying that he has said it all before; there is nothing to add. If they did not believe him before, no further words will enable them to do so now.

What the Father Said

Jesus goes on to refer to other things he has to say to them. If he is going to say no more about himself, he has a lot more to say about *them*. And those other things concern judgment. This is one of the great themes of this Gospel, as we have seen in our previous studies. He does not develop the thought at this point, but it recurs (cf. 8:50; 12:48; 16:8, 11, etc.). Jesus did not come primarily for judgment (8:15; 12:47), but judgment is one of the important truths. Jesus' hearers were responsible people. One day they would give account of themselves to God, and they should not complacently shelter themselves under the security blanket of the conviction that they belonged to the people of God. Nor should we.

Jesus goes on with "he who sent me is true" (v. 26). He does not say "the Father" but "he who sent me." Once again we see that the mission of Jesus is important. Again and again we find him referring to the great truth that the Father "sent" him. John will not let us miss the truth that in Jesus we see not merely human wisdom, but one sent from none less than God the Father. Truth is a very important concept in this Gospel, and it is connected with Jesus (14:6) and the Spirit (14:17) as well as with the Father. Here the thought is that the Father is utterly real and completely reliable. Jesus' hearers might quibble about the things he said and might fancy that they knew more about spiritual realities than he did. But he is pointing them to God as real truth. The trouble with the hearers was that they were substituting their ideas about God for the reality. No matter what they might say and no matter what we may say, no matter what their or our contemporaries may say, the truth of God still stands.

And it is that truth that Jesus proclaims because what he says are the things he heard from the Father. Again we have a consistent thought in this Gospel. Again and again John reports words of Jesus that bring out the truth that his message is not of human origin. He brings a revelation from none less than the Father.

And this revelation he speaks "to the world" (v. 26). This means that the message is worldwide in its scope. As it is the message of God's way of salvation obviously it has no restricted application. Jesus spent his earthly life in Palestine and his preaching was very largely restricted to the Jews. It was only after his ascension that the Holy Spirit came at Pentecost and led the church to proclaim the gospel among the Gentiles. But words such as these make it clear that the worldwide application of the gospel was in view from the first. It moved out in God's good time to the lands outside Israel, but the nature of the message is such that it is meant for all and in due time must go to all.

We should also bear in mind that "world" has another meaning. It can mean the worldly-minded, those whose horizon is bounded by the things of here and now. It is not unlikely that, as is the case with so many expressions in this Gospel, we should see "world" here as having a double meaning. It points to people in the lands beyond the sea but also points to those who would normally take no notice of a religious message. The gospel is to be preached not to the converted but to the unconverted, and Jesus is setting the example with his preaching.

There is yet another possibility. The word I have translated "to" also means "into" and in New Testament times was sometimes used in the sense of "in." It is possible that we should see Jesus as saying that this is what his message is as he speaks "in the world."

But the Jews did not understand. They did not know God nor did they know that he is in a special sense Jesus' Father (v. 19). So it is not surprising that they did not catch the allusion to "the Father" (v. 27). With their views about Jesus they did not care who his father was; they had no idea that he had been sent by the heavenly Father. Their spiritual blindness meant that they did not recognize the mission of Jesus. Indeed, it is the basic fault of the enemies of Jesus right through this Gospel that they lacked spiritual perception and failed to recognize the wonderful thing that had happened in their midst, when the Son of God himself came to live among them. When Jesus spoke about his "Father" they did not recognize that the message came from the One they called God. So can prejudice blind people.

Lifting Up the Son of Man

So Jesus took the discussion further. He spoke of the time when they would have "lifted up the Son of man" (v. 28). John uses this verb *to lift up* in an unusual way (as we saw in our study on 3:14). The word means "to raise on high" and is used of elevating physical objects, as when Moses lifted up the bronze snake in the wilderness (3:14). It could also be used figuratively, as it is when it is used of Capernaum's thinking it was "lifted up to heaven" (Matt. 11:23). Similarly Jesus said that "everyone who exalts himself will be abased," while it is "he who humbles himself" who "will be exalted" (Luke 18:14).

This idea of exaltation in the heavenly realm is often the meaning of the word in the New Testament. It is used of Jesus' being exalted to God's right hand in heaven (Acts 2:33) and of God's exalting him to be a Prince and Savior (Acts 5:31).

John, as we have seen, uses the word of Moses' lifting up of the bronze snake in the wilderness. He has it four times more, and on each of these four occasions it refers to Jesus' crucifixion. In a sense that was a physical lifting up, so we can understand it being used of death in this way. Yet at the same time we should bear in mind that what was so obvious to John was far from obvious to his contemporaries, and the word was not normally used of crucifixion at all. John probably chooses the term because of its other associations. It could refer to the physical elevation of Jesus on the cross. But John also surely has in mind the truth that it was this being "lifted up" on the cross that was Jesus' supreme glory. We have seen that John has the great idea that to serve in a lowly place when one could readily take a higher place is real glory. That is surely his idea here. Presumably Jesus spoke in Aramaic, but when John put his words into Greek he chose to use a verb that spoke of physical exaltation but also of exaltation in the heavenly region.

Jesus used his favorite self-designation, "the Son of man." This is a title that is used by no one in the Gospels except Jesus, but he uses it again and again. It is generally agreed that it points us back to "one like a son of man" in Daniel 7:13. It was not a recognized title of the Messiah, and Jesus seems to have used it as a way of both concealing and revealing his messiahship. Those who did not heed his message would see nothing in the expression, but to Jesus himself it expressed something of his mission and his relationship to the Father.

When this "lifting up" takes place, Jesus says, "you will know that I AM" (v. 28). This means that the cross is not only the means of our redemption, but that it has a revelatory function. We have seen a number of times that "I AM" is a title of divinity and points to the highest place. The cross, where the Son of man died to bring salvation, shows who he is.

There is a problem in that many of those at the crucifixion did not come to know anything of the sort. There were mockers there who did not take Jesus seriously and there were his enemies who rejoiced in his death. It seems that what Jesus means is that the cross forces people into a final decision. Face to face with the cross his hearers would come into either a place of salvation or of final condemnation. They would accept him as God's own Son and the Messiah who was bringing salvation. Or they would turn away from him with finality.

The cross always does that. When we come face to face with it, when we see the One who died on it for us, then either we respond with penitence and faith and so enter salvation, or we harden our hearts, reject the revelation, and shut ourselves up to the eternal consequences of our action.

The Father and the Son

From the cross Jesus moves on to another thought we meet many times in this Gospel: that he does not act independently of the Father. "I do nothing of myself," he says (v. 28). Most translations take "and I do nothing of myself" as part of the previous sentence, and this must remain a possibility. In that case Jesus is saying that part of the revelation that the cross would bring is that Jesus does nothing alone. Always the Father is with him.

But it seems more likely that the revelation is simply "that I AM." Then Jesus goes on to say that now, long before the cross, it is true that he does nothing in isolation from the Father (cf. 5:19, etc.). We misunderstand his whole life if we see him merely as someone who set out to follow high ideals and to do things of which the heavenly Father would approve. For Jesus (and for John who records it) it is important that he had never been at work in separation from the Father. He could do nothing apart from God. There was a close unity between them right through his earthly life.

This is brought out first with respect to his teaching. His message was not an earthly message on which God was pleased to set his seal of approval. It was a message right from God. It was only what the Father taught him that he spoke (v. 28).

Then he moves on to his fellowship with the Father. Jesus lived an earthly life with all that this means in terms of trials and tribulations, of joys and sorrows, of achievement and opposition. But he was never left to do all this by himself. The Father, who is again characterized as "he who sent me" (v. 29; the thought of mission keeps coming up), is with him. The thought that God will be with his people is one that is found often in the Old Testament and is carried on in the New. People of faith can rely on that presence. But especially is that presence given to Jesus, and he says here that God has not left him. The Father never leaves the Son. Even in the shadow of the cross, with the malignancy of his enemies at its worst and with his closest followers about to desert him, Jesus could say that he was not alone (16:32). The Father never deserts the Son.

The third thing is that the Son always does the things that please the Father. His life is spent entirely in doing those things of which the Father approves. Christians often speak of the sinlessness of Jesus, which is a fact and an important fact. But it is negative; it tells what Jesus did not do. Here we have the positive. Not only did he avoid evil, but he actively did the good. Always he did the things that please the Father.

Faith

As Jesus spoke, "many believed in him" (v. 30). John does not tell us whether these were people from among Jesus' opponents who had been changed as a result of what he said to them or whether they came from among the uncommitted who were listening to what was going on. Either way the point is that not all who heard him were hostile or indifferent. Even in a chapter like this, where there is so much opposition to Jesus and all he stood for, many came to trust him. And, in a world that is as hostile and indifferent as ours is, it is heartening to reflect that there are still many who come to believe. It encourages all God's servants to persist in their mission as Jesus did in his and to trust the same heavenly Father who did such things in and for and through him.

40

Freedom

Jesus therefore said to the Jews who had believed him, "If you remain in my word you are truly my disciples and you will know the truth and the truth will set you free." They answered him, "We are Abraham's seed and have never been slaves to anyone; how do you say 'You will become free'?" Jesus answered them, "Truly, truly, I tell you that everyone who commits sin is the slave of sin. Now the slave does not remain in the house forever; the son remains forever. If then the Son makes you free, you will be really free" (John 8:31–36).

This passage is a dialogue between Jesus and some Jews who "had believed him" (v. 31). It is plain from the exchange that their faith did not go very deep. In fact it can scarcely be called faith at all. We are reminded that there are degrees of conviction. Evidently these people had been impressed by some of Jesus' sayings. They believed them, and they counted themselves as followers of Jesus. This may mean only that they agreed that some of Jesus' teachings were true. The Greek construction John uses could mean no more than that they accepted as true what Jesus had said. Some scholars press this literal meaning. But John uses a variety of constructions when he refers to believing, and he does not seem to put much difference between them. It is better to see these people as folk who claimed to be disciples of Jesus, but whose commitment did not go very deep. Jesus now speaks to them about the meaning of true discipleship.

323

The first point is that it is necessary that they "remain." Discipleship is not a sudden enthusiasm, not something that flares up quickly but is soon over. Discipleship means remaining with Jesus. It means remaining in his "word," too. The "word" of Jesus means his whole teaching, not this aspect, nor that, but the teaching as a unity. The teaching of Jesus is to be taken seriously. Many of us delight to call ourselves Christians but then go on to manufacture a religion of our own, perhaps taking up some aspects of what the Master said and which we find attractive. But we like to keep firmly in control. What we approve we see as right, and what we find uncomfortable we reject as no part of authentic Christianity. We decide what we think is suitable and do not dream of comparing that with the teachings of the Lord we profess to obey. So we evolve a religion of respectability or, if we are younger, of non-respectability, and label that Christian.

Jesus is insisting that this is not the way to go if we really want to be disciples. That involves the discipline (do not miss the connection of "discipline" with "disciple") in the first place of learning what the teaching is, and in the second of putting it into practice. Discipleship means taking with full seriousness the fact that Jesus is the Master.

Free

It is easy to grasp this part of Jesus' teaching and to go on from there to the thought that being a Christian is a grim business in which we are shut up on a kind of treadmill. It means, we so easily think, that we are always trying to learn a little more and then to put that into practice. And as soon as we have done this some further demand is made of us. We are never able to escape the grind of learning and then trying to put what we learn into living. We make our Christianity into a very trying, very unpleasant, and very grim way of being right with our Maker.

Wherever we got that idea, it was not from the teaching of our Lord. It is, of course, true that there is always something more to learn and something more to do in Christian service. But this is no dull grind. Rather it is an ever-new adventure. To remain in Jesus' word is to know the truth, and to know the truth is to be free. Truth is an important concept in John's writings and is used especially about the truth of God, the truth that is expressed in the gospel and finds its embodiment in Jesus who said, "I am the truth" (14:6). It is the truth that God sent his Son to live for us and to die for us. It is the truth that we reach our full potential and enjoyment of life only when we live in harmony with God who made us. It is the truth that it is the Son's death on Calvary's cross that puts away our sins. It is the truth that it is only as we trust him that we know the calm of sins forgiven and the entrance into a life of satisfying service of God and man. This final truth we never know apart from Jesus. His "word" brings us the knowledge of things eternal that was forever beyond our unaided grasp.

"And the truth will set you free" (v. 32). Jesus was well aware of the fact that sin binds people, shuts them up to a cramped, narrow experience and prevents them from enjoying real freedom. Jesus' words are often misunderstood in modern times by people who see them as a charter for liberty in research and in intellectual pursuits generally. Truth is then seen as the one compulsory quest; to follow the way of truth is a liberating experience.

It is not to be denied that there is a sense in which this is true. Dedication to the quest for knowledge, for a better understanding of truth, is a liberating thing. But that is not what Jesus is saying. His concern when he uttered these words was not for science or philosophy or the like, but for the deep needs of the soul. He was not even speaking of freedom from sin in the sense of a way of liberation from what we see as shackling us, so that we could use his teaching to get free from something that we could not defeat in any other way. Jesus is not a tool to enable us to get personal success, even in respectable, religious ways.

Jesus is talking about liberation from the whole way of the world, with its concentration on the things of here and now. He is talking about the liberation that brings us near to God, so that our concern is with him, with the doing of his will. We no longer are caught up in our own selfish concerns, in the darkness of sin and evil, of alienation from God, of concentration on "the world." The liberation of which Jesus speaks brings us into fellowship with the Father.

Abraham's Seed

Jesus' hearers did not like this at all. It seems pretty clear that they did not really understand what he was saying. Perhaps their gorge rose at the suggestion that they were not free. Sometimes the use of a word riles us so that we find it difficult to pay attention to the flow of an argument because of our resentment at the word we do not like. It seems that it was something like this that happened to the Jews, because they did not reply to what Jesus was saying but to something that they thought up themselves.

"We are Abraham's seed," they said, "and have never been slaves to anyone" (v. 33). "Seed," of course, means "descendants," and the Jews took great pride in being descendants of the great patriarch Abraham, the man whom God called "my friend" (Isa. 41:8). There is a saying of Rabbi Akiba (who was a little later than this; he died about A.D. 135):

325

"Even the poorest in Israel are looked upon as freemen who have lost their possessions, for they are the sons of Abraham, Isaac, and Jacob." The whole nation, Akiba felt, had a dignity that rested on relationship to the great patriarchs and not to any worldly wealth. This attitude was undoubtedly to be found in the days of Jesus as well as in the next century.

There is something admirable about this patriotic view, for those who held it were not going to be too depressed about life's little troubles. But it all too easily led to a depraved kind of patriotism whereby one's own nation is regarded as the only one that counts and all others are despised. And it could lead to a failure to reckon with reality. Thus on this occasion the Jews showed a superb disregard for the facts of life as typified by the presence of the Roman soldiers in their very midst. They were not slaves in the sense of being the personal possession of any one Roman or group of Romans. But they were slaves in that their destiny was not in their own hands. It was what the Romans said that dictated Jewish conduct. It is unrealistic to call a nation occupied by enemy troops free. But that is what these Jewish leaders did.

They also disregarded their history. We have "never" been slaves, they said. Not when they were in Egypt before Moses led them out? Not when the Philistines invaded their land and, in their determination not to allow weapons, regulated even the way axes and sickles were sharpened (1 Sam. 13:19–22)? Not when the Assyrians carried off as captives the people of the northern kingdom (2 Kings 17:6–7)? Or when the Babylonians did the same to those in the kingdom of Judah (2 Kings 25:11)? So can prejudice blind people to the truth.

It is one of the melancholy facts of life that the spiritually blind think that there is nothing to see and the spiritually bound deny that there is any freedom beyond their condition.

Slavery

Jesus' answer begins with the solemn "truly, truly" (v. 34). This is a formula that Jesus uses often to prefix statements of special importance and solemnity. It is a warning to take very seriously the words that follow. There is a division among the manuscripts as to exactly what follows, but the best reading is probably "everyone who commits sin is a slave." Other manuscripts have "is the slave of sin," but the longer reading appears to be the result of an attempt by some scribes to make unmistakably clear what they saw as Jesus' meaning. Now there cannot be any doubt that Jesus is referring to slavery to sin. But the way he puts it gives emphasis to "slave." The sinner is not free.

The more we think about it, the more we see that it is true. The first time anyone commits a particular sin there may have been a terrible struggle with temptation. But if the person gives way, then the next time there is not such a hard struggle. And if he continues in that path, there comes a time when there is scarcely a ripple of temptation. The person has become the slave of the sin that once was so strongly resisted.

We see the same thing if we reflect on what happens when we try to break a bad habit. It is not easy. We are well aware that we are in the power of the evil thing. It may be that by God's grace in the end we succeed, but that does not alter the fact that until God helps us we are in the grip of the habit. In our own experience we know what it is to be enslaved to evil.

Our very attempts to assert our freedom all too often lead to a worse bondage. One of the saddest features of modern life is the growth of violence over almost the whole of the world. People decide that they will not be bound by the petty restrictions that they find so frustrating and so limiting. So they assert themselves to the maximum of their strength to get what they want by the exercise of their power. But that does not lead them into a glorious life where they can get all they want. It provokes other people to be violent in return, and the end result is the loss of peace for all. Evil never brings freedom. It brings bondage.

The drug habit is another illustration. For an increasing number of people, life seems impossible without the use of heroin or some other drug. The habit was begun in all probability as an attempt to assert freedom, to show that one is not bound by the petty conservatisms that govern the lives of the "straight." But the freedom is illusory. It leads straight into slavery.

The list could go on and on. There is an almost endless number of evils to which we in modern times have made ourselves slaves as we assert our freedom. But we are no more free than the previous generations against whom we rebel. We have simply exchanged one form of conformity for another; we have found a new kind of slavery to take the place of an old one.

The Son

Jesus goes on to point out that there are differences between a son in a household and a slave. He begins with tenure. "The slave," he says, "does not remain in the house forever" (v. 35). A given slave, of course, might remain in the one household all his life. But that is an unusual occurrence. It depends on the nature of the services he can render, on the character of his owner and his own character, and on a host of other things. The point is that he has no security. He can be removed at any time. He can be transferred temporarily or permanently. He can be retained by the present owner or given away or sold.

But the son is always a son. Normally he will remain in the house as an honored member all his life. Should he journey abroad or should he be expelled from the household, he is still a son. His status as a son is permanent. He has his responsibilities and his privileges and in both is distinctively different from a slave.

There is a story of an old man and a twelve-year-old boy who passed through customs in New York after a trip to France. A friendly customs man asked if they had enjoyed the trip, whether they had seen the Louvre, Versailles, and the like. The man replied that he was blind and had seen nothing. He went on, "I want my son to see as much as he can, so that his life will be rich and full. But first he has to tell me all about what he sees. That ensures that he sees much. And in a way I see them, too, as he tells me about them." The boy carried his notebook in which he had written all the things he wanted his father to "see." For both of them the relationship (and the trip) was meaningful. There is a permanent link between father and son.

A Son and *The* Son

In Jesus' saying the son in question is the human son, the son in any household. But John's interest is in *the* Son, the Son of God, and, while he uses an expression that has its application to any human family, in the fullest sense it applies to Jesus. He is the Son who "remains forever." His sonship is a heavenly sonship and it is never-ending.

And just as his sonship is distinctive, so the freedom he brings is distinctive. The person who is made free by Christ will be "really free" (v. 36). John uses a word for "really" that he uses nowhere else. It carries the idea of "in essence"; there is that about Christ that means he can give a freedom that is qualitatively different from the lesser freedoms people enjoy.

This will be connected with the slavery to sin that Jesus has been speaking about. That is a slavery that no man can break. No man can give another freedom from sin, because he himself is caught up in the same bondage. But Jesus is not, and the great thought that John hammers at over and over again is that Jesus came to bring salvation, a salvation that may be understood in terms of freedom from the sin that besets us all.

41

Children of the Devil

"I know that you are Abraham's seed; but you are seeking to kill me because my word has no place in you. I speak the things I have seen with my Father, and you therefore do the things you have heard from your father." They answered him saying, "Abraham is our father." Jesus says to them, "If you were children of Abraham you would do the deeds of Abraham. But now you are seeking to kill me, a man who has told you the truth which I heard from God. Abraham did not do this. You are doing the works of your father." They said to him therefore, "We were not born of fornication; we have one Father, God." Jesus said to them, "If God were your Father you would love me, for I came out from God and have come; and I did not come of my own accord, but he sent me. Why do you not understand my speech? Because you cannot hear my word. You are of your father, the devil, and the lusts of your father you will to do. He was a murderer from the beginning and did not stand in the truth because the truth is not in him. When he speaks the lie he speaks of his own, because he is a liar and the father of it. But because I speak the truth you do not believe me. Which of you convicts me of sin? If I speak the truth why do you not believe me? He who is from God hears my sayings; for this reason you do not hear them, that you are not from God" (John 8:37–47).

The Jews had claimed that they were "Abraham's seed" (i.e., descendants of Abraham, v. 33). This was a matter of great importance to many of their race. They looked back with pride to their great ancestor, but this was more than a matter of being thrilled at the wonder of their connection with so great a man. They held that it brought them many blessings.

Sometimes they connected this with the inspiration it gave them to be worthy of so great an ancestor. Thus in the tractate "Aboth" ("The Fathers") we read: "He in whom are these three things is of the disciples of Abraham our father; but [he in whom are] three other things is of the disciples of Balaam the wicked. A good eye and a humble spirit and a lowly soul—[they in whom are these] are of the disciples of Abraham our father. An evil eye, a haughty spirit, and a proud soul—[they in whom are these] are of the disciples of Balaam the wicked" (Danby's translation). There are other such sayings drawing attention to other qualities, such as compassion.

Now to see oneself as a descendant of Abraham in matters like these is a very good thing. It is to take delight in the outstanding merits of Abraham and to model oneself on the great patriarch. It is to see Abraham as one whom it is important to imitate. When the Jews took pride in Abraham in this way it meant that they were striving to be better people, to be more like Abraham in the things they did day by day.

But it was possible to fasten attention on the advantages people thought they would get from belonging to Abraham. Thus the saying we were looking at a moment ago goes on to ask how the disciples of Abraham differ from those of Balaam and, instead of answering in terms of upright conduct or of careful attention to the service of God or the like, says simply: "The disciples of Abraham our father enjoy this world and inherit the world to come. . . . The disciples of Balaam the wicked inherit Gehenna and go down to the pit of destruction." To belong to Abraham means the blessings of heaven, whereas to belong to anyone else (like Balaam) means hell.

This attitude is the end of any genuine attempt to serve God, and it was this attitude that was characteristic of the Jews to whom Jesus was talking. They took pride in their connection with the great patriarch and were confident that because they were descended from him they were sure of God's blessing in the here and now and also of a place in heaven in the hereafter. Since Abraham would take care of them, they saw no need to be very much in earnest about their service of God. They could thus ignore the challenge in Jesus' teaching and refuse to take him seriously. They simply refused to think about what Jesus was saying and to ask whether it was true.

Murder

Jesus agrees that they are "Abraham's seed." They were the patriarch's physical descendants and in this sense were certainly his seed. But conduct is another matter. We have just seen that among the Rabbis there were those who saw descent from Abraham as a reason for cultivating qualities of character: because they were Abraham's seed they must be humble, compassionate, and the like. But this meant nothing to the people to whom Jesus was speaking.

He brings this out by saying "you are seeking to kill me" (v. 37). This has come before us several times in this part of the Gospel. John mentioned it in his narrative section (7:1), Jesus referred to it himself (7:19), the people spoke about it (7:20, 25), and attempts were made to arrest him (7:30, 32, 44). Plainly his life was in danger and equally plainly it was people like those to whom he was speaking who were responsible. A little later they would take up stones to stone him (v. 59). They may have been descendants of Abraham in the sense that they were his physical progeny, but in spirit they were as far from Abraham as was conceivable. At heart they were murderers.

The reason for their rejection of Jesus, he says, was that "my word has no place in you." Jesus' "word," as we have seen, was his teaching; it is a short way of referring to the essential message that he brought from God. And the tragedy of his hearers was that they had no room for this message. Their hearts were too full of pride and self-sufficiency, too taken up with their own importance to give consideration for a moment to the possibility that a teacher from the provinces, and from an obscure village in the provinces at that, could possibly have anything to say that would be worth hearing for these grand folk who lived in the capital city, in God's own Jerusalem.

Yet what Jesus said came directly from God. Interestingly he does not speak of the things he "heard" from the Father, but says, "I speak the things I have seen with my Father" (v. 38). His vision of God is unobscured and constant. He speaks because his message reflects this vision. He brings a message direct from God.

Another Father

Notice Jesus' "therefore." It is precisely *because* his message came directly from God that they did not receive it. His message was one of love and humility and compassion, and it was because it was the kind of message it was that they would not receive it. The way Jesus puts it is "you do the things you have heard from your father" (v. 38). Their conduct reflects their parentage. Jesus does not say who their father is; he leaves it that they are acting as they are because their father is who he is. Now what father would lead his sons to plan murder?

This is a question his hearers do not attempt to answer. It was fundamental to these Jews that they were descendants of Abraham. For them everything depended on that. Their hope for this life and the next did not depend on God's grace or their piety or their moral achievement or anything of the sort. It depended on their relationship to Abraham. No descendant of that great patriarch, they thought, could ever be lost. Because of their father, they were safe.

So they gratefully go for the opening they think Jesus has left them. "Abraham is our father," they say simply (v. 39). For them that was all that mattered. If they were doing the things they had heard from their father, then all was well because Abraham was their father.

Consistently Jesus is taking the position that what we do shows who our real father is. So he immediately retorts that their deeds show that it is not Abraham who is really their father. If they were Abraham's children, they would do Abraham's deeds. This, of course, was recognized by the better minds in Israel, people who said things like those we noticed earlier about the disciples of Abraham being humble and compassionate. But these people were too self-opinionated for that, too certain that they had to be right and Jesus had to be wrong.

So Jesus goes on to say, "But now you are seeking to kill me" (v. 40). He is aware of the intention to murder him and brings the plot out into the open. And who are they trying to murder? "A man who has told you the truth which I heard from God." This is as far as could possibly be conceived from doing what Abraham did. It shows that it was not Abraham who was their father but someone else. And for the second time Jesus says that they are doing the works of their father. If they thought about what they were doing, they might possibly come to see who their real father was.

God's Children

That leads the Jews to change their position in a hurry. Somewhat curiously they say, "We were not born of fornication" (v. 41; Moffatt translates "We are no bastards"). Their "we" is emphatic: "we, in contrast to others." It is not easy to see why they say such a thing. Possibly they had heard something about the virgin birth of Jesus. They would not have accepted this for a moment, but, recognizing that there was something unusual about the way Jesus came into the world, they may be putting the worst possible construction on it. So they took the opportunity of being scornful of him, while at the same time they asserted their own superior position.

Another possibility is that they were thinking of the way the Old Testament prophets so often denounced idolatry by likening it to adultery or fornication. False religion is faithlessness and may be illustrated by thinking of faithlessness in marriage. These Jews were perhaps beginning to see something of the way Jesus' argument was running and they tried to counter it. That may be why they ceased to call Abraham their father and said instead, ". . . we have one Father, God" (v. 41). Malachi had asked, "Have we not all one Father? Did not one God create us?" (Mal. 2:10). It was a nice thought to fall back on.

But it drew the response "If God were your Father you would love me" (v. 42). The way in which this is expressed in the Greek implies that both propositions are wrong: "If God were your Father (as he is not) you would love me (as you do not)." There runs right through Jesus' teaching in this exchange the thought that our conduct reflects our paternity. It was nice that these people claimed now that God was their Father. But would the claim stand up to the test of facts? Did their deeds show that this was true or false? Jesus begins with love. John tells us in his first Epistle that "God is love" (1 John 4:8, 16), and it follows that those who are God's children will be distinguished by the love they show to others. These Jews were not characterized by love; it followed that it was not God who was their Father.

It is critical that they did not love Jesus, for he "came out from God" (v. 42). His divine origin is emphasized throughout this Gospel, and those who belong to God, those who are God's children, will recognize this. He adds "and have come," which is somewhat curious. But there is some evidence that this second verb was used by people claiming to have come from a deity or even when the heathen said that one of their gods had "come." It may be that Jesus is asserting by his use of the word that his origin was divine.

It goes with this that he was not self-impelled. That he came from God meant that he was on a mission from God (as John says so often). Jesus did not come completely of himself. God sent him. It was this that was so basic for Jesus and this that his opponents so consistently refused to see.

There is a problem in the difference between Jesus' "speech" and his "word" (v. 43). Both terms can denote what anyone says. Rieu seems to give us the meaning with his translation, "Why do you not understand my language? Because you cannot comprehend my thought." They are not in tune with Jesus' basic position. They do not comprehend what he means by coming from God, by being sent from God and the like. And, because they never get to grips with what is basic in his teaching, they

find the words of a particular discourse impossible to understand.
They can "hear" in the sense that the words fall on their ears and are
registered. But this is not the same thing as appreciating the meaning
of what is said. It is in this latter respect that they fall short.

The Devil and His Sons

Now Jesus says bluntly, "You are of your father, the devil" (v. 44).
When he has previously spoken of their father he has clearly meant the
evil one, but this is the first time he has said this explicitly. Consistently there has been the thought that parentage dictates actions.
Those who are of God do the things that please God. Those who are
sons of Abraham do the deeds of Abraham. And those who are of the
devil do the devil's deeds. So, Jesus says, "the lusts of your father you
will to do" (v. 44). The word *lusts* means any strong desire. It can
occasionally be used of good desires, but mostly it speaks of a yearning
for evil. Clearly that is the meaning in this verse. The evil desires that
are characteristic of the devil are characteristic also of his sons. Jesus
says not only that they do such evils, but that they "will" to do them.
They have set their wills on the evil course they have chosen, a course
that is identical with that of the devil. In this way they show that he is
indeed their father. As John says in his first Epistle, "He who does what
is sinful is of the devil, because the devil has been sinning from the
beginning . . ." (1 John 3:8).

The devil "was a murderer from the beginning." This takes us back
to the story of Eden. There the devil tempted our first parents and
caused them to do what God told them not to do. God said plainly to
Adam and Eve, "You must not eat from the tree of the knowledge of
good and evil, for when you eat of it you will surely die" (Gen. 2:17). Eve
had this in mind when the devil approached her (Gen. 3:3), but the evil
one threw doubt on this and led her and Adam into the sin that brought
death to them both and thus to the whole human race. The evil one was
thus a murderer on quite a scale. And in a different sense he was the
murderer of Adam's son Abel. When Cain was angry at Abel's acceptance with God, God said to him, ". . . sin is crouching at your door; it
desires to have you, but you must master it" (Gen. 4:7). But Cain did not
master it. He yielded to it and murdered Abel. Right from the beginning the devil has brought about murder.

Jesus moves to the thought of truth. We have seen before that truth is
an important idea throughout this Gospel and that it is to be seen as a
quality of action as well as of speech (3:21). It is closely linked with
Jesus, who would in due course say, "I am the truth" (14:6). But the
devil had nothing to do with the truth. He "did not stand" in it. He took

up his stance elsewhere, for he had nothing to do with truth. He found truth utterly alien.

It is an easy step from there to the thought that the devil has a natural affinity for lying. "When he speaks the lie he speaks of his own" (v. 44). He is a natural liar "and the father of it." The Greek here could be translated "and so is his father," from which some have engaged in curious speculations about the devil's father. But we have no information about such a being and there is no real reason for thinking that this is the meaning of Jesus' words. Rather he is saying that falsehood takes its origin in the devil. He is utterly false and he deals in falsehood. He moves people to be as false as he is.

Truth

That puts Jesus apart from his hearers. He speaks the truth, he says, and because he speaks the truth they do not believe him (v. 45). Notice that he does not say "although I speak the truth . . ." but "because I speak the truth. . . ." The presumption all God's people make is that when the truth is spoken people will believe. And so they will if they are from God.

But Jesus is speaking of evil people. Because they are who and what they are, because they are the children of the devil, because the devil and all his helpers are false and love falsehood, therefore they do not believe the truth when they hear it. They have nothing to do with truth. We should be clear that good and evil are separated by a great chasm. We must not expect that the evil will believe the good. They will not believe unless there is a miracle of grace wrought in them.

Jesus goes on to challenge his hearers. They are opposing him and maintaining that he is not from God. So he asks them, "Which of you convicts me of sin?" (v. 46). It is interesting that none of them replies. This is striking, and we may well say that if even Jesus' enemies could not find sin in him, then his life must have been really outstanding.

But perhaps it is the issue of the challenge rather than the silence of the hearers that is the really wonderful thing. It indicates that Jesus had a perfectly clear conscience. He knew that there was no sin in him. Even a good man, a man far better than the average among God's servants, could not ask such a question if he knew that there was sin in him, even if his enemies did not know about it. A good man would not rely on the ignorance of his opponents. For Jesus, then, to ask such a question means that he knew that there could be no answer. Only one who lived very close to the Father could utter such words.

In the light, then, of the fact that they could not bring evidence of even one sin, in the light of the fact that he spoke the truth, Jesus can ask, "Why do you not believe me?" They ought to have believed one who came in the way Jesus did.

Jesus rounds off this section of the discussion by pointing to the two groups of people we so often find in this Gospel. The one who is "from God" hears Jesus' sayings. This group of people do not hear them because they are not "from God" (v. 47). They have argued that Abraham was their father. Then they shifted their ground a little and said that God was their "Father." These are both ways of saying that they were faithful Israelites, loyal members of the people of God, and Jesus emphatically denies their claim. They do not recognize God's messenger. They are therefore shown to be not God's people.

42

Before Abraham Was

The Jews answered him saying, "Do we not say well that you are a Samaritan and that you have a devil?" Jesus replied, "I have no devil, but I honor my Father and you dishonor me. But I do not seek my own glory; there is One who seeks and judges. Truly, truly, I say to you: if anyone keeps my word he will certainly not see death, not for ever." The Jews therefore said to him, "Now we know that you have a devil. Abraham died, and the prophets, and you say, 'If anyone keeps my word he will certainly not taste death, not for ever.' Are you greater than our father Abraham, who died? And the prophets died; whom are you making yourself?" Jesus answered, "If I glorify myself my glory is nothing. It is my Father who glorifies me of whom you say that he is our God. And yet you do not know him, but I know him. And if I should say that I do not know him I would be a liar like you. But I do know him and I keep his word. Abraham, your father, rejoiced to see my day, and he saw it and was glad." The Jews therefore said to him, "You are not yet fifty years old, and you have seen Abraham?" Jesus said to them, "Truly, truly, I say to you, Before Abraham was, I AM." Therefore they took up stones to throw them at him. But Jesus was hidden, and went away out of the temple (John 8:48–59).

Why did the Jews say that Jesus was a devil-possessed Samaritan? We can see why they said he had "a devil." They did not like his teaching and it suited them to ascribe it to the evil one. But

"Samaritan"? There is no serious suggestion that Jesus was anything other than a Jew, born in Bethlehem of a Jewish mother and brought up in Nazareth in a Jewish home. But we have seen that the Jews did not like the Samaritans. Though the two groups worshiped the same God, the Jews felt that the Samaritans were too ill-informed about him and too lax in the way they approached him. So they had as little to do with them as they could.

There is a saying reported in the Talmud in which three scholars criticize someone who has picked up some learning but has not been to one of the rabbinical schools. One Rabbi says that this man is just one of "the people of the land" (i.e., the common people who did not observe the religious regulations properly), a second that he is "a boor" and a third that he is "a Samaritan." Clearly the scholars had no high view of the Samaritans.

It is probably something like this here. Jesus' opponents may well have in mind the fact that he did not go along with them in observing their detailed regulations. They are saying in effect, "You are no better than a Samaritan! And a demon-possessed Samaritan at that." It is a way of repudiating his teaching and, by classing him with a despised nation, saying that what he taught would not be accepted by any right-thinking person.

Honoring God

Jesus completely ignored the charge that he was a Samaritan. It was not important. The Jews of his day might be narrow nationalists, but he was not. He was quite ready to pass through Samaria and talk with a Samaritan woman (chapter 4). He told a parable about a good man from Samaria. So it probably did not worry him in the slightest that he should be accused of being a Samaritan.

But he did deny that he was demon-possessed. So far from following the dictates of a demon he said, "I honor my Father" (v. 49). It was important that he had come to do the will of God, and he did not allow the accusation that he was demon-possessed to stand for a moment. He uses emphatic pronouns for "I" ("*I* have no devil, but honor my Father") and "you" ("*you* dishonor me"). This sets the Jews apart from him. He consistently gave honor to the Father, but they gave no honor to the one the Father sent. They are in opposite camps.

Jesus further differentiates himself from his opponents when he says, "But I do not seek my own glory" (v. 50). There is the implication that they do seek their own glory: he is not like them. "Glory" is a complex concept in this Gospel and Jesus will return to it later in this conversation. Here the point is that there are people who continually try to get others to think well of them. His Jewish opponents are like that. But Jesus is saying that this is not true of him. His aim is to do the will of God and it is God who "seeks and judges." The language is that of the law court. A just judge would seek out the truth of a matter and give a true and just verdict on the basis of the evidence. The implication is plain. It is his opponents and not Jesus who will be condemned by God. His enemies have not understood the situation in which they find themselves. They think that they are able to hound Jesus with their accusations of being a Samaritan and having a devil. But in fact they are people who stand under judgment, and it is God who will pass judgment on them in due course.

Death

Consistently in this Gospel Jesus' teaching is derived from God, and it is the revelation God gives whereby people enter life. So Jesus moves to the point that his teaching brings life. It is life that his opponents are refusing by taking up their attitude of hostility to him. He prefaces his words with "Truly, truly," which we have seen is his common way of introducing something that is both solemn and important. And with an especially emphatic form of expression he says that anyone who keeps his "word" will never die: "not for ever" (v. 51). His "word" stands for the whole body of his teaching (as in vv. 31, 37, 43). To give heed to that teaching, to accept it and act on it, is to enter God's salvation and that means no eternal death.

Far from impressing them, these words confirm the worst suspicions of these Jews. "Now we know that you have a devil," they say (v. 52). They take Jesus' words to apply to this physical life and see it as quite impossible that his "word" can prolong this life indefinitely. Since this is so, what he says must be wrong, they reason, and to make such a farfetched claim without any real basis proves that he has a devil.

They appeal to the example of Abraham, their great ancestor. Abraham had been a wonderful servant of God (was he not even called God's "friend" [Isa. 41:8]?). If anyone could avoid death, they seem to say, it would be this man. But did he?

No, he did not. Abraham died, as everyone else dies. For good measure they add the prophets. The prophets were the nation's great heroes. The Jews, almost alone among the nations of antiquity, saw the prophets (rather than warriors of some kind) as their great ones. And these, the Jews now say, are all dead. If the great ancestor of the nation died and if the great teachers of the nation died, then what is this heresy that anyone who keeps Jesus' word will never die? To them it was nonsense.

They ask, "Are you greater than our father Abraham?" and "Whom are you making yourself?" (v. 53). The recording of these words is another example of John's irony. He knows, and his readers know, that Jesus is greater by far than Abraham and the prophets. But he leaves the objection in the form in which it was made. It is ironical that the Jews are drawing attention to the really significant point, though without realizing its significance.

"My Father Glorifies Me"

Jesus has already said that he does not seek his own glory (v. 50). He repeats more or less the same point in slightly different language by saying that if he were to "glorify" himself that glory would be nothing (v. 54). But the important point, the point that his opponents were missing, was that it is the Father who glorifies Jesus.

Notice that Jesus sees his own relationship to God as very different from that of his antagonists, when he speaks of "my Father . . . of whom you say that he is our God." He enjoyed such a close personal relationship to him that he could speak of him as "my Father." They could not and did not; they called him "God." The manuscripts are divided, some reading "our" God and some "your" God; but it is the noun and not the adjective that is important. Where Jesus found the intimate relationship expressed in the word *Father* they were more at a distance.

But even when they called him their God they were not being accurate. They did indeed call him God, and it was their proud boast that there is only one God and that he was their God. They were sure that they had a relationship to the one God closer by far than that of any other nation on earth. It was a point of national pride as well as of religious exclusiveness.

And in this they were wrong. "You do not know him," Jesus says (v. 55). Far from having a good relationship to the one God, they did not even know him. They were self-deceived and could not grasp what was really the situation.

They remind me of a teacher in a school whose pupils almost all came from very wealthy homes. The teacher tried to help them see the problems of people who were in a very different situation from their own. One day she asked them to write an essay on the subject "A Poor Family." It would make them think hard, she thought, of how the other half lives. One child wrinkled his brow and began: "Once there was a very poor family. The father was poor, the mother was poor, the children were poor." Then really entering into the spirit of the thing he went on, "The butler was poor, the chauffeur was poor, the maids were poor, the gardener was poor. . . ." The child clearly had no conception whatever of what poverty means.

And these Jews had no conception whatever of who God is. They had their own pet ideas about God and they stuck firmly by them. They did not allow the facts to intrude on their beautiful illusion. They claimed to know God but had no real knowledge of him at all. Jesus was in a different position. He really did know God, and he points out here that if he were to deny that (and take up a position like theirs), he would be a liar, as they are. "But," he says, "I do know him and I keep his word" (v. 55). That is a truth insisted on throughout this Gospel. Indeed, the whole gospel is written out of the conviction that God had acted in Christ for the world's salvation and nothing matters alongside this.

Abraham

The Jews had brought Abraham into the conversation earlier (v. 52). Jesus did not follow that up straightaway, but now he returns to the great patriarch and says some strange words: "Abraham, your father, rejoiced to see my day, and he saw it and was glad" (v. 56). By saying "your father" Jesus is perhaps indicating that the Jews ought to behave differently. If they really were the true children of Abraham, they would act towards Jesus in a way very different from the way they were behaving. They would welcome him as Abraham did.

There are two specially difficult problems about what Jesus said: the meaning of Abraham's rejoicing and the meaning of Jesus' "day." The "day" of Jesus in the New Testament often is clearly the great day when Jesus will return in glory to end this whole world order and to bring in God's new order (e.g., Phil. 1:10; 2:16). But such a meaning does not suit the context here as well as the view that it is Jesus' first coming that is in mind, his coming to make atonement and to open the way to salvation for sinners. That was the critical thing in the working out of salvation. Abraham rejoiced at the coming of Jesus to be our Savior.

When did Abraham rejoice at this day? Jesus is not saying that Abraham is rejoicing now in heaven, but that he "rejoiced." It is a past event, and it is not easy to see when it could have been. We may get a little help if we consider some of the things the Rabbis said about Abraham. Take, for example, the way they understood some words uttered on the occasion of the great patriarch's first appearance in Genesis. God said to him (among other things): ". . . all peoples on earth will be blessed through you" (Gen. 12:3). The Rabbis took this as

341

a prophecy of the coming of the Messiah and held that Abraham rejoiced at this prospect. Another passage they saw as messianic was the vision narrated in Genesis 15. Here Abraham is told that his descendants will be as numerous as the stars in heaven (v. 5), and subsequently God made a solemn covenant with him (v. 18). The Rabbis understood this passage, too, as messianic and a cause for joy.

A third relevant passage is that in which God promised Abraham that he and Sarah, his wife, would have a child. The old couple were incredulous and both laughed at the prospect, Abraham as told in Genesis 17:17 and Sarah in Genesis 18:12. Curiously the Rabbis interpreted Abraham's laughter not as an incredulous reaction, but as joy at the prospect of having a child by Sarah. That is an incredible piece of exegesis; they did not really take notice of what the words meant.

People sometimes miss the point, and some statements must be interpreted with great care. I like the story of a man who worked for a great film actress who was somewhat temperamental and a great trial to those unfortunate enough to have to work with her. She demanded that they agree with her in everything and was quite put out if they did not. But she liked to put on a good face with the press and at an interview one day said, among other things, "I always have great respect for those who differ from me." These words were relayed to the man we are speaking of, and he was asked his opinion. He replied, "Sure. So I differ from her and she respects me. But where do I get my next job?" We are left feeling that the man did not put the same interpretation on the words as the actress did.

The lady's words were all right, but they did not correspond to reality. It is something like that with the rabbinic interpretation. The view sounds attractive, but it is not the meaning of Scripture.

We should think of yet another rabbinic interpretation, this time of Genesis 24:1, where the New International Version tells us that Abraham "was now old and well advanced in years." More literally this last expression means "gone into the days," and our translators have simply said this in the way English speakers would naturally express it. But it is possible to understand "gone into the days" in more ways than one, and the Rabbis took it to mean that Abraham, being an inspired man, was able to go in thought through all the days up to the coming of the Messiah. Once again we may feel compelled to conclude that this is not exegesis. This is not what the passage means. The rabbinic interpretation tells us little about the meaning of Genesis, but much about the way the Rabbis thought.

But it helps us to see the force of what Jesus was saying to the Jews. They had brought up Abraham. Very well, let us think about Abraham, Jesus is saying. From their understanding of a number of passages the

Jews were ready to say that Abraham rejoiced. Jesus is saying that Abraham's joy was real enough, and that it concerned the Messiah, as Jewish tradition held. The things that were taking place before his opponents' very eyes were the things at which Abraham rejoiced. He looked for the coming of God's Messiah and it was this that made him happy. But God's Messiah was now before them; if they really accepted what Abraham was saying, they would rejoice with him at the presence of the Messiah.

"Before Abraham Was—"

The Jews scarcely look at the claim that Abraham *rejoiced;* they are preoccupied with the thought that *Abraham* rejoiced. They are quite prepared to agree that Abraham looked for the coming of the Messiah, but they could not for one moment countenance any view that there was a connection between Abraham and Jesus. So they seize on the question of age. "You are not yet fifty years old," they say to Jesus, which leads us to wonder why they fixed on this figure. Luke tells us that when Jesus began his ministry he was about age thirty (Luke 3:23). Nobody tells us how long the ministry lasted, but it is usually accepted that it covered a span of no more than about three years. Of course a man who was in his early thirties is "not yet fifty," but that is not the way he would usually be described. But fifty was the age when the Levites were considered to have finished their life's work (Num. 4:3), and it may be that they are saying, "You are far too young to have seen Abraham. He lived a long time ago and you have not even completed a normal working life!" Or it may be that they were simply making every allowance without seriously estimating the actual age of Jesus.

They are saying that when you add on every possible year you can think of there is no way of taking Jesus' past back nearly far enough for Abraham to have seen him. Actually, considering the way the Rabbis interpreted the passages we were looking at, this was not strictly necessary. When they said that Abraham had gone into all the days they did not mean that the Messiah had actually been alive at the time of Abraham's vision. They meant that the patriarch had seen the Messiah prophetically. But these Jews were not trying to make allowances for Jesus. They were trying to condemn him; a connection with Abraham looked like an outrageous claim, and that is the way they saw it.

Jesus quite realizes that this was the way what he had said appeared to them. But he makes no attempt to modify it or to make it more acceptable in any way. Instead he introduces his words with the solemn "Truly, truly." What he is about to say is very solemn and very important. Then he says, "Before Abraham was, I AM" (v. 58). This is emphatic speech in the style of deity, which we have seen Jesus using before. There is a claim to deity in the form of words he uses and there is a claim to deity in the meaning we must give them. Jesus claims to have existed not only in the time of Abraham (who could thus have seen him and rejoiced), but before that time. Jesus' "I AM" is timeless. He existed long before Abraham. We should probably understand the words to mean that he has always existed. This is a tremendous claim.

It was a claim that outraged his hearers. To them it was nothing less than blasphemy. In the face of that claim there are only two possibilities. We may accept it and open our hearts to Jesus so that he becomes our Lord and we live to do his will. Or we will reject him. There is no middle course. And if we reject him, we may well take action against him and that was what these Jews did. "They took up stones to throw them at him" (v. 59). Stoning was the Jewish punishment for blasphemy, and these people did not wait for the verdict of some court. Had they not heard him themselves? They saw no reason to delay but attempted to carry out an execution in the traditional style.

But they could not do it. Jesus "was hidden," which may mean that he hid from them in some way. Or the passive may be taken with full seriousness and we then see in it the thought that the Father hid him so that these evil people could not carry out their plan. The will of God is done. Jesus would die on the cross, but it would be in God's good time. There would be no precipitate execution.

Let us finish this meditation with some words from Augustine, a great Christian from an earlier age: "As man, He fled from the stones; but woe to those from whose stony hearts God has fled."

43

Sight to the Blind

And as he passed by he saw a man blind from birth. And his disciples asked him, "Rabbi, who sinned, this man or his parents, that he was born blind?" Jesus replied, "Neither did this man sin nor his parents, but (it happened) so that the works of God might be made manifest in him. We must work the works of him who sent me while it is day; night comes when no one can work. As long as I am in the world I am the light of the world." When he had said these things he spat on the ground and made clay of the spittle, he smeared his clay on his eyes and said to him, "Go, wash in the pool of Siloam (which interpreted means 'Sent')." He went off and washed and came seeing (John 9:1–7).

During the course of the discussions that followed this healing the formerly blind man said, "From of old it was never heard that anyone opened the eyes of a man born blind" (v. 32), and as far as we know the man was accurate. There is no example of the giving of sight to any blind person (let alone one born blind) throughout the entire Old Testament. And in the New there is no example of any of Jesus' followers being instrumental in bringing about such a miracle. As near as we come to it is the occasion when Ananias laid hands on Saul and prayed, with the result that the temporary blindness that followed his vision on the Damascus Road gave way to normal sight. But this is nothing like the miracle that Jesus did on the man who had never seen throughout his entire life.

It is all the more interesting that there are more accounts of the giving of sight to the blind in Jesus' ministry than of any other form of healing. It is never said why this should be so, but perhaps we should think here of the Old Testament prophecies that link the giving of sight to the blind with the activity of the Messiah. "In that day," writes Isaiah, "the deaf will hear the words of the scroll, and out of gloom and darkness the eyes of the blind will see" (Isa. 29:18). And again we read, "Then will the eyes of the blind be opened . . ." (Isa. 35:5), while God says of the Servant of the Lord, "I will . . . make you to be . . . a light for the Gentiles, to open eyes that are blind . . ." (Isa. 42:6–7). There are passages, too, where it is said that "the LORD gives sight to the blind" (Ps. 146:8; see also Exod. 4:11), We should probably understand the writers of our Gospels to be telling us that the giving of sight to the blind shows us Jesus fulfilling messianic prophecies and doing things that God alone can do.

The Problem of Suffering

John introduces this story by saying that Jesus "passed by" but does not say what or where or whom he passed by. Evidently he did not think it important to place the story exactly in a chronological sequence or to tell us precisely where the incident took place. He simply says that Jesus saw a man "blind from birth" (v. 1). That was the important thing. Evidently it was well known that this man had been blind from birth, for John does not mention any discussion of the topic nor does he say that anyone told Jesus or the disciples this fact. It is assumed that they all knew and John takes the story from this point. And, of course, a blind man would be a beggar; as such his story would tend to be known and he would probably be found in a regular spot where pious and generous citizens would be likely to give him money.

The disciples address Jesus as "Rabbi" (v. 1); the word means "my great one" (like the French *monsieur*). Theoretically it might have been used of people in a wide variety of occupations but in practice was confined to teachers, and that is its meaning here. "Teacher," they say, "who sinned?" They do not argue the point as though there was any doubt about it. The man had been blind all his life. Therefore, they reasoned, someone had committed a terrible sin.

There is a rabbinic saying, "There is no death without sin, and there is no suffering without iniquity" (the Rabbis held that this was proved by two texts from Scripture, Ezek. 18:20 and Ps. 89:32). Evidently this view was widely held and the disciples assume it without question. There had to be sin somewhere behind the man's blindness. For the disciples the question was not whether it was sin that had brought about this terrible affliction, but rather "Whose sin was it?"

Never to have seen is a frightful hardship. It deprived this man of much that is valuable and enjoyable in life and meant that the only occupation that had ever been open to him was that of a beggar. In those days there was no other option. Why had such a punishment been inflicted on him? Was it due to some sin of his own? It was not easy to see how this could be. What sin could a person commit before being born that was so dreadful that its punishment was lifelong blindness? But if the man had not committed the sin himself, his parents must have been responsible, and it was not easy for the disciples to see what they could possibly have done that would have brought this punishment not on them but on their son. It was all very puzzling.

Actually it was not beyond the ingenuity of the Rabbis to find an answer. The sin might well have been that of the man himself, as they saw it. Some of them held that the soul existed before it came into the body. Thus, in the apocryphal book *The Wisdom of Solomon,* the author says that "a good soul fell to my lot; or rather, being good, I entered an undefiled body" (8:19–20). Since that author claims that he was good before he entered the body, it is clear that the possibility had to be allowed that other people were bad before they began their lives on earth. The view was apparently not widely held, but certainly some people thought that way. Thus the man might have sinned before he came to earth. But could he have sinned so greatly that he would merit the punishment he had received?

More common was the thought that children might sin in the womb. We read in Scripture that when Rebekah was pregnant with twins "the babies jostled each other within her" (Gen. 25:22). This opened up the possibility that unborn babies were active and could thus do what was wrong as well as what was right. So prenatal sin was thought to be quite possible. Only, in this case, it seemed that a very great punishment was being inflicted for what could scarcely be a very great sin.

That left the possibility that it may have been the parents who sinned. One Rabbi held that a man should not gaze at a woman, "and he who looks even at a woman's heel will beget degenerate children," while another maintained that this was true of a man's own wife during menstruation. Yet another held that if anyone who "has had a blood-letting has marital intercourse, he will have epileptic children." There are many such sayings, and it is clear that the Rabbis were firmly of the conviction that it was quite common to have the sins of the parents punished by various defects in the children, defects for which the children would have to suffer all their lives.

So the disciples were not manufacturing an imaginary problem. It is clear that among the religious teachers of the Jews there were some who thought a person might well be punished for sins he had committed before birth, and there were some who held that even very serious afflictions might be the punishment of parental sins. So this blind man presented them with a problem. It was not easy to see how he could have sinned before birth a sin serious enough to merit such a heavy punishment. Nor could they see why the heavenly Father of whom Jesus had taught them so much would punish a man in this terrible fashion for the sins of someone else. But in their culture these seemed the only possibilities. So they ask Jesus. Whose sin was it?

The Works of God

Jesus immediately dismissed both possibilities (v. 3). There are still mysteries about the afflictions that trouble us in this life, but we must not seek the answers along the lines that the disciples were pursuing. Jesus did not say that sickness and the like are never the consequence of sin. In a previous incident he said to the man he had cured of lameness, "Sin no longer, lest something worse happen to you" (5:14). Sin can have damaging consequences. But it is a great mistake to think that all our afflictions and illnesses are due to sin.

This blindness, Jesus said, was "so that the works of God might be made manifest in him." I do not think that Jesus means that the man was made to go through all his life up to this point without ever having been able to see, simply in order that Jesus might effect a cure and thus manifest "the works of God." Rather he is saying that the blindness is something in and through which God's "works" are manifest.

It is important that we recognize that God's hand is in all our afflictions as well as in those good things that we recognize as his blessings. Christians are not shielded from the hardships and difficulties of life so that they are freed from the afflictions that trouble other people. On the contrary. They live on the same terms as do other people; they have the same kind of troubles, illnesses, accidents, and the like. There are some differences; perhaps a Christian, to take an example at random, is not very likely to find himself incapacitated as the result of driving a car while he was drunk. But, setting such consequential sufferings apart, Christians live their lives with the same kind of problems as other people have.

The difference is that, as God's children, Christians look to God for the grace to see them through. In their troubles they manifest the fact that, as Paul found out, God's grace is always sufficient and that his power "is made perfect in weakness" (2 Cor. 12:9). They do not com-

348

plain bitterly at every trial, for they know that the heavenly Father has his purpose in everything that happens in life.

And, of course, sometimes "the works of God" are made manifest in the removal of an affliction. So it is in this case. What God had done through the man's blindness in past days we do not know. But we do know that the removal of that affliction was a manifestation of the divine power and resulted in both physical and spiritual blessing to the man.

That the works of God are made manifest has its consequences for the people of God: "We must," said Jesus, "work the works of him who sent me" (v. 4). God chooses to do his mighty works through those on earth, at least as a general rule. He can do mighty miracles without human participation, but normally he chooses to let his people have a part in the great works he is doing. So now. It is not certain whether Jesus said "we must work" or "I must work"; some of the manuscripts have one reading, some the other. But "I must work" is the reading of most of the later manuscripts, while the earlier ones for the most part have "we must work." Scribes would be tempted to alter "we must work" to "I must work" because Jesus immediately goes on to refer to the time while "I am in the world"; with those words to follow it would be easy for scribes to reason that "we must work" must be wrong. So most scholars accept "we must work" as the true reading and think of "I must work" as a scribal alteration.

That means that Jesus was associating his people with himself in this obligation. He did the miracle himself, of course, though even here we should bear in mind that Jesus did not simply speak a word of power as he often did in his healing miracles. He put clay on the man's eyes and told him to go and wash in Siloam. The man was given a part to play. But in general God calls his people to work with him when he does his mighty works. We are given a great privilege, which Paul expresses by saying that we are God's "fellow-workers" (1 Cor. 3:9). There is a dignity about Christian service, a dignity such as attaches to nothing else on earth.

Notice further that Jesus says that we "must" work. The term means that there is a compelling necessity about this. He is not saying that it would be a good idea for us to do some work for God. He is saying that it is necessary that we do this work. Salvation by God's grace is not an invitation to spiritual laziness. The fact that we do nothing to merit our salvation should not lead us to reason that it does not matter what we do with our lives. Rather it should impel us to do the best we can in living out what salvation means. It should motivate us to do the works of God "while it is day."

349

We might expect that after "we must work" we would have a reference to "him who sent us" (which indeed we find in some manuscripts; the scribes were apparently uneasy with the change from "we" to "me" and while some altered "we" to the singular, others altered "me" to the plural). But very few scholars doubt that "me" is correct here. John makes a great deal of the fact that the Father sent the Son. It was the sending of the Son that altered everything. Jesus' death on the cross is the great central fact. It brings us salvation and it reveals to us the magnitude of God's love. So when Jesus is speaking about the work of God that his followers must work he links it with the mission on which he had come. All Christian work is connected in one way or another with the fact that the Father sent the Son.

The Light of the World

Jesus says that we all must work "while it is day"; he contrasts the day with the night that is coming, when "no one can work." He does not define the day and the night here, but we must surely see them as the time while we have the opportunity of working and the time when work is done. In Jesus' own case there is the approach of the crucifixion, when his earthly work would be done. There is a sense in which it was indeed "night" when Jesus died, and this is symbolized in the darkness that the Synoptists tell us was over all the land while he was on the cross (Matt. 27:45; Mark 15:33; Luke 23:44). All the work that Jesus was sent to accomplish had to be done before the "night"; after the cross there was none of the earthly life left in which to do anything.

In the case of the servants of Christ there is an equivalent. It is true of us, as it was of him, that when our earthly life is done our earthly work is done. We must not put off doing service until it is too late. We must also bear in mind that for particular pieces of service there is an earlier "night"; before our lives are over the opportunity for doing them will have gone. In other words, opportunity must be grasped while it is there; every opportunity passes away sooner or later and if we miss it we cannot bring it back.

With this encouragement to get on with the work we are given to do, Jesus links the words: "As long as I am in the world I am the light of the world" (v. 5). These words bring out the shortness of the incarnation. The time when Jesus was in the world was definitely limited and, therefore, he must act decisively. And throughout that time he was "the light of the world." Of course he still is and always will be. But in a special sense he was light to the world during the days of his life, and it is in that sense that he now says, "I am the light of the world." As long as he lived here on earth it was his function to be light to the dwellers on earth.

The Giving of Sight

Jesus proceeded to give sight to the blind man. It is interesting that John says nothing about any initiative from the man himself. He did not ask for sight, for example. Nor is there any conversation with him as there was with the lame man in chapter 5. John says nothing about whether the man had faith in Jesus or not, or even whether he knew who Jesus was. We are probably right in thinking that he had no faith as yet, because at the end of the incident John records Jesus as asking him whether he believed on the Son of man, only to have the man ask, "Who is he?" (vv. 35–36). It seems that he became a believer only after the miracle. It is also to be noted that on this occasion Jesus invited the man's cooperation. Just as he had said to the lame man, "Get up, pick up your pallet and walk" (5:8), so he could have said to this man, "Open your eyes and see." But he did not. He asked him to do something.

Jesus spat on the ground and made a little bit of clay. Then he smeared the clay on the eyes of the blind man. The ancient world thought highly of the curative values of spittle, but it is impossible to think that it was spittle itself as a medical method that brought about the cure. Jesus healed many people without resort to such means (though Mark tells us that he used spittle on two other occasions: Mark 7:33; 8:23). It is probable that Jesus used spittle on this occasion because of the way the man himself would view it; it may have been a help to him to have this method used in his own case.

Having put the clay on the man's eyes, Jesus sent him off to the pool of Siloam and told him to wash (v. 7). John explains the meaning of Siloam as "Sent." King Hezekiah had a tunnel dug from the Virgin's Fountain (which was outside the city) to this pool to bring a water supply into the city, so that the water was "sent" along by this tunnel. The name properly belongs to the conduit but was given to the pool and that at quite an early date (Neh. 3:15; Isa. 8:6). John probably includes an explanation of the meaning of the name because of the large place he gives to the concept of Jesus as having been "sent" by the Father. Now a blind man is cured by means of the "sent," basically by Jesus but in a secondary manner by the pool. The word for "pool" is connected with the verb "to swim"; it was quite a large pool, not some ornamental pond.

The man did as Jesus told him. He went off to the pool and washed and "came seeing." He found that he had received the gift of sight. "The light of the world" was meaningful to him.

44

Friends and Pharisees

*The neighbors, then, and those who formerly had seen him that
he was a beggar said, "Is not this the man who sat and
begged?" Others said, "No, but he is like him." He said, "I am
he." They said to him therefore, "How were your eyes opened?"
He replied, "The man called Jesus made clay and smeared it on
my eyes and said to me, 'Go to Siloam and wash.' So I went
off and when I had washed I saw." And they said to him,
"Where is he?" He says, "I do not know."*

*They bring the formerly blind man to the Pharisees. Now it
was the Sabbath on the day when Jesus made clay and opened
his eyes. Therefore the Pharisees too asked him how he received
his sight. He said to them, "He put clay on my eyes and I
washed and I see." So some of the Pharisees said, "This man is
not from God because he does not keep the Sabbath." But
others said, "How can a man that is a sinner do such signs?"
and there was a division among them. So they said to the blind
man again, "What do you say about him, because he opened
your eyes?" And he said, "He is a prophet."*

*The Jews did not believe about him that he was blind and
had received sight until they called the parents of him who had
received sight. And they asked them, "Is this your son, of whom
you say that he was born blind? How therefore does he now
see?" So his parents replied saying, "We know that this is our
son and that he was born blind. But how he now sees we do
not know, or who opened his eyes we do not know. Ask him, he
is of age; he will speak for himself." His parents said these
things because they were afraid of the Jews, for the Jews had
already agreed that if anyone should confess him to be the*

*Christ he should be put out of the synagogue. For this reason
his parents said, "He is of age; ask him."*

*So a second time they called the man who was blind and
said to him, "Give glory to God; we know that this man is a
sinner." He therefore answered, "Whether he is a sinner I do
not know. One thing I know, that I was blind, now I see." They
said to him therefore, "What did he do to you? How did he
open your eyes?" He answered them, "I told you already and
you did not listen; why do you want to hear it again? You don't
wish to become his disciples, too, do you?" And they abused
him and said, "You are a disciple of that fellow, but we are
Moses' disciples. We know that God spoke to Moses, but as for
this man, we don't know where he is from." The man answered
them saying, "Why in this is the marvelous thing that you do
not know where he is from and yet he opened my eyes! We
know that God does not hear sinners but if anyone is devout
and does his will, him he hears. From of old it was never heard
that anyone opened the eyes of a man born blind; if this man
were not from God he could do nothing at all." They answered
him saying, "You were altogether born in sins and are you
teaching us?" And they threw him out* (John 9:8–34).

T he man born blind doubtless was a very happy man as
he exulted in his new gift of sight. But it was not long before he found
himself in conflict with some of the highest in the land—a most unexpected result of what he must have seen as the most wonderful thing
that had happened to him in all his life. The inquisition the Pharisees
carried out when it was all reported to them shows the man as a sturdy
character, one who would not be stampeded by the opposition of those
in authority but was ready to give a good account of himself as he stood
by the facts of the situation. He knew what had happened and was not
going to let himself be browbeaten into a criticism of the healer who
had given him the wonderful gift of sight.

John begins with a paragraph in which he tells of the man's reception by his friends and neighbors (vv. 8–12). He was obviously sighted,
a fact that caused a division of opinion among those who saw him. He
was recognizably the same man, and that was what impressed some
who saw him. But blind men do not see, and that was what impressed
others. The man was able to resolve that problem and he announced
his identity.

That raised the question "How were your eyes opened?" (v. 10) to
which he gave a concise answer, explaining how Jesus had healed him.

But to the question "Where is he?" he could reply only "I do not know" (v. 12). He had left Jesus in response to the command to go off to the pool of Siloam, and when he found that he could see he had evidently gone off home straightaway. He had had no opportunity for knowing where Jesus was.

The Sabbath

The excited group brought the man to the Pharisees (v. 13). John does not say why they did this, nor when. It may have been a spontaneous, immediate reaction. But from the subsequent conversation it seems more likely that it was some time later. It is interesting that they brought the man to the Pharisees, not to the priests or any official body. But in popular esteem it was the Pharisees who were the religious experts and, in any case, many of them were members of the Sanhedrin. They were prominent in the life of the nation and evidently were regarded at least by this little group of ordinary people as the kind of leading people who could give a decision on matters that troubled them.

John does not tell us what they said when they came to the Pharisees. But the giving of sight took place on the Sabbath, and the subsequent discussion shows that it was this that troubled the religious leaders and presumably also some of the people who brought the man before them. It may be that it was not so much the cure in itself as the cure on the Sabbath on which they wanted the verdict of the learned Pharisees. In any case it was the Sabbath that loomed large, and John now tells us that it was on that day that the cure took place (v. 14).

Throughout this section of the Gospel the Sabbath is stressed. The healing of the lame man took place on the Sabbath (5:1–18), as, according to some manuscripts, did the teaching in the synagogue at Capernaum (6:59). At the Feast of Tabernacles there was a discussion about the bearing on Sabbath observance of the regulation that circumcision be carried out on that day (7:22–23), and now we have a further work of healing on the holy day. Clearly the right use of the Sabbath formed a large part of Jesus' conflict with the authorities in Jerusalem. They saw the day as one on which not the slightest risk should be taken of doing anything that profaned its holiness. Accordingly they ringed it about with a multitude of restrictions, with the praiseworthy intention of bringing glory to God but with the unfortunate practical result of making the Sabbath a burden.

Jesus called people back to an understanding of what God meant when he called on people to keep the day holy. It was wrong to see God as simply calling for abstention from all sorts of work. This misunderstanding led the Pharisees and others into a close examination of exactly what constituted work (and which accordingly could not be done) and what could be seen as not coming under the heading "work" (and thus was permissible). God created everything in six days and rested on the seventh, and this was the basis of the Sabbath. But his "rest" did not mean cessation from all activity. If God did not continually sustain his creation on the Sabbath it would cease to exist. It was therefore proper for people to do things on the Sabbath that would bring honor to God, things like circumcising a child, or healing a blind or lame man.

It was this failure to understand the ways of God that led the Pharisees into their bitter and continuous hostility to Jesus. They saw him as giving teaching that cut at the heart of service to God as they understood it. He saw them as blind to what God was saying to them. Throughout this part of his Gospel John is emphasizing the importance of the right use of the Sabbath as opposed to the way the Pharisees observed it.

Signs and Sinners

The Pharisees began quite properly by asking the man what had happened (v. 15). They had not been there at the time and wanted him to tell them exactly what had occurred. We have already seen that the man had a gift for saying things concisely, and once again we have a very short but very clear account of the miracle.

Immediately the more hidebound of the Pharisees trotted out their doctrinaire verdict. Their views on the Sabbath were clear, and equally clear was it that what Jesus had done did not fit in with those views. Therefore, reasoned this group, Jesus "is not from God" (v. 16). If he did not keep the Sabbath according to their rules, how could he be?

They were not prepared for anything outside their normal approach. I am reminded that it is said that during his time as a recluse Howard Hughes would often demand the same meal day after day. At one time he ate two scoops of banana-nut ice cream at every meal. There was consternation among his staff when they learned that the manufacturer had decided to discontinue the line. But they got in touch with him and persuaded him to make a special batch. As 1,325 liters was the smallest amount he would make, they felt that they were well provided for, for quite some time. But when they served the millionaire his next meal he said, "That's fine ice cream, but it's time I changed. From now on I want French vanilla."

Like the aides of Howard Hughes these Pharisees were prepared for what could be expected. But something outside the normal did not fit

355

into their rules, and they could not recognize it as anything other than wrong.

But that was not the only opinion. Others asked, "How can a man that is a sinner do such signs?" These men were impressed by the miracle. They recognized that Jesus had given sight to a man born blind, and they saw that this called for a mighty divine intervention. No quack or charlatan could call forth the power of God in this way. Sabbath rules or no Sabbath rules, for them this was clear evidence that Jesus was not the sinner their comrades claimed he was.

We very often overlook this section of Pharisaism. The Pharisaic system was such that it all too easily degenerated into a keeping of rules, and that meant a process of defining with the greatest precision what constituted a fulfillment of the rules and what constituted a breach. With a great variety of exceptions open to those who were learned in these definitions, it was all too easy to give attention to the letter rather than the spirit, and thus for us Pharisaism has become synonymous with hypocrisy. But it is well to remember that there was another side to Pharisaism. There were Pharisees who were more open-minded and who were genuinely pious people. While those who opposed Jesus received the emphasis in the Gospels, there were those who agreed with him, and we should not forget that in the early church there were Pharisees who believed and who were heard in the councils of the church (Acts 15:5).

So on this occasion there were some who saw that it was simply not possible for a sinner to do "such signs." It was, of course, possible for Satan to disguise himself as an angel of light, and they were not dismissing the possibility of the evil one's deceit. But they were talking about "signs," about mighty works that taught people about God and his ways and brought them near to God. Miracles like that are not possible for evil people. And it was miracles like that that Jesus kept doing.

The result was division. Neither group could accept the position of the other. So they called the blind man into the discussion again. He had told them what had happened. Now they wanted to know what he thought about Jesus (v. 17). Normally these religious experts would never have dreamed of asking an opinion about a religious teacher from a beggar. It shows us how perplexed and divided they were that they should ask such a thing of such a man.

Progress and Regress

The man's instant response was "He is a prophet" (v. 17). We may feel that this is inadequate, but we should bear in mind that it was probably the highest religious title that the man was able to give at that instant. He was no theologian; he had lived all his life in the world of darkness and had known no occupation other than that of a beggar. So he could not be expected to know all about Jesus from the very brief contact he had had with him.

One of the intriguing things about this chapter is the way the blind beggar grew in understanding, while at the same time the Pharisees with all their advantages became progressively more limited in their understanding of Jesus. Evidently the blind man was quite intelligent and was a man of character. The result was that he came to see more and more of who and what Jesus was.

The blind man's first description of Jesus was "the man called Jesus" (v. 11). By now he has gone on to see him as a prophet. During subsequent discussions he came to see that he was a leader, one whom it was well to follow, and he spoke of disciples (v. 27). Toward the end he says that Jesus could not do what he does if he were not "from God" (v. 33). This means, since Jesus does in fact do these things, that he *is* "from God." Finally, when Jesus seeks him out, he comes to see him as the Son of man, as Lord, and as one who may fitly be worshiped (vv. 35–38). It is an interesting spiritual progression.

But the Pharisees went the other way. They started with the conviction that Jesus was "not from God" (v. 16), then went on to question the reality of the miracle he had done (v. 18). They declared their certainty that he was a sinner (v. 24) and made statements arising from this that showed them to be ignorant in matters spiritual (v. 29). Finally they were shown to be both blind and sinful (v. 41).

People do not stand still. As we go through life we either make progress in spiritual things or we slip back. The two parties in this discussion press an important lesson on us.

The Blind Man's Parents

For some reason John drops his references to "the Pharisees" (they are mentioned specifically again only in v. 40). He reverts to the name he usually used for Jewish leaders in opposition to Jesus, "the Jews," but we need not think that anyone other than the Pharisees mentioned in the earlier part of the chapter are in mind. They could not believe that Jesus had worked such a striking miracle and looked at ways of discrediting the report.

They began with the parents of the man. They summoned them to the discussion and asked whether this sighted person was their son and, if so, how he had received sight (v. 19). We have already seen that the formerly blind man was ready to stand up to the Pharisees, but this was not true of his parents. Evidently they were humble people and did not want to come into conflict with those in high places. So they are prepared to identify their son and to attest the fact that he was born blind (v. 20). But they will not go beyond that. They were not there when the cure took place and thus could not testify of their own knowledge that it was Jesus who had given him sight. So they say, "But how he now sees we do not know."

They could scarcely be blamed for this. It was no more than the truth. But they went on to say that the Pharisees should direct their questions to the man himself. They said, ". . . he is of age; he will speak for himself" (v. 21). It is clear that they discerned danger in this inquiry. The leaders were clearly displeased with their son. He might be punished severely. They wanted to make sure that whatever happened, they were safe. So they put all the responsibility on their son.

John adds a little explanation (vv. 22–23). The Jews had agreed to excommunicate anyone who confessed Jesus to be the Christ. Some writers go into detail as to what this meant, while others deny that any form of excommunication existed at this time. Both extremes seem to be wrong. Excommunication in some form is as old as the time of Ezra (Ezra 10:8), though little is known of precisely what this involved at the time of Jesus or of just how it was carried out. But the withdrawal of any synagogue privileges would be a serious matter to anyone from such a religious community as the Jews of that day, so it is not surprising that the man's parents did not want to incur the punishment. That must be said, but it is still surprising that they did not give more support to their own son in his difficulties just as he was beginning to find his way in the sighted world.

Give Glory to God

Not being able to make much progress with the parents, the Pharisees went back to questioning the man himself. This time they began with "Give glory to God" (v. 24), the precise bearing of which is not clear. They may mean, "You have been lying. We know that. This man Jesus did not give you sight. You have done wrong in saying so. Now we invite you to leave your sinful path and do what is right. Give glory to God and tell us the truth" (Joshua made a somewhat similar plea to Achan, Josh. 7:19).

Another way of taking their words is to see them as reasoning that Jesus did not do the work of healing. All he did was put clay on the man's eyes. If there was healing, then it was God who did it and all the glory should be given to him.

They reinforce their exhortation by informing the man that they know that Jesus is a sinner. Their "we" is emphatic; whatever be the case with ignorant people like blind beggars, these religious experts have knowledge and they lay it down categorically that "this man is a sinner."

But the former blind beggar is not a man who can be easily moved from a position he knows to be right. He does not know anything about Jesus and thus does not know whether or not he is a sinner. But he has one important certainty: "I was blind, now I see" (v. 25). Nobody is going to shake a man out of a certainty like that. And, as it was Jesus who gave him his sight, nobody is going to make him take sides against Jesus.

All this must have been quite unexpected. The Pharisees did not usually discuss religious matters with common people like a beggar, and when they did they expected that what they said would be accepted without question. It was very unusual to have anyone react like this man.

I am reminded of a little old lady who went into a shoe shop and asked for a pair of shoes with platform soles. This was high fashion at the time, and the little old lady looked a long way from being glamorous. The assistant, however, did not argue. She produced a number of platform soles and eventually sold the most stylish of them all, with platform soles twelve centimeters high. As she was wrapping them she asked, "Are you buying these for some special occasion?" "Good heavens, no," said the little old lady. "They're for when I do my washing. I'm not tall and the sheets touch the ground when I'm trying to get them onto the clothesline. Now I'll be high enough to keep them out of the dirt."

It was a quite unexpected reaction (and an unexpected use for high-fashion shoes). So with the blind man. The Pharisees did not quite know how to proceed. So they went back to the beginning: "What did he do to you? How did he open your eyes?" (v. 26).

But the man wanted nothing to do with going over the story again. He reminded them that he had told them all this already. And perhaps with a mischievous twinkle in his eye he asked whether they wanted to become Jesus' disciples, too (v. 27). The way he put his question shows that he expected a negative answer. He knew that this kind of person was not going to become a disciple, but it was fun suggesting it. We should notice his "too." He is already counting himself as a disciple of Jesus.

Disciples of Moses

The Pharisees clearly are angry. They take up this mention of discipleship and distance themselves from the blind man. They use emphatic pronouns to say, "*You* are a disciple of that fellow, but *we* are Moses' disciples" (v. 28), and speak contemptuously of Jesus. They want there to be no doubt of their repudiation of the blind man and also of Jesus. They clinch their position (so they think) with the assertion that God spoke to Moses but that they have no knowledge of Jesus' origin (v. 29).

The formerly blind man comes up with an interesting piece of reasoning. He begins by referring to "the" marvelous thing: more astonishing even than his miraculous cure is the ignorance of the Pharisees in the face of convincing evidence. He marshals his arguments: (1) Jesus opened his eyes; (2) God does not hear sinners (they had said, "We know that God spoke to Moses" and he retorts with another "we know," this one referring to God's refusal to bless sinners); (3) God hears the devout who do his will; (4) In all the history of the world no one has opened the eyes of a blind man; and (5) If Jesus were not from God he would be powerless.

It is a convincing case and all the more remarkable in coming from a man who could have had little experience in this kind of discussion. But the Pharisees took absolutely no notice. Their minds were made up and they refused to receive enlightenment from one who was "altogether born in sins" (v. 34). They had no answer to what the man said and took refuge in getting rid of him. To the end they resisted the light.

45

Faith in the Son of Man

Jesus heard that the Pharisees had thrown him out and when he had found him he said, "Do you believe in the Son of man?" That man replied, "And who is he, sir, that I may believe in him?" Jesus said to him, "You have both seen him and it is he who is talking with you." And he said, "Lord, I believe"; and he worshiped him.

And Jesus said, "For judgment I came into this world, so that those who do not see might see and those who see might become blind. Some of the Pharisees who were with him heard these things and they said to him, "We're not blind, are we?" Jesus said to them, "If you were blind, you would not have sin; now you say, 'We see'; your sin remains" (John 9:35–41).

The giving of sight to the man born blind must have caused a great deal of interest. People would have taken notice, too, of the attitude of the Pharisees. There is no suggestion that the proceedings we were looking at in our last study took place in secret. The Pharisees evidently interrogated the man quite openly and it would be common knowledge that in the end they had "thrown him out," whether this means something like excommunication or simply exclusion from their assembly. By no stretch of the imagination could it be called a friendly act, and all Jerusalem would know that the Pharisees, while unable to deny that a most unusual miracle of healing had taken place, had rejected the man. What they did about the minority of their own group who had spoken up on his behalf (v. 16) we do not know. They may have censured them or they may have ignored them. What we know is that the Pharisees did not act in accordance with the views of that minority.

Since it was common knowledge that the man had been rejected, Jesus sought him out. It is interesting that John says simply "when he had found him" (v. 35); John evidently felt that it was not necessary to tell his readers that Jesus looked for him. He was a person who had been helped by Jesus and then had been subjected to some form of persecution by the religious establishment. John knew Jesus well enough to know that his Lord would never desert a person in such a situation. He would certainly look for him and support him and do whatever needed to be done for him. So he says no more than "when he had found him." We are probably to understand that Jesus did not conduct a perfunctory search. The man was in some difficulty. Therefore Jesus continued looking until he found him.

Faith

Then he asked him the question "Do you believe in the Son of man?" This is the first time faith has been mentioned in connection with this miracle. (In v. 18 the verb *believe* is used as we are told that the Jews did not believe that the man had been born blind and had received sight until they spoke with his parents; but this is clearly something quite different from faith in the sense in which Jesus is using the term.) In the synoptic Gospels we often find Jesus saying, "Your faith has saved you," or the like. We tend to get the idea that faith was the necessary prerequisite to healing: no faith, no healing!

But that does not seem to be the correct way of understanding it. The divine Son of God is not dependent on people's help before he can do mighty works. We have seen that he once cured a man who had been lame for thirty-eight years and who did not even know Jesus' name (5:1–18). There was no possibility of faith there. Jesus commonly responded to faith, but there was no absolute necessity for it.

In the ancient world there were religious "quacks" who managed to get quite a good living by demonstrating "miracles" of some sort. At this distance in time it is not possible to say exactly what it was that they did, but we know from experience in our own days that any good conjurer can do things that to the uninitiated look suspiciously like miracles. We cannot understand them and we just marvel. It appears to have been something like this in the first century. People could not explain how these "miracle workers" did their act, and they responded with some form of veneration (and, of course, financial assistance).

Now Jesus was not that sort of "miracle worker." He did not work spectacular but purposeless miracles. Mark tells us that when Jesus went back to Nazareth he "could do no mighty work there" and that "he was astonished at their unbelief" (Mark 6:5–6). Luke says that in his synagogue sermon in that village Jesus recognized that they wanted him to do miracles like they had heard he had done in Capernaum (Luke 4:23). These people were not humbly looking for the presence and the power of God. They wanted no more than what we want when we see a good conjurer at work. To gratify that desire and class himself among the "miracle workers" was quite impossible for Jesus. He "could not" do that kind of miracle. This does not mean that he lacked the power. Of course not. Even in Nazareth he healed a few sick people (Mark 6:5).

The impossibility lay in the kind of person he was and the kind of work he had come to do. Being the kind of person he was, and having come to do the will of God as he did, he could not do the kind of "miracle" that would brand him as a publicity-seeker.

But where there was faith, where people believed in him, there was not that possibility of misunderstanding. So it was in such an atmosphere that Jesus did most of his miracles.

The blind man of whom we have been reading seems not to have been a believer. At any rate he did not know who "the Son of man" was and this was Jesus' favorite way of referring to himself. But he had a spiritual need as well as a physical one, so Jesus came to him with a question about believing. In some of our earlier studies we have seen that John has a number of ways of expressing what "believing" means. Here he uses the construction that means wholehearted faith, literally "believing into," the faith that makes the believer one with Christ. John later has a good deal about "abiding in" Christ, and the faith of which he writes here has that flavor. Jesus asks whether the man has that kind of faith.

The Son of Man

He does not ask, "Do you believe in me?" but "Do you believe in the Son of man?" Jesus mostly called himself "the Son of man," an expression that is used in all four Gospels and is always used by Jesus himself. There is only one passage in the whole New Testament where anybody else used the expression and that is when Stephen said that he saw the heavens opened and "the Son of man" standing at God's right hand (Acts 7:56). It was Jesus' own way of referring to himself.

Most scholars agree that when he used this term Jesus was referring back to the vision in Daniel 7, where "one like a son of man" came with the clouds of heaven, was brought into the presence of "the Ancient of

Days," and "was given authority, glory and sovereign power" (Dan. 7:13–14). It was not an accepted name for the Messiah, and thus when Jesus used it people would not think that he was claiming messianic status. Of course, when they came to know him they would recall the passage in Daniel and see in it a fullness of meaning.

Jesus commonly used this expression, it would seem, as a way of both asserting and concealing his messiahship. It asserted it, for that was what the term meant in Daniel 7. It also concealed it, for this was not the way the passage was normally interpreted. What would the formerly blind man understand by the term? It is impossible to say.

A New Believer

But he knew the voice of Jesus. Never in all his life would he forget the voice that had told him to go and wash in Siloam! And, from the way Jesus put it, it was obvious that he looked for people to "believe in the Son of man." And, if Jesus wanted it, the formerly blind man was willing to believe in that Son of man. But there was a problem. Throughout his discussion with the Pharisees it had become abundantly clear that this man was fundamentally honest and was not now going to profess faith in someone he did not know. He was willing, but he needed more information. So he asked, "And who is he, sir, that I may believe in him?" (v. 36).

He addresses Jesus as "sir." This is the translation of the Greek word *kurios*, which has several meanings. It may denote the owner of a vineyard (Matt. 20:8) or other property. It may mean someone in high authority, and Festus uses it when he speaks of writing to his "lord" (the emperor) about Paul (Acts 25:26). It was used commonly of anyone in high place, but it was also frequently employed as a form of address in polite society. In this it was not unlike the English word *Sir*. This is a very common form of polite address, but in England it is also a way of designating a knight.

So the healed man's "sir" is here probably no more than this polite way of speaking. He is willing to go along with what Jesus is suggesting, providing that he understands it a little better. But he as yet does not know enough to understand that it is Jesus who is "the Son of man" and that he is far more than just a man. He asks for information "that" (his word means "in order that") he may believe. There is purpose in the way he puts this.

Jesus says, "You have both seen him and it is he who is talking with you" (v. 37). This self-disclosure is decisive for the man. John Marsh puts it this way:

. . . in the pause between one sentence and the next, it is almost possible to see the once blind man take a new look at his interrogator, and see precisely the same phenomena as he had seen before, as even his previous questioners had seen as they looked on Jesus—face, hair, clothes, hands, gestures all the same, and like those of any other man—and yet! Yet now, with power of sight given to him by Jesus in a humanity that was a new creation, he can see beyond or through the phenomena that are but signs and symbols to the reality inherent in them. . . .

The words of Jesus have brought a new enlightenment. He sees now something that he had not seen before.

The result is seen in both words and action: "And he said, 'Lord, I believe'; and he worshiped him" (v. 38). He uses the same word *kurios* that he had used before. But then he did not know Jesus for what he was and had surely used the term in nothing but a normal, polite way. But now he uses it with fuller meaning, and we must translate "Lord" to bring this out. Where before he saw Jesus as an honored acquaintance, the leap of faith enabled him now to see him as Lord. What form his worship took John does not say. It does not matter. What matters is that it was worship, and this enables us to know that the man had entered into a satisfying relationship with his new Lord. He was a believer. He does not say, "I believe in you." He lets "believe" stand by itself. It is of course the case that it is Jesus in whom he believes, but he speaks simply of believing. He had become a man of faith.

Judgment

John does not say whether the dialogue of this final paragraph (vv. 39–41) took place right then or whether it was somewhat later. A later time seems more likely, because Jesus would surely not have had the conversation that led the formerly blind man to faith in the presence of hostile witnesses. It seems best to hold that John has added at this point a short conversation that arose out of the miracle and its results.

It is somewhat startling to find Jesus saying that he came into this world "for judgment" (v. 39), especially since at an earlier time he said that God did not send him into the world to judge it (3:17). But the offer of salvation necessarily means judgment. What are we to say about those who reject God's offer of salvation and go their own careless way? The fact that they have rejected God's good gift means in itself that they have pronounced their own judgment; they have chosen to be lost, to be condemned. It is not the purpose of the shining of the sun to cast shadows. But where the sun shines on opaque objects, shadows are inevitable. It is not the purpose of the coming of the Son of God to bring condemnation. But when his offered salvation is rejected, condemnation is inevitable.

Jesus explains this in two ways. First, he came "so that those who do not see might see." This presents us with no problems. We have had an excellent example of what Jesus means in the man who had been healed first of physical blindness and then, more importantly, of spiritual blindness. He had really entered into light.

But Jesus also says that he came "so that . . . those who see might become blind." This is a difficult saying. But both the words themselves and also the subsequent conversation indicate that Jesus is speaking of people like the Pharisees, people who claimed to be religiously enlightened but were not. He is saying that he came to expose the sham and show these people for the blind folk they really were. The way of salvation is not that of religious pretension, outward conformity to a series of rules, pride in one's own standing before God, and all the rest of what made up the Pharisaic system.

It is not only the Christians who were critical of the Pharisees. Some of the Rabbis were very conscious of the faults of these people. The Rabbis could say, "There are seven types of Pharisees," and go on to describe them. The first type is the Pharisee who is circumcised from an unworthy motive; the second, they said, walks with exaggerated humility; the third is so anxious to avoid looking at women that he keeps knocking his head against walls; the fourth is the "pestle" Pharisee—he is bowed like a pestle in a mortar (in ostentatious humility); the fifth keeps saying, "What further duty may I perform?" (implying that he has fulfilled every obligation); the sixth is the Pharisee because he loves rewards; and the seventh is the Pharisee because he fears punishment. It is obvious that those outside the Pharisaic party were well aware of their faults.

There were Pharisees with Jesus at this time. These may have been some of the Pharisees who believed in him, but the subsequent conversation makes that unlikely. It is much more probable that these were typical Pharisaic critics of what Jesus was doing and teaching. Such people had to be near him to find out what he was saying; secondhand reports tend to be unreliable!

These people took up the word *blind* that Jesus had just used and asked whether they were blind in this sense (v. 40). They put their question in a form that expects the answer "No." Whoever might be spiritually blind, they were sure it was not such religious people as they. Surely no one in his right mind would suspect them of a religious defect like this?

People have a way of being blind to their own defects even if they are very conscious of those of other people. I like the story of the district council clerk in a certain English town who decided that the municipality was run far too inefficiently. He met waste and bungling every day and was very conscious of the unnecessary expenditure the council was incurring. So he persuaded the councilors to hire some efficiency experts to look into the problem and make recommendations. The experts did their task faithfully. They looked into everything and did a thorough survey. Then they reported that the most expedient saving would be made by firing the district clerk.

These Pharisees were a bit like that district council clerk. They could discern faults in all the people around them but did not realize their own shortcomings. So they ask their question of Jesus out of an attitude of conscious rectitude: "We're not blind, are we?"

Jesus' reply must have been totally unexpected. They would have been ready for him to say, "Of course you are blind!" or even (perhaps) to agree with them that they were not. But he says that their claim to sight puts them in the wrong (v. 41). There is one kind of spiritual blindness that is not blameworthy, the blindness, for example, of a person in a primitive society who has never heard of Jesus and knows nothing of the way of salvation. Such a person is not a sinner in the sense of rebelling against the commandments of God. He will have other sins, but his blindness means that his sins are not sins against the light, since his eyes have not yet been opened.

But people who have been brought up to know that God has revealed himself and that this revelation is recorded in Holy Scriptures are not in the same position. They know what God has revealed. They say, "We see," and therefore, Jesus says, their sin remains. The Pharisees were apt to appeal to the Law, both as a means of justifying what they were doing and as a means of condemning Jesus. But their very appeal to the Law of God took away every possibility of saying, "We know no better." They did know better. They knew the Law of God.

It is, of course, easy to condemn the Pharisees, but in doing so we run the danger of repeating their sin. Light shows us our own shortcomings and gives encouragement to us to seek forgiveness and amendment. To use it instead as a means of congratulating ourselves that we are not as other people is simply to repeat the sin of the Pharisees. Light demands of us a better attitude than that.

46

The Sheep and the Door

"Truly, truly, I tell you he that does not enter the courtyard of the sheep through the door, but comes up some other way, that man is a thief and a robber. But he who enters through the door is the sheep's shepherd. To him the doorkeeper opens; and the sheep hear his voice and he calls his own sheep by name and leads them out. Whenever he puts all his sheep out he goes in front of them and the sheep follow him because they know his voice. They will not follow a stranger but will run away from him, because they do not know the voice of strangers." Jesus spoke this parable to them but they did not understand the things he was saying to them.

So Jesus said to them again, "Truly, truly, I tell you that I am the door of the sheep. All who came before me are thieves and robbers, but the sheep did not listen to them. I am the door; if anyone enters through me he will be saved; he will go in and out and find pasture. The thief comes only in order to steal and kill and destroy. I came so that they may have life and have it abundantly" (John 10:1–10).

Sheep are peculiarly helpless animals. They have little in the way of offensive mechanisms, so they cannot fight with attackers with any hope of success. Their association with humans, bred into them over many generations, means that they are dependent animals. Unlike goats (who can look after themselves much better), they are not good foragers; unless they are brought to the place where the pastures are they are in trouble. They are not good at seeking out water either. Early in my ministry I had an extensive parish in the Australian outback and I recall one sheep station where I used to drive through a paddock measuring ten miles by ten miles. The men on the station told me that when they put a flock of sheep (a "mob" they called it) into such a paddock, for some days they had to come out and drive the animals to the water troughs. There was no shortage of water in the troughs. But, left to themselves, the animals did not know how to find it. (Does not the Shepherd Psalm say "he leads me beside quiet waters" [Ps. 23:2]?). After a while, of course, they learned where the water was. But they had to be taught.

Sheep can be incredibly stupid. I have seen sheep moving along when one thought he saw an obstacle and jumped over it. Those that followed leaped over the same imaginary obstacle at the same place. Again, there may be difficulty in getting sheep through a gate. Apparently they wonder what perils may lurk on the other side. So they will mill round in a mob and refuse to go through. But, after the drover pushes one or two through, the rest follow without any trouble. They can be exasperating.

The helplessness of sheep and their complete subservience to their shepherds has led to sheep imagery being used at many times and in many places. Rulers have often seen themselves in the capacity of "shepherd," and people have often longed for a real "shepherd" so that their needs for leadership and sustenance might be met. We find this often in the Old Testament. The outstanding example, of course, is the great psalm that begins "The LORD is my shepherd, I shall lack nothing" (Ps. 23:1). But there are also passages in which the shepherd imagery is applied to human shepherds, often, alas, to bewail their failures.

Thus "Israel's watchmen" are castigated for a number of reasons, culminating in the words: "They are shepherds who lack understanding; they all turn to their own way, each seeks his own gain. 'Come,' each one cries, 'let me get wine! Let us drink our fill of beer! And tomorrow will be like today, or even far better'" (Isa. 56:10–12). There is a powerful denunciation of Israel's shepherds in Ezekiel 34, where we read: "Woe to the shepherds of Israel who only take care of themselves! Should not shepherds take care of the flock?" (v. 2). The prophet goes on to show how those in places of responsibility in Israel had signally failed to fulfill their vocation as shepherds.

Jesus' words about "the Good Shepherd" are to be understood against this background. All too often those in the position of "shepherd" to the people of God were interested only in their own welfare,

369

not in that of the flock. But God knew what they were doing and God said, "I will save my flock, and they will no longer be plundered. I will judge between one sheep and another. I will place over them one shepherd, my servant David, and he will tend them; he will tend them and be their shepherd" (Ezek. 34:22–23). It is this shepherd of whom Jesus speaks in John 10.

Both Matthew and Luke record a parable about the shepherd who was not content with the ninety-nine sheep in the fold, but went out into the wilderness to search for the one that was lost and bring it back (Matt. 18:12–14; Luke 15:3–7). It is a wonderful picture of God's love and care for his own and marks a significant advance on the Judaism of the day. Among the Jews it was accepted that if a sinner repents, God will receive him, but there is nothing corresponding to this thought of a God who loves so much that he goes out looking for the lost and brings them home.

It is clear, then, that Jesus used the shepherd imagery more than once and to teach different lessons. But perhaps nowhere does he do this as powerfully as in this passage where we read of the Good Shepherd, the one who lays down his life so that the sheep may live.

The Door

Jesus begins this discourse with his solemn "Truly, truly" (v. 1), which emphasizes that what follows is important and is to be taken with full seriousness. He distinguishes between the person who enters a courtyard through the proper door and one who climbs over the fence. The word Jesus uses is *aule*, which properly means a courtyard and is used, for example, of the courtyard at the high priest's house (Matt. 26:3; Mark 14:54, etc.). Here he may mean that sheep were kept in the courtyard of a house (which makes a lot of sense—why waste a courtyard?). Or he may use the word that properly means a courtyard round a house for a structure that was similar but was erected in the wilderness where the sheep grazed and was used to keep them safe at night. There were wild animals in Palestine at that time and sheep could not safely be left in the pastures overnight. So they were herded into enclosures. It is either one of these enclosures or a courtyard round a house of which Jesus is speaking.

He says that you can tell a man's business by the way he gets into such an enclosure. If he does not use the door, but climbs over the fence (or wall), he has no right to be there. The manner of his entrance shows what kind of person he is. Jesus calls him "a thief and a robber." These two words for dishonesty can be distinguished. The word for "thief" is *kleptes* (from which we get our "kleptomaniac"), which properly means a petty thief. It is used, for example, of Judas Iscariot, who took money from the common stock of the little group round Jesus (12:6). The "robber" is *lestes*, which strictly means a brigand; it points to a member of a robber band, a much more interesting character. The word is used of Barabbas (18:40). In this place there is probably no great difference in mind. Jesus simply uses two different words for a dishonest person to make his point that the manner of entrance points to someone who has no business being there.

But the man who "enters through the door" is a different kind of person altogether (v. 2). The fact that he comes through the door shows that he has the right to be there. He is the shepherd, one who stands in a relationship to the sheep such as nobody else does. His open manner of entry shows that he has legitimate business there and that he has no need to be furtive.

This is shown also by the fact that the "doorkeeper" opens to him (v. 3). A small flock in a small sheepfold would not need such an official, but if the courtyard was a large one and if there were several flocks of sheep in it, such a person would perform a useful function. That is apparently what is in mind here, for Jesus goes on to speak of the sheep as hearing the voice of their shepherd.

Perhaps we should notice here a little grammatical point about the way John uses the Greek verb for "to hear." When it is used of hearing a person he uses one construction (the genitive case), and when it is used of a sound (for example, a voice or a cry) he uses another (the accusative). But sometimes John uses the usual construction for a person when he is referring to a voice, and each time he means not only that the voice is heard, but that it is heard with understanding and acceptance. That is what he has here. The sheep not only hear the sound of the shepherd's voice; they understand that it is their shepherd (and not someone else) and they respond to it.

The shepherd "calls his own sheep by name," which is something a modern Australian finds hard to understand. In my country flocks of sheep tend to be large. I recall seeing a few drovers move a flock of over five thousand. I don't know that it was particularly large; I simply mention it as one I have seen. When you are talking about numbers like that it is impossible to think of the sheep as individuals. They simply belong to a huge undifferentiated mass. But a Palestinian shepherd would have a small flock, maybe twenty or thirty, or perhaps a hundred. Nathan spoke of a flock whose number was the irreducible minimum: "one little ewe lamb" (2 Sam. 12:3). In small flocks individual sheep could be recognized and the shepherd could call them "by name."

But the emphasis here is not so much on the individual sheep as on the individual shepherd. Travelers tell of modern-time Palestinian shepherds whose flocks have been brought together (perhaps for shelter overnight). Then in the morning the sheep have been separated when one and then another of the shepherds gives his own call. The sheep recognize the voice and respond to it.

When such a shepherd moves his sheep he does not drive them but leads them (v. 4). Even in modern times this happens. I have seen a flock being moved in Palestine in this way. The shepherd went on ahead, and the sheep followed him. (In this case he prudently had a rear guard; an assistant followed the last of the sheep to make sure they did not stray! I have no idea how common that is.) The reason given here is that "they know his voice." The reassuring voice of their own shepherd keeps them in line.

But an alien voice is different: "They will not follow a stranger" (v. 5). Presumably from time to time a dishonest stranger would try to get sheep to follow him, but, says Jesus, they will not go. On the contrary, they will run away, for they do not know his voice. It is not simply any voice, but the voice of their own shepherd that they follow.

John rounds off this section by saying that Jesus spoke this "parable" (v. 6), but his word is not that used for "parable" in the well-known stories in the synoptic Gospels (*parabole*, a word not found in John). The word here (*paroimia*, not used in the other Gospels) is often used of a short, pithy saying like a proverb. But it is not easy to find a difference between them. The passage here is not quite the same as the parables in the Synoptics, but it is more like them than like a proverb, so I have translated it "parable." However we translate, John is speaking of an illustration Jesus used as he taught the people. "But," John adds, "they did not understand the things he was saying to them."

The Door

I like the story of Dr. Andrews, who was giving a public lecture on his explorations in Mongolia and referred on a number of occasions to the "Gobi desert." An expert in the field rebuked him afterwards for using the redundant expression. "Gobi means 'desert,'" he said. "You should not say 'Gobi desert.'" "Well," replied Dr. Andrews, "you know that and I know that. But few of my audience are fluent in Mongolian. I address them in language they will understand."

The good teacher accepts the limitations of his audience. That is what Jesus does here. The people do not understand. Very well. He puts it another way. Again there is the solemn "Truly, truly." This is important and is to be taken seriously. He makes clear the application to himself: "I am the door of the sheep," he says (v. 7). What he has been saying is not just so much instruction in animal husbandry. He is teaching spiritual truth.

"Door" is used figuratively elsewhere in the New Testament, as when Jesus speaks of entering the narrow door (Luke 13:24), or when we read of the "door of faith" that God opened to the Gentiles (Acts 14:27). But this is the only passage in which Jesus is himself spoken of as "the door." Elsewhere he is said to be like a ladder connecting earth and heaven (1:51) or "the way" (14:6). These are similar thoughts, but Jesus calls himself "the door" only here. The expression "of the sheep" is unusual in such a connection, but it probably means the door by which the sheep enter. There is something exclusive about "the door." Jesus is not suggesting that there are several doors to salvation and that he is but one. He says that he is "the" door. We are not to think of many ways of coming to God. Jesus is saying that he is the one way, the door by which all the sheep enter.

Thieves and Robbers

Jesus goes on to speak of those who preceded him, and he speaks of them all as "thieves and robbers" (v. 8). This presents us with something of a problem. He has already spoken of people who get into the sheepfold other than by the door with the use of just these words (v. 1), and this is probably part of the same imagery. The people who enter the sheepfold by climbing over the wall are up to no good and are seeking their own profit rather than the welfare of the flock. But who are they? Those "who came before" Jesus, if taken strictly, would refer to teachers of Old Testament days and those between the Testaments. But Jesus always speaks respectfully of Old Testament teachers, as when he said that Moses wrote of him (5:46) or that Abraham rejoiced to see his day (8:56).

In any case we should notice that he says that these predecessors "are" thieves and robbers, not "were." We should take "before me" as part of the general picture of the fold and not as indicating strict chronology. The thieves and robbers are surely people of Jesus' own day. They may have been teaching before he started his mission, but it is their error and their motives rather than the precise time of their appearance that are important. Some think of revolutionary leaders like Theudas or Judas the Galilean (Acts 5:36, 37), but there seems no reason why Jesus should be referring to men of violence like these. Others think of the Teacher of Righteousness of the Qumran scrolls, but Jesus does not seem ever to refer specifically to the men of this community, and it is hard to see a reference to one or more of them here. It is much more likely that he is referring to the Jewish teachers in general, those who so consistently opposed him and refused to recognize that he had come from God. Jesus is saying that they are dishonest leaders and are not to be followed.

Abundant Life

Jesus repeats the words "I am the door" (v. 9), this time without the addition "of the sheep." It is Jesus' function that is of central importance and it is this that stands out. Anyone who goes through this door enters salvation. John does not use the verb *to save* very often (six times in all), certainly not nearly as often as the other Gospel writers (Matthew has it fifteen times, Mark fifteen times, and Luke seventeen times with another thirteen in Acts). Nor does he use it in the same way. The others often use the verb for the healings Jesus performed, but John does not use it in that way. For John it denotes much the same as eternal life (the two are linked in 3:16–17). It seems that Jesus is here giving expression to a thought we find often in this Gospel, namely that the way to eternal life is through Jesus. That means a lot to John and he brings it out in all sorts of ways.

The saved person, the one who enters through Jesus, will have real freedom ("he will go in and out"). Other ways of life are restricted in one way or another. Sin is always a limiting factor. But Christ brings us a genuine and complete liberty. With that he links "and find pasture." This is not defined, but it surely refers to spiritual nourishment. Just as a sheep finds all its needs met when it is securely in the fold with a caring shepherd, so the sinner will find all the nourishment his soul needs when he enters life eternal through Jesus.

This is a contrast with the teachers whom Jesus is castigating. "The thief," he says, "comes only in order to steal and kill and destroy" (v. 10). The verb translated "kill" seems to mean either kill for sacrifice, or kill for food, the second meaning developing naturally enough from the first, for in a sacrifice part of the victim was usually eaten by the worshipers. Here we probably have the second meaning, so that the three possibilities are "steal," "kill for food," and "destroy." None is very attractive from the point of view of the sheep, and the combination brings out the thought that the false teachers are interested in getting what they can out of the people they teach and that in the end their pupils must suffer loss.

Jesus, by contrast, is not interested in any personal profit. He came "so that they may have life." Right through this Gospel there is this thought: Jesus came into this world in order that he might make eternal life available for those who trust him. In due course he would die on the cross to put away their sins and to open wide for them the way into life. And this life is wonderful. Jesus speaks of believers having it "abundantly." Put negatively, there is nothing cramped and limiting about the life Christ gives. Believers have an "abundant" life. (How, I wonder, have Christians so often given the impression that the life they live is a negative affair, full of occasions when they must say, "Christians must not do this," "Christians never do that," and lacking in sheer enjoyment?)

The Christian life is an exuberant affair, full of the joy of the Lord and the power of the Holy Spirit. The early-church Fathers often thought that it is life in the world to come that is meant. True, that is an abundant life. But surely those Fathers had missed the wonderful thing Jesus is saying here. Not only does he give believers the best of things in the life to come; he also gives them the best of things here and now. There are difficulties and troubles for the believer. Sure. That, in the modern phrase, is part of the deal. But the wonderful joy that comes from constant fellowship with the Lord far outweighs any such inconveniences. The life Christ gives is the abundant life.

47

The Good Shepherd

"I am the Good Shepherd; the Good Shepherd lays down his life for the sheep. The hired man (and one who is not a shepherd), whose own the sheep are not, sees the wolf coming and leaves the sheep and runs away—and the wolf seizes them and scatters them—because he is a hired man and he does not care about the sheep.

"I am the Good Shepherd and I know my own and my own know me, even as the Father knows me and I know the Father; and I lay down my life for the sheep. And other sheep I have which are not of this fold; I must bring them too and they will hear my voice and there will be one flock, one shepherd.

"For this reason the Father loves me that I lay down my life for the sheep so that I may take it again. Nobody took it away from me, but I lay it down of myself. I have authority to lay it down and I have authority to take it again. This command- ment I received from my Father."

There was again a division among the Jews on account of these words. Many of them were saying, "He has a demon and is mad. Why are you listening to him?" Others were saying, "These words are not those of a demoniac; does a demon open the eyes of blind people?" (John 10:11–21).

When Jesus called himself "the Good Shepherd" he used a title that has meant much to Christians through the centuries. It makes a universal appeal. Even people who are strangers to pastoral

376

pursuits and have never seen a sheep (or a shepherd) in their lives find this an attractive title and respond to it. It is a title that emphasizes Jesus' care for his own. We saw in our last study that sheep need a good deal of care; left to themselves they are apt to fare badly. They do not seem well equipped to face life's hardships and need a shepherd to lead them to pasture and to water and to defend them against life's dangers. So when Jesus speaks of himself as the Good Shepherd he is saying that he will provide for all the needs of those who are his sheep. Life often finds us at our wit's end, but if we belong to Jesus we may confidently look to him to lead us in the way in which we should go. He will see that we get all that we need (though not necessarily all that we want!).

There is another implied claim in this statement. As we saw when we were thinking of words like "I am the bread of life" and "I am the door," the "I AM" is the language of deity. It is not the normal way people would say these things, but the way God would say them. So, in claiming to be the Good Shepherd in this way, Jesus is using the language of deity. He is more than just a man, and this is involved in his claim to be the Good Shepherd and to do what the Good Shepherd does.

We may notice an interesting point that arises from the fact that Jesus uses the word *kalos* for "good." Greek has a number of words that may convey the idea of goodness and very often they do not differ greatly. But Abbott-Smith's lexicon informs us that while *agathos* points to "inner excellence" and *dikaios* refers to the person "who merely measures up to a high standard of rectitude," *kalos* "properly refers to goodliness as manifested in form." In other words it refers to what is beautiful as well as what is good (we have taken this over into our language; we speak of beautiful handwriting as "calligraphy" while "callisthenics" combines strength with beauty). E. V. Rieu, a classical Greek scholar, some years ago produced a translation of the Gospels and here has "I am the shepherd, the Shepherd Beautiful," which brings out this aspect of what Jesus was saying. I see no reason for departing from the usual translation, "the Good Shepherd," but we should bear in mind the point made by William Temple that "it is possible to be morally upright repulsively!" There was something attractive about Jesus' goodness, a point we should bear in mind as we seek to serve him.

The Death of the Shepherd

Jesus might have gone on to quite a lot of things that a good shepherd does for his sheep. As we saw in our last study, a shepherd can be a very busy person, for the sheep are so helpless that he must look to all their needs. But, interestingly, Jesus passes over all that and goes straight to one unexpected thing: "the Good Shepherd lays down his life for the sheep."

A shepherd's life had its dangers, and we must not overlook the fact that in biblical Palestine there were wild animals, some of which have since died out. David mentions his fights with a lion and with a bear while he was looking after sheep (1 Sam. 17:34–36; cf. Isa. 31:4) and Amos speaks of the shepherd who rescued two legs or a piece of an ear from a lion's mouth (Amos 3:12). At an earlier time Jacob said, "I did not bring you animals torn by wild beasts; I bore the loss myself . . ." (Gen. 31:39), which brings before us another aspect of the shepherd's life.

It is plain enough that dangers could arise for the shepherd at any time. But the Palestinian shepherd did not reckon on dying; he thought he would survive. The job had its dangers, certainly. But men have never been deterred from jobs simply because there are dangers (as we can see from modern life as well as any other). Men always think that there are ways of dealing with the danger and never expect the dire results to follow for them—it is always other people who get caught! So with the shepherd in antiquity. Allowing for the fact that there would be problems as he looked after the sheep, he thought he could cope; otherwise he would not be a shepherd. He knew that there was the possibility that he would be wounded or even die, but he knew the resources he had and was optimistic. No man willingly dies for animals like sheep.

But the one thing Jesus says he will do for people in his capacity as Shepherd is die for them. That for him was the central thing. He had come to bring salvation, and that meant death on behalf of his sheep.

A Palestinian shepherd might sometimes die in the exercise of his duty as a shepherd, but that was always a mishap, something that occurred as a result of some miscalculation. If he was thinking of the welfare of his sheep, the shepherd thought of what he could do by his life, not of what he could do by his death. Jesus' attitude was quite different. He put his death in the forefront. That is what the Good Shepherd would do.

The Hired Help and the Wolf

Jesus contrasts the attitude of the hired help (v. 12). The man who does not own the sheep and who simply looks after them for pay is different from a true shepherd. As I have said, even a true shepherd will not willingly die for sheep, but he will certainly run into danger for them and put up a fight for them. But the man whose interest is in his pay rather than the sheep in his care will think of his own skin and take no risks.

When he sees the wolf coming he simply runs away. Actually he is wrong in doing that, for according to the Mishnah he is required to defend the sheep against one wolf. But, continues the regulation, "two wolves count as unavoidable accident." A man who was simply a hired shepherd was not expected to cope with more than one wolf; there was a limit to what could be asked of such a person. And Jesus' words show that the hired man might well do less than he was supposed to, rather than more. That one wolf could do considerable damage to the flock. Quite apart from the sheep that he seized and ate, his coming would scatter the remainder, and in due course they would have to be found and brought back.

The hired man runs because of what he is—a man who is interested in his pay (v. 13). Jesus does not mean that there were no paid shepherds who did more than this. Of course there were. But typically the hired man did less than the shepherd who owned the sheep. And Jesus is saying that this arises from the nature of the case: the man whose interest is in pay will always react differently from the man whose interest is in sheep.

One Flock and One Shepherd

Jesus repeats his words, "I am the Good Shepherd," and this time adds "I know my own and my own know me" (v. 14). We saw in our last study that the Palestinian shepherd of Jesus' day commonly knew his sheep very well, and they knew him so well that they would respond to his call and follow him, while they would not respond to the call of other people (v. 5). There is a difference between those who are genuinely the sheep of a given shepherd and those who are not.

Genuineness is important over a wide range of life. I like the notice I read about that is supposed to hang in one of the museums given over to memorabilia of the Wild West. The notice is reputed to say: "We do not have the gun that killed Billy the Kid. Two other museums have it." The museum asserted its own rectitude and its own regard for what is genuine, though it did not find this universal in its competitors.

Genuineness matters when we are talking about the sheep of Jesus' flock. It is not what we say that matters, but what is really the case. Jesus sees through shams and knows exactly who really belong to his flock and who do not. He goes on to liken the mutual knowledge between him and his sheep to that between him and his Father (v. 15). There is no possibility of mistake in that knowledge. The Father and the Son know each other intimately. Jesus is saying that the mutual knowledge of the Good Shepherd and the sheep is something like that. I do not think that he means that the sheep know the Shepherd as well as the Son knows the Father. We are all prone to mistakes, though he is not. It is the reciprocal knowledge that Jesus is stressing. It is not only that Jesus knows us, but that we know him, and it is this that is likened to the fact that the Father and the Son know each other.

It is significant that Jesus goes on to say again, "I lay down my life for the sheep." This is the characteristic thing and he leaves his hearers in no doubt of its importance. The teaching of Jesus is wonderful and his people have been grateful for it through the centuries, but it is not the teaching that is of central importance. It is the atoning death, the death "for" the sheep.

And this has meaning, not only for the few people that had so far followed Jesus. He goes on to speak of "other sheep" not of the "fold" of Judaism (v. 16). In all four Gospels there is mostly a concentration on the people who were with Jesus at the time, as we might expect. But now and then there are glimpses of the wider application of the gospel and we have one here. The death of Jesus would be for people everywhere, not only for those in Palestine who had so far heard his voice and followed him.

Notice that he says "I *must* bring them too." There is the thought of a compelling necessity. He had come on a mission of salvation, which meant dying for sinners. It also meant that those sinners must be informed of what had happend and invited to put their trust in the crucified Savior. In other words, he *must* bring them. That was in the divine plan and in due course it would inevitably come about.

These "other sheep" would be on the same footing as those already in the fold. "They will hear my voice," Jesus says, which means that they will be in the same intimate relationship to the Shepherd as those who were already following him. There were those in the early church who apparently thought that the Jews had a privileged position in the church. When Gentiles were converted such people wanted them circumcised and made full members of Judaism. But Jesus is saying no such thing. For him the important thing was that these sheep would hear his voice.

And when they do "there will be one flock, one shepherd." There is a play on words in the Greek, which we cannot easily reproduce in English: one *poimne*, one *poimen*. The important thing is that the two go together. The unity that links all believers is not due to their coming from any particular nation, to their being the same kind of "religious" people, to their position in society, to natural affinity, or anything of the sort. It is a unity that arises because of their relationship to the one Shepherd who "brings" them all.

Authority to Die and
Authority to Rise

Jesus goes back to the thought of his death (which, of course, is what would make them all members of the one flock). He says that the Father loves him for it (v. 17). This does not mean that the Father did not love him until he died for people. The Father always loved the Son. Jesus is saying that this love was connected with the cross. His death for sinners was an expression of the love of the Father as well as that of the Son (cf. 3:16). We should never think of the cross as though it meant that the love of the Son was triumphing over the wrath of the Father. That is not the way of it at all. The love of the Father and the love of the Son were both there, and the Father loved the Son because of his death for sinners.

Sometimes, when people have been married for many years or have been friends for many years (or both!), one will do something that wins the approval of the other and will get the response "I love you for that!" The love was there before the deed. But the deed calls forth the love yet once more.

And on this occasion the deed was the laying down of the life. Throughout this passage this is brought out repeatedly. It is central to the teaching of this Gospel and indeed central to Christianity. John will not let us miss it and he keeps recording words that bring it out. Perhaps in part at least this is because God does not act as we do. It is natural for people to try to avoid hardship and to take the easiest way. We do it constantly.

There was a time in World War II when the American army launched a strong attack and drove back the central part of the enemy line quite a distance. But then the enemy counterattacked and the Americans were in danger of being completely surrounded. In this emergency everyone was pressed into service. Even those whose normal duties were routine office work found themselves called up into defense. One pusher of typewriters found himself instructed to dig foxholes in very hard ground. He was making heavy weather of it, so made a suggestion to his superior officer: "Sir, wouldn't it be better if we attacked and made *them* dig the foxholes?"

That corresponds to something deep down in the heart of most of us. We don't want to do the hard things and like to discover some easy way round. But we must not read our own attitudes into the way our salvation was brought about. The road to Calvary would be hard, but the Good Shepherd would tread it resolutely. So Jesus says that he will lay down his life "for the sheep" and do this "so that I may take it again." "So that" indicates purpose. We are to see the resurrection as in mind long before the death took place on the cross. Jesus is saying that his attitude to life and to death is different from ours. He will go to death, but it will be a voluntary act and he will rise in due course triumphant over death.

He makes this clear by saying, "Nobody took it away from me" (v. 18). It was true that in due course people like Judas, the Jewish high priestly party, and the Romans, especially Pilate, would all play their part. But if Jesus had not allowed them to put him to death, he would not have been killed. He is supreme over life and death. So he repeats that he lays his life down of himself. Many manuscripts read "Nobody takes it away from me," and this may well be the right reading. But it corresponds to what we would expect and looks like a scribal "correction" to make an easier reading. I think that this Gospel text did read "took" and that Jesus is regarding his death as so certain that he can speak of it as already accomplished.

He makes clear his lordship over life and death by saying that he has authority to lay down his life and to take it again. The repetition of "authority" gives the word some emphasis (as is the case when Pilate repeats the same word later in this Gospel, 19:10). Some translations prefer the word *power* but that is not the meaning of Jesus' word. It is true that he has power over death, but it is also true that this is not simply naked power. Being the Son of God, he has the right to die and to rise, and it is of right rather than of power that Jesus is speaking.

He concludes this part of his address by saying that he has received a command from the Father. Once again we have the typical teaching in this Gospel that the Father and the Son are at one in this matter of salvation. There is no division in the Godhead.

Division

But there was "division" among the hearers (v. 19). Some were for Jesus and some against. Those against were saying, "He has a demon and is mad." The accusation that he had a demon was made before (7:20; 8:48, 52); indeed, in this Gospel the only times demon-possession is mentioned is when this accusation is being made or refuted. Apparently these people saw demon-possession and madness as much the same thing, though elsewhere the two seem to be distinguished. Thus Matthew tells of an occasion when people brought to Jesus for healing "demon-possessed and lunatics" (Matt. 4:24; some translations have "epileptics" instead of "lunatics," but Phillips is surely right when he renders "the insane"; *The Living Bible* also has "insane"). The separate mention of the two groups shows that they were different; the demon-possessed and the insane were not the same. But these determined opponents of Jesus are refusing to take him seriously. They are convinced that he is in error and simply throw out accusations: "he has a demon" and "he is mad." They produce no reason for what they are saying and indeed they could not.

But others are more balanced. They have listened to what Jesus said and are clear that words such as Jesus has spoken are not the words of a demoniac (v. 21). And it was not only the things he said. What about his deeds? Can a demoniac open the eyes of the blind? They find both his words and his deeds convincing.

The contrast between the two groups is instructive. We find such division again and again in the history of the human race. Where people are blinded by prejudice they will always find some "reason" for rejecting Jesus: demoniac, madman, anything will do. But where people listen to what he says and where they take notice of what he does there is always a different verdict.

48

"I and the Father Are One"

Then it was the Feast of the Dedication in Jerusalem. It was winter and Jesus was walking in the temple in Solomon's colonnade. The Jews stood around him and asked him, "How long are you going to keep us in suspense? If you are the Christ, tell us plainly." Jesus answered them, "I told you and you do not believe. The works that I am doing in my Father's name, these bear witness about me. But you do not believe because you are not of my sheep. My sheep hear my voice and I know them and they follow me, and I give them life eternal. They will never perish and no one will snatch them out of my hand. What my Father has given me is greater than all and no one can snatch them out of my Father's hand. I and the Father are one" (John 10:22–30).

John moves to the Feast of the Dedication, an eight-day festival that began on 25th Chisleu, which means somewhere in November–December in our calendar (the Jews had a lunar calendar, not a solar year like ours, and thus a given day on the one calendar will not always fall on any one given day in the other). It was an important feast, for it commemorated the last great deliverance the Jews had known.

There was a time when Antiochus Epiphanes, the king of Syria, conquered Palestine. This king set out to make Hellenistic culture a unifying bond, which he thought would unite the diverse peoples in his empire. Among other things this meant imposing the same heathen religion on them all, and the Jews were not allowed to continue their characteristic religious practices. Thus they were forbidden to circumcise their children, to observe the Sabbath, and to do many other things that they valued highly in connection with their religion. They were required to offer sacrifice to heathen gods. There were, of course, some people who conformed to the Syrian edicts, not only because they were told to, but also out of a desire to be up with the latest fashions: Hellenism was the "in" thing. Others did so from fear.

But it was a time of indescribable horror for those who took their religion seriously. There were pious and patriotic people who would not do what Antiochus required of them at any price. This led to the Maccabean rebellion, which started in a very small way but in the end was successful in liberating the Jewish people, giving them rulers of their own and the right to worship according to the teachings of the Bible. There came the great day when the Jewish warriors liberated Jerusalem and the heathen altar that had been set up in the temple was removed. There was a joyous celebration as the temple was restored and rededicated, and this wonderful event was commemorated in an eight-day festival that was held each year. This was the Feast of the Dedication of which John writes. It was a feast that reminded everybody of the way God had delivered the people out of a situation that had seemed hopeless, and this must have been an encouragement to those who looked and longed for the day when they would be delivered from the Romans.

It was not necessary for John to mention the time. But he has a habit of referring to the Jewish feasts, and he mentions more of them and mentions them more often than do any of the other Gospel writers. It seems that he sees Jesus as the fulfillment of all that the feasts symbolized. If that is the reason he mentions this one, it will surely be to make the point that the hopes that people had of freedom, hopes that centered on resistance movements and leaders like Barabbas, would be filled in Jesus and in him alone. He would bring deliverance from sin and thus a liberty far more significant than any that warriors could envisage, let alone accomplish.

Jesus was in Solomon's colonnade (v. 23). This was a structure with a roof supported on pillars. It would have given some protection in the winter weather and would have been open to the sun if it was shining. It was a very old structure, and the people in general thought it had been built by Solomon, though that was not very likely. But evidently it was a pleasant place to be on a winter's day.

Suspense

"The Jews" (John's way of referring to Jewish people, especially those in leading positions, who were hostile to Jesus) surrounded Jesus

(v. 24). Phillips translates "The Jews closed in on Him," which brings out the truth that they had no friendly intent. By surrounding him they apparently thought that they could compel Jesus to give them the answer they were looking for. I have translated the question they put to him as "How long are you going to keep us in suspense?" and it is not easy to find an alternative. But it is not certain that this is what they meant.

The words John records mean "How long do you lift up our soul?" The usual translation takes this to mean that Jesus' teaching was such that his hearers' "soul" was disturbed, raised from its resting place so to speak, and not given a new one. It is this that enables us to translate "keep us in suspense." This may be the correct way of understanding it.

If so, at least they were honest in confessing their ignorance. People are not always like that. There is the story of a wife who asked her husband, "What makes the stock market go up and down?" There was a thoughtful silence, then the reply, "There are several factors like inflationary pressures, fiscal instability and, of course, political pressures and national imbalance." The wife thought about this for a moment, then said, "If you don't know, why don't you just say so?"

Unlike the man in the story, the Jews may have been honestly admitting that they did not know what Jesus' teaching meant. But their words could be understood in other ways. To "lift the soul" might mean that the soul is set adrift, so to speak. The words could mean that the hearers felt that Jesus was upsetting their cherished beliefs without giving them any satisfactory alternative. "Why do you trouble us?" would give credence to this view.

The Christ

We should also bear in mind that the word for "soul" also means "life," and the question might mean "Why are you taking our life away?" This view would be supported by the fact that nobody doubts that Jesus was talking about death when he used the same verb together with a reference to the same noun no farther away than verse 18 (where "it" refers to "life" in v. 17). In that passage Jesus was referring to his life being taken away, and it is quite possible that the Jews have a similar meaning here. A little later Caiaphas was to say that if they left Jesus alone they would be destroyed; the Romans would come and take away their place and their nation (11:48). The Jews may have had a dim perception that Jesus' teaching meant the end of things as they knew them. To accept and act on his teaching, they may have thought, would be to put an end to Judaism as they knew it. It would be to destroy their whole way of life. "Is this what you are trying to do?" they may be asking. They want to be clear on Jesus' program.

Their supplementary request is easier to understand: "If you are the Christ, tell us plainly." But it was not an easy question to answer because there were different ideas of what "the Christ" meant. To follow the thought of the last paragraph for a moment, Jesus has just been envisaging followers from outside the fold of Judaism (v. 16), and he had earlier raised the possibility that his Jewish hearers might die in their sins (8:21, 24). Does this mean that being the Christ means putting no difference between Jew and Gentile when we stand before God? That some Gentiles must be brought into the fold? That some Jews will die in their sins and therefore be excluded? What sort of Messiah is this? Most Jews of the day did not think that the Messiah would treat the Gentiles with favor and judge the Jews in this way. They usually saw the Messiah as a Jewish deliverer of some sort. Many thought he would be a warrior who would raise an army and drive the Romans out of the land. Had not the Maccabean warriors done just that to a very mighty conqueror at the time they were commemorating in the Feast of the Dedication they were even then observing?

The Works Bear Witness

With different ideas of messiahship in circulation, obviously the question the Jews asked was not easy to answer. They asked Jesus to answer "plainly"; clearly they wanted a straight "Yes" or "No." But because the meaning of "Messiah" was understood in so many different ways it was impossible to give the short, clear answer they looked for. Even so, Jesus' reply must have been completely unexpected: "I told you" (v. 25). John has not recorded any plain statement that Jesus has made to the Jews on this subject. He has informed us that Jesus told the woman of Samaria that he was the Messiah (4:26). Again, although that term is not used, we might well think that it was the meaning of what he said to the man born blind (9:35–38). From the beginning, at least some of his followers had recognized that he was the Messiah (1:41). But John has not told us of any occasion when Jesus has used the word of himself when he was talking to the Jews generally.

Jesus may mean that his teaching had been plain enough. After all, there was a group of people around him who followed him as the Messiah. They were in no doubt about it, and the Jews had access to the same teaching as they did. If they had really wanted to know whether or not Jesus was the Messiah, they had before them the kind of teaching that would have told them. The trouble was not that they had not been told enough; the trouble was that they had not given attention enough.

Or Jesus may mean that some of the things he had said to them and to which they had taken exception were plain enough. For example, he had said, "Before Abraham was, I AM" (8:58). On that occasion they had taken up stones to stone him. They had a clear enough answer. On an earlier occasion they had recognized that the way Jesus spoke of God as his Father was in fact a way of "making himself equal to God" (5:18). They had heard enough and understood enough to have an answer to their question if they really and sincerely wanted one.

Jesus draws attention to "the works" that, he says, "I am doing in my Father's name." He had done a series of miracles such that no mere man could have accomplished them. And, as we have seen before, in this Gospel Jesus often calls his miracles "works," a term that applies also to his non-miraculous deeds. The word is wide enough to include his whole manner of life as well as the astonishing miracles he did. He is inviting his questioners to contemplate the kind of person he was and the kind of deeds he did. There was their answer.

"My Sheep"

But they did not believe (v. 26). The word "you" is emphatic: it puts them in strong contrast with other people who did believe. This Gospel has recorded many examples of people who came to believe, and John is constantly using this verb, "believe." Jesus is making it clear that it was lack of faith, not lack of evidence, that led to these questioners being uncertain. They cannot in all honesty complain that there was not enough evidence. There was evidence that convinced other people. Why not them?

Jesus gives an answer to that: "you are not of my sheep." These words link this conversation with the discourse earlier in the chapter. The sheep who belong to a particular shepherd hear his voice and respond to it, but those who belong to another shepherd do not. These Jews are showing quite plainly by their attitude and their questions that they do not belong to the flock of which Jesus was the Good Shepherd, the Messiah. Of course they could not recognize him as their Messiah when they followed all sorts of other shepherds.

"My sheep hear my voice" (v. 27). It is still the case that those who are Christ's hear his voice in all the circumstances of life, while those who are not his do not. For them life is simply a succession of haphazard happenings with no meaning and no pattern. For Christ's sheep there is always the thought of the Good Shepherd, who gave his life for them and who constantly leads them into the places where they should go. His voice gives meaning to all of life.

We might have expected him to go on with "and they know me." That was what happened with flocks of sheep and their shepherds. The sheep hear the voice of their own shepherd; they know that voice and they respond to it. But, instead of saying that the sheep know him, Jesus says that he knows the sheep. He is moving on to the thought of the security of his sheep, and it is more important in this connection that he knows them than that they know him. His knowledge of them is part of his watching over them and providing for their every need.

"They follow me," Jesus goes on. He has referred to this in the realm of the ordinary Palestinian shepherd and his sheep. When that shepherd calls his sheep there are results. The sheep know his call and follow the shepherd when they hear it. This has its equivalent with the people who hear Jesus' call. If they really are his sheep, they will certainly respond and will follow him as the disciples had done.

Security

Jesus moves from the illustration taken from pastoral life to the facts of spiritual life. He says that he gives "life eternal" to those who follow him (v. 28). As we have seen in previous studies, this expression means the kind of life that is appropriate to the age to come, when this world has ceased and Christ has returned to bring in the final state of affairs. That life does not end and thus may be called "everlasting." But its real characteristic is not this but the fact that it is the kind of life people will enjoy in the final shape of things. It is the quality of this life rather than its quantity that is the significant thing.

That said, it seems that in the present passage there is some emphasis on the "everlasting" aspect. Jesus goes on to say that those who receive this life "will never perish." His verb points to the ultimate disaster. The German scholar A. Oepke says that this verb means "definitive destruction, not merely in the sense of the extinction of physical existence, but rather of an eternal plunge into Hades and a hopeless destiny of death in the depiction of which such terms as wrath, anger, affliction and distress are used." We should be clear that perishing is a terrible fate and to be delivered from it is a priceless gift. Oepke also says that this idea is not found in the apocryphal writings, nor in those of the Rabbis. This is distinctive of Christianity. People often think of Christians as being sure that the life after this is one of joy and bliss. So it is for those who are Christ's sheep, but we should be clear that his salvation is from real peril, real disaster, and that Jesus made this clearer than did contemporary teachers.

389

Jesus further brings out his people's security by saying that "no one will snatch them out of my hand." The verb *to snatch* is often used of violent activity, but no matter how strong the force arrayed against us, Jesus says, it will not be enough to snatch us out of his hand. Christians have always found it an immensely encouraging thought that our eternal security does not depend on our own ability to retain a hold on Christ, but on the fact that he holds us within his strong hand. This is real security.

Our earthly securities are often all too fallible. I like the story I picked up somewhere of a bomber crew during World War II. On a raid over enemy territory they ran into heavy flak and were hit a number of times. There was a problem with steering, and the pilot asked the rear gunner if there had been a hit at the rear of the plane. The gunner replied, "There's a three by five hole in the left horizontal stabilizer and elevator." He added an anxious query, "Will we be able to make it home?" "No sweat," the pilot assured him. Eventually they made it, though as they landed the plane skidded and skewed alarmingly. When they got out and the pilot viewed the damage he exploded: "When you said three by five I thought you meant inches, not feet!" "I thought you might have gotten that impression," said the gunner, "but you were busy with the aircraft and I didn't want to bother you with details."

A good deal of our earthly security is like that: it is far from being as secure as we imagine. Sometimes things turn out all right for us and sometimes they don't. We learn that uncertainty and trouble are part of this life. But the wonderful thing about eternal life is that it is absolutely secure. Jesus holds his people in his own firm grasp, and they can trust his assurance that they will never perish.

The manuscripts differ a little about the text of verse 29. Some have "My Father, who has given them to me, is greater than all" and there are other readings. It seems likely that the true text is as I have translated and that the scribes made small alterations to make the reading more acceptable. It is, of course, true that the Father is greater than all, and in the absolute sense that must be accepted. But it seems that what Jesus is saying here is that, among things and people here on earth, the church ("what my Father has given me") is the greatest. This is not due to the wonderful excellence of church members, because they are but sinners. What makes them so great is what God has done in them. They are sinners, indeed, but forgiven sinners, sinners whom God has transformed and to whom he has given of his Holy Spirit. They are those through whom he does much of his work on earth and those he will keep eternally.

Since these transformed sinners are so much involved in what God is doing in the world, it is not surprising that Jesus says that "no one

390

can snatch them out of my Father's hand." This is similar to the statement about himself in verse 28, but it is not the same. Jesus has said that no one "will" snatch them from his hand. Now he says that no one "can" snatch them from the Father's hand. Here is a reference to the power of the Almighty Father. He is so strong that the sheep need never fear. Nobody has the power to take them from the hand of the Father. The two thoughts, that nobody will snatch them from the Son's hand and nobody can snatch them from the Father's hand, combine to give us the strongest assurance of our security throughout all time and all eternity.

The Unity of the Father and the Son

"I and the Father are one" (v. 30) is a statement whose full meaning is beyond us. We can say that in the Greek "one" is neuter, not masculine: "one thing" and not "one person." Jesus is affirming a deep, basic unity, but he is not saying that the two are identical. Some point out that later in this Gospel we have Jesus' prayer that his followers may be one as he and the Father are one (17:11, 21). They suggest that the unity that binds Christians is a unity of love and it is this that binds the Son to the Father. There is truth here, of course, for there is a bond of love between the two, but it is not easy to think that this is all there is to it. C. K. Barrett remarks, ". . . the oneness of Father and Son is a oneness of love and obedience even while it is a oneness of essence." We need something like this for a full understanding.

It is true that there is a unity of love. It is also true that there is a unity that proceeds from Jesus' constant obedience to the Father. A further aspect of unity consists in the fact that Jesus is the perfect revelation of the Father (1:18), and there is a unity between the Son who reveals the Father and the Father he reveals.

But, as Barrett says, there is also "a oneness of essence." What that means we cannot understand here and now and perhaps shall never understand it. We are created beings and we are talking about the Creator. But we can know that there is such a unity of being between these two as exists nowhere in all creation. And in the context that is a reassuring and encouraging thought, for Jesus has been speaking about what the Father does and specifically about what he does in keeping us safe within the fold. There is no division between these two over the keeping of their people secure.

49

Unbelief—and Faith

*The Jews again brought stones in order to stone him. Jesus
answered them, "I have shown you many good works from my
Father; on account of which of them are you stoning me?" The
Jews answered him, "We are not stoning you for a good work
but for blasphemy, and because you, being a man, make
yourself God." Jesus answered them, "Is it not written in your
law, 'I said, "You are gods"'? If he called them gods to whom
the word of God came, and the Scripture cannot be broken, do
you say of him whom the Father sanctified and sent into the
world 'You are blaspheming' because I said 'I am the Son of
God'? If I do not do the works of my Father do not believe me.
But if I do, even if you do not believe me believe the works so
that you may come to know and keep on knowing that the
Father is in me and I am in the Father." Therefore they were
trying again to arrest him, and he went off out of their hand.
And he went away beyond the Jordan back to the place
where John had been baptizing at first and he stayed there. And
many came to him and said, "John did no sign, but all things
that John said about this man were true." And many believed
on him there (John 10:31–42).*

Jesus had just made his great assertion, "I and the Father are one" (v. 30). This has brought enlightenment, comfort, and
inspiration to Christians through the centuries, but for those Jews it
was an incredibly wicked thing to say. They regarded it as blasphemy

and were so incensed that they got ready to stone Jesus. In this way they were being as wicked as they claimed Jesus was, because they were preparing to kill a man without giving him the opportunity of defending himself. They were setting aside all due process and taking the law into their own hands. It is a measure of their anger and of their abhorrence of what they saw as blasphemy that they should be ready to engage in a lynching.

There were actually a few offenses for which action of this kind was encouraged. If a man stole a sacred vessel, for example, we read in the Mishnah that "the zealots may fall upon him." There is no indication of a trial. This is the case also when a priest served at the altar in a state of uncleanness. This was seen as a very horrible thing, cutting at the heart of much of the Jewish understanding of the way to approach God. In this case the Mishnah tells us that his brother priests did not bring him to the court. Instead, "The young men among the priests took him outside the Temple Court and split open his brain with clubs." It was a horrible offense and brought a horrible punishment. So the action of the crowd on this occasion cannot be said to lack precedents of a sort. But it was still illegal. On their own understanding of the law they should not have done it.

The Jews had tried to stone Jesus before (8:59), which is the point of John's "again." The word I have translated "brought" really means "carried"; there would have been no stones lying round in Solomon's colonnade, and they would have had to go elsewhere to get them. So they found stones and brought them back. One would not have expected a stoning in such a place, but evidently the Jews were so angry that they did not stop to think about such a thing. It was there that Jesus had committed the offense, they may have reasoned, and it was there that he would suffer the penalty for it. They may even have thrown a few stones, for they say, "We are stoning you," not "We are going to stone you" (v. 33). But clearly the stoning did not get far. Jesus spoke to them and they got caught up in further discussion.

Jesus responded to the attempt by drawing attention to his deeds (v. 32). He reminded them that he had done "many good works" and asked for which they were stoning him. In this Gospel the word "works" is the one Jesus usually used when talking about his miracles, so he may well be drawing their attention to the fact that he had accomplished many great deeds that were quite beyond the power of men. Should they stone someone who had done such unusual deeds? But since the word is broad enough to cover the non-miraculous, Jesus may well be drawing attention to his whole manner of life. He had once asked them, "Which of you convicts me of sin?" (8:46), and no one had responded. Should they stone a man who lived a life they could not fault?

Those good works, Jesus says, were "from my Father." It is consistent with his whole approach throughout this Gospel that he does not ascribe the "good works" (whether miraculous or non-miraculous) to himself. He is not speaking of his own unaided achievement. He is speaking of what the Father was doing through him. He has earlier spoken of his works as the works the Father gave him to do (5:36), and in the upper room he would in due course say "the Father dwelling in me does his works" (14:10). He has just said that he and the Father are one (v. 30), and it follows that the works he is doing are in a very meaningful sense the Father's works. They are not to be understood apart from the Father.

Perhaps we should notice also that the word Jesus uses for "which" is not the normal relative pronoun, but a word that has the notion of quality about it. It is often translated as "what kind of." The kind of works Jesus did, the quality apparent in them, showed to discerning people something of their origin. The works were not the kind of works anyone could do. There was a quality in them that showed their divine origin.

Blasphemy

The Jews deny that they are stoning him for anything good. The reason, they say, is "blasphemy," and they explain this in the words "you, being a man, make yourself God" (v. 33). It is sometimes objected that these words cannot be authentic, because blasphemy as the Jews defined it meant that a person had pronounced the divine name in what he said about God. Jesus had not done this, so whatever he had done, it was not blasphemy. It is not necessary to take this seriously. It is true that blasphemy was narrowly defined in the Mishnah, but this represents a development of Pharisaic thought and it may not have been defined as early as this. In any case the Pharisaic view was not the only one in Judaism and there was a wider view of what constituted blasphemy. Whatever the basis in law, these people were angry. For them what Jesus had said was blasphemous and they were not going to be deterred by legal hairsplitting.

They had discerned accurately enough the thrust of Jesus' teaching. They recognized that what he was saying was not the kind of thing that any mere man, one who was no more than a created being, could legitimately say. That for them was enough. The man was a blasphemer and must suffer the fate of blasphemers.

There is a nice piece of Johannine irony here. "You, being a man, make yourself God," they say. But John knows, as do his informed readers, that the real truth is something like the opposite: he, being God, made himself man! John does not dwell on the thought, but as he has brought it out throughout his Gospel he could trust his readers to see it.

"The Scripture Cannot Be Broken"

Jesus' reply was to direct their attention to a passage of Scripture that he speaks of as "your law" (v. 34). The passage he quotes is from the Psalms, which strictly speaking was not in the law. "The Law" as the Jews understood it was the books from Genesis to Deuteronomy. These books they saw as Scripture par excellence; they excelled all else and to these books they gave special honor. But sometimes they extended the name that strictly meant these five books so as to include all of Scripture and that is what Jesus is doing here.

He speaks of "your" law. This does not mean that he himself repudiates it. On the contrary, he recognized all Scripture as being God's word and he goes on to say that it "cannot be broken" (v. 35). But it was Scripture on which the Jews based their position. When they opposed Jesus they did so because they could not reconcile what he was saying and doing with what they understood Scripture to teach. Consistently Jesus points out that if they really understood what the writings to which they gave so much honor were saying, they would recognize that he has been sent from the Father. Here he is saying something like: "This is not merely what I am saying. It is what the Scripture that you praise so highly is saying."

The passage Jesus quotes is from Psalm 82:6. This psalm is one that deals with the problem of unjust judges. "How long will you defend the unjust and show partiality to the wicked?" asks the psalmist and then goes on to urge them to defend the weak and uphold the rights of the poor (vv. 2–3). The words Jesus quotes use the word *gods* of these people and thus bring out their very great dignity. Judges have a great responsibility and are to be seen as very significant people. "Gods" though they were, the psalm goes on, they would "die like mere men"; they would "fall like every other ruler" (v. 7).

The point Jesus is making is that the word of which the Jews were complaining was used of the judges in the Scriptures they recognized and to which they gave such honor. How, then, could they complain when it was used of "him whom the Father sanctified and sent into the world"? If it was rightly used of the judges of old, how much more did it apply to Jesus?

He speaks of himself as "sanctified," a word used again in this Gospel only in 17:17, 19. In the great prayer in the upper room Jesus prays that the Father will sanctify his disciples and goes on to say that for their sake he sanctifies himself. His sanctification of himself clearly means his setting of himself apart to die for sinners. It is a word with solemn overtones. It suits the context of the Feast of the Dedication (when the people remembered the sanctification of the temple) that Jesus should speak of himself as "sanctified." What the feast symbolized was fully accomplished in Jesus. With this is joined the thought of mission, a concept we have seen again and again and which is very characteristic of this book. John will not let his readers forget that Jesus was sent by the Father.

This passage is sometimes misinterpreted as though Jesus was simply classing himself with men in general. He appeals to the psalm that speaks of men as "gods," so runs the reasoning, and thus justifies his speaking of himself as Son of God. He is "god" in the same sense as others. But this is not taking seriously enough what Jesus actually says. He is arguing from the less to the greater. If the word *god* could be used of people who were no more than judges, how much more could it be used of one with greater dignity, greater importance and significance than any mere judge, one "whom the Father sanctified and sent into the world"? He is not placing himself on a level with men, but setting himself apart from them.

The justification of his appeal to Scripture is "the Scripture cannot be broken." This is important for our understanding of the Bible. Notice that Jesus' argument depends on the exact word used. The psalmist could have used any one of a number of words for "judge" to make his point. After all, there are several ways of bringing out the dignity of important people like judges. Had any one of these ways been used, Jesus could not have used the passage in the way he did. Everything depends on the fact that it was the word *gods* that the psalmist used. But it is with respect to this passage from the Psalms that Jesus says that "the Scripture cannot be broken." It is a strong affirmation of the reliability of the Bible.

The Father's Works

Jesus refers to his having said, "I am the Son of God," although John has not recorded a claim made in just these words. Jesus may mean that this is the thrust of what he has said. After all, he has called himself "the Son" on a number of occasions (e.g., 5:19; 6:40) and once, "the Son of God" (5:25), and he has used language that shows that there was a special relationship between him and the Father (5:19–20). It may be, too, that this is Jesus' way of answering the charge the Jews had made against him (v. 33). The Jews did not understand the relationship existing between him and the heavenly Father. If they had understood this, they would have seen both the truth and the error of what they had said. There was truth, because Jesus was claiming to be divine. But there was also grievous error, because he was not "making" himself God. He did no more than accept the facts as they were. He could not deny his essential nature, but that did not mean that he was "making" himself anything. He was simply accepting the facts that he was who he was and that he had been sent by God on a mission to this earth. That meant that he was not to be put in the same category as his opponents. They were simply refusing to face the facts and because of this were imagining blasphemy when there was no blasphemy.

Jesus accordingly invites his opponents to face the test of "works." His life was an open book; they could see as well as anyone the things that Jesus did so habitually. He invites them not to believe him if the things he did were not "the works" of his Father" (v. 37). It was basic to the Jewish position that people should live lives in accordance with the commandments of God; they should do the service (the works) of God continually. Well, then, let them see what Jesus was doing. His whole life was a life of service, service of God and service of mankind.

The works he did were very important. Jesus goes on to say that even if they did not believe the things he taught, they ought to believe the evidence of "the works" (v. 38; actually he says "believe the works"). They might conceivably find some of Jesus' teaching incredible, not because it was in error but because nothing in their experience had prepared them for teaching that came so directly from God. But the things Jesus did were another matter entirely. When he healed the sick, when he gave sight to the blind or enabled the lame to walk, when he was found constantly doing the service of God, then that was evidence that they could believe and ought to believe. It did not need a degree from the rabbinical schools to enable them to say that the person who did these things was a good man, to say the least. Their refusal to face the test posed to them by the life of Jesus was their condemnation. The works could have been the means of bringing home to them important truths about both Jesus and the Father.

He goes on to speak about knowledge. Most translations have two different verbs for "knowing" (e.g., NIV: "that you may learn and understand"). Actually John uses the same verb both times but in different tenses. On the first occasion he has the aorist, which has a meaning like "come to know," "begin to know" (and which is the basis of NIV's "learn"). The second time the tense is present continuous, with the meaning "keep on knowing." It is not enough to have a brilliant flash of insight and then let the knowledge gained fade away. It is important both to come to know things about Jesus and about the Father and also to keep on knowing these things, to retain them in our memory. If they had really considered what his works taught them, they would have enlightenment and abiding knowledge.

And that knowledge concerned the mutual indwelling of Jesus and the Father. That is a truth that runs through this Gospel and we find it taught over and over. It was of central importance, and Jesus is saying that if his enemies had considered what his life was teaching them, they would find this truth.

But they did not. Their only response was to try to arrest Jesus again (v. 39; at least that was a small improvement on trying to stone him!). The tense of John's verb implies that they kept trying, though he does not tell us in what the persistence consisted. But Jesus escaped. How he did it John does not say. For him that was not important. What mattered was that Jesus was steadily moving on towards his "hour." When that time came he would die to bring salvation to the world (3:16). Until that time came no enemy could destroy him. They could plot and rage as they liked; they could not overthrow the plan of God.

The Witness of John the Baptist

Probably because of the hostility that this incident revealed, Jesus went away to the other side of the Jordan (v. 40). There is an ambiguity here, arising from the fact that there is a Greek word that may mean either "again" or "back." Many translations have "again" here, but it seems more likely that John is telling us that Jesus went back to the place where he had had his early ministry, "the place where John had been baptizing at first." We should not understand this withdrawal as due to fear. Jesus was quite ready to die, and in due course he would die for our salvation. But he would die at the right time in the purposes of God. It would be at his choosing, not that of his enemies. Clearly those enemies were angry and were ready to take extreme action. So Jesus removed himself from the possibility of trouble until the right time had come.

In the first chapter of this Gospel we read of John the Baptist's testimony to Jesus and of how Jesus first met some of his disciples. There must have been some very happy memories for both Jesus and the disciples when they went back to where this had happened.

John the Baptist was well remembered in those parts. He had called for people to repent and be baptized, and it is this for which we often remember him. But in this Gospel the one thing the Baptist did was to bear his witness to Jesus. The Fourth Evangelist says nothing about the things John the Baptist did and not very much about what he said. The one thing he is interested in is the Baptist's testimony to Jesus, and that he makes very clear. Now we find that the people in this area remembered that testimony, too. The Baptist had been so forthright in his witness that his hearers knew well that one greater than he would come. They looked forward to that greater one and now that he was among them they welcomed him. John had left them eager to find out about Jesus.

I am reminded of a story about a ringing telephone. A harried housewife picked it up and shouted, "Sorry, I can't talk now. Our white mouse is loose in the kitchen and I have to catch him before the cat does." She left the receiver dangling, and sundry strange noises filtered through for the next five minutes or so. Then she took up the phone and heard a strange voice say, "Excuse me, lady, I know I have a wrong number. But I just had to find out. Who got the mouse?" The housewife's speech had not been brilliant, but it left the hearer eager to find out what happened. It was a bit like that with John the Baptist. He spoke about Jesus in such a way that his hearers wanted to find out about him. And when Jesus came among them they did.

So they said, "John did no sign, but all things that John said about this man were true" (v. 41). "Sign," of course, is used in the sense "miracle." The Baptist had been a witness, a forerunner. He disclaimed being the bridegroom and said he was simply the friend of the bridegroom (3:29). He did not do spectacular things like the miracles Jesus did.

But he did bear his witness. And now that they met Jesus the people could see that what John had said was quite true. They in turn bear their witness to the truth of what the Baptist had said. The result was that "many believed on him there" (v. 42).

There is an important lesson for all Christian workers here. It is not easy to be the servant of God in days like these. In all our Christian organizations and in all our Christian churches there are great demands on those who serve Christ. The need is tremendous, and the resources always seem too limited for us to accomplish what we would like to do. Whenever a new pastor is appointed, or the secretary or president of an organization, or the leader of a youth group, we expect miracles of that person. Perhaps in a few cases our verdict is that some small miracle has occurred. But that is very rare. And it does not matter. What matters is that we so live and so speak as to bring people to Jesus.

We will probably never be able to do the miracles people expect of us. But at the end of the day it will not matter much whether we can walk on water. It will matter everything, however, that people should be able to say of us, "All things that John [or whatever our name is] said about Jesus were true."